On Sacks

This book is devoted to the reintroduction of the remarkable approach to sociological inquiry developed by Harvey Sacks. Sacks's original analyses – concerned with the lived detail of action and language-in-interaction, discoverable in members' actual activities – demonstrated a means of doing sociology that had previously seemed impossible. In so doing, Sacks provided for highly technical, detailed, yet stunningly simple solutions to some of the most trenchant troubles for the social sciences relating to language, culture, meaning, knowledge, action, and social organisation. In this original collection, scholars working in a range of different fields, including sociology, human geography, communication and media studies, social psychology, and linguistics, outline the ways in which their work has been inspired, influenced, and shaped by Sacks's approach, as well as how their current research is taking Sacks's legacy forward in new directions. As such, the collection is intended to provide both an introduction to, and critical exploration of, the work of Harvey Sacks and its continued relevance for the analysis of contemporary society.

Robin James Smith is Senior Lecturer in Sociology at Cardiff University, UK. His research is concerned with the ethnomethodology and ethnography of interaction in public space and mobile embodied practices. His work is influenced by, and contributes to, developments in the analysis of categorisational practices. He has also published on qualitative research methodology more generally and is the current editor of *Qualitative Research* and associate editor of *SAGE Research Methods Foundations*. He is co-editor of *Urban Rhythms: Mobilities, Space and Interaction in the Contemporary City* and *The Lost Ethnographies: Methodological Insights from Projects That Never Were*.

Richard Fitzgerald is Professor of Communication at the University of Macau, China (SAR). He has researched and written extensively on methods of qualitative discourse analysis with a particular focus on membership categorisation analysis (MCA) and ethnomethodology. His recent publications on MCA include *Advances in Membership Categorisation Analysis*, with W. Housley, and a co-edited issue of the *Journal of Pragmatics* with S. Rintel and W. Housley under the title *Membership Categorisation Analysis: Technologies of Social Action*.

William Housley is Professor of Sociology at Cardiff University, UK. He has published extensively on qualitative and social research methods, sociological theory, the study of practical reason, ethnomethodology, membership categorization analysis, social interaction and digital sociology. He is co-editor of *Advances in Membership Categorisation Analysis* with Richard Fitzgerald.

Directions in Ethnomethodology and Conversation Analysis

Ethnomethodology and conversation analysis are cognate approaches to the study of social action that together comprise a major perspective within the contemporary human sciences. Ethnomethodology focuses upon the production of situated and ordered social action of all kinds, whilst conversation analysis has a more specific focus on the production and organisation of talk-in-interaction. Of course, given that so much social action is conducted in and through talk, there are substantive as well theoretical continuities between the two approaches. Focusing on social activities as situated human productions, these approaches seek to analyse the intelligibility and accountability of social activities 'from within' those activities themselves, using methods that can be analysed and described. Such methods amount to aptitudes, skills, knowledge and competencies that members of society use, rely upon and take for granted in conducting their affairs across the whole range of social life.

As a result of the methodological rewards consequent upon their unique analytic approach and attention to the detailed orderliness of social life, ethnomethodology and conversation analysis have ramified across a wide range of human science disciplines throughout the world, including anthropology, social psychology, linguistics, communication studies and social studies of science and technology.

This series is dedicated to publishing the latest work in these two fields, including research monographs, edited collections and theoretical treatises. As such, its volumes are essential reading for those concerned with the study of human conduct and aptitudes, the (re)production of social orderliness and the methods and aspirations of the social sciences.

Embodied Family Choreography
Practices of Control, Care, and Mundane Creativity
Marjorie Harness Goodwin and Asta Cekaite

Establishing Shared Knowledge in Political Meetings
Repairing and Correcting in Public
Hanna Svensson

On Sacks
Methodology, Materials, and Inspirations
Edited by Robin James Smith, Richard Fitzgerald and William Housley

For more information about this series, please visit: www.routledge.com/Directions-in-Ethnomethodology-and-Conversation-Analysis/book-series/ASHSER1190

On Sacks

Methodology, Materials, and Inspirations

Edited by Robin James Smith, Richard Fitzgerald and William Housley

Routledge
Taylor & Francis Group
LONDON AND NEW YORK

First published 2021
by Routledge
2 Park Square, Milton Park, Abingdon, Oxon OX14 4RN

and by Routledge
52 Vanderbilt Avenue, New York, NY 10017

Routledge is an imprint of the Taylor & Francis Group, an informa business

British Library Cataloguing-in-Publication Data
A catalogue record for this book is available from the British Library

Library of Congress Cataloging-in-Publication Data
Names: Smith, Robin James, editor. | Fitzgerald, Richard, 1965- editor. | Housley, William, 1970- editor.
Title: On Sacks : methodology, materials, and inspirations / edited by Robin James Smith, Richard Fitzgerald and William Housley.
Description: Milton Park, Abingdon, Oxon ; New York, NY : Routledge, 2021. | Series: Directions in ethnomethodology and conversation analysis | Includes bibliographical references and index.
Identifiers: LCCN 2020034332 (print) | LCCN 2020034333 (ebook) | ISBN 9780367111038 (hardback) | ISBN 9780429024849 (ebook)
Subjects: LCSH: Sacks, Harvey. | Social interaction. | Ethnomethodology.
Classification: LCC HM1111 .O57 2021 (print) | LCC HM1111 (ebook) | DDC 302–dc23
LC record available at https://lccn.loc.gov/2020034332
LC ebook record available at https://lccn.loc.gov/2020034333

ISBN: 978-0-367-11103-8 (hbk)
ISBN: 978-0-429-02484-9 (ebk)

Typeset in Times New Roman
by River Editorial Ltd, Devon, UK

Contents

Notes on contributors

Jack Bilmes is Emeritus Professor of Anthropology at the University of Hawaii, Manoa. He is the author of *Discourse and Behavior* and *The Structure of Meaning in Talk: Explorations in Category Analysis* and of articles on various subjects, including microanalysis of verbal interaction, category analysis, narrative, public policy, social theory, and Thai social organization. Currently, his primary interest is in what he calls 'occasioned semantics', focusing primarily on taxonomic and scaling relations in interactive talk.

Andrew P. Carlin is a visiting fellow at the University of Macau, in Macau SAR, China. His central concern is the social organisation of scholarly communication. His current projects are on equipmentally mediated instructed action, discipline-specific teaching and learning in the higher education sector, and parent-child interaction. He has published in a range of international journals.

Susan Danby is Professor in the School of Early Childhood at the Queensland University of Technology, Australia, and Director of the Australian Research Council Centre of Excellence for the Digital Child. Her research applies ethnomethodological and conversation analysis perspectives to investigating social interaction in children's peer groups as well as between children and adults in a range of settings that involve family, classroom, helpline, and medical interactions.

Derek Edwards is Emeritus Professor in the School of Social Sciences and Humanities at Loughborough University. His interests are in the analysis of language and social interaction in everyday and institutional settings. He specialises in discursive psychology, in which relations between psychological states and the external world are studied as discourse categories and practices, including accounts of actions, events, and intentionality in everyday conversation, and in various specialised settings, including school classrooms, police interrogations, telephone calls, and counselling. His books include *Discursive Psychology*, with Jonathan Potter, and *Discourse and Cognition*.

Richard Fitzgerald is Professor of Communication at the University of Macau. He has researched and written extensively on membership categorisation analysis and forms of discourse analysis. He is currently Editor-in-Chief of the journal *Discourse, Context and Media* and Senior Research Fellow at the Institute of Advanced Studies in Humanities and Social Sciences, University of Macau.

Elliott M. Hoey is a postdoctoral researcher at the University of Basel, in the Department of Linguistics and Literature. He completed his PhD research at the Max Planck Institute for Psycholinguistics. His research interests include conversation analysis and usage-based linguistics, with particular emphasis on multimodality and emotion. He is the author of *When Conversation Lapses: The Public Accountability of Silent Copresence.*

William Housley is Professor of Sociology at Cardiff University, Wales, UK. He has published extensively on qualitative and social research methods, sociological theory, the study of practical reason, ethnomethodology, membership categorization analysis, social interaction and digital sociology. He is co-editor of *Advances in Membership Categorisation Analysis* (Sage, 2015) with Richard Fitzgerald.

Bogdana Huma is a lecturer in psychology at York St John University. Her research uses inductive methods for analysing social interaction – discursive psychology, conversation analysis, ethnomethodology, and membership categorisation analysis – applied to the examination of social psychological topics in and as part of everyday talk-in-interaction in ordinary and institutional settings. Her current research interests revolve around exploring the interactional mechanisms that underpin social influence – in particular, persuasion and resistance.

Sara Keel is currently a researcher at the School of Health Sciences, Vaud, Switzerland. She holds an MA in Sociology from the University of Geneva and a PhD in Human and Social Sciences from the University of Neuchâtel (Switzerland) and the University of Lyon II (France). Adopting ethnomethodology and conversation analysis, she carries out research projects on naturally occurring interactions in family, political, and healthcare settings.

Christian Licoppe is Professor of Sociology, alumnus of the Ecole Polytechnique, and acting head of the Social Science Department at Telecom Paristech. He is interested in conversation analysis and multimodal interaction analysis and, more generally, ethnographic studies of multi-participant interaction in mobile and institutional settings. He is currently engaged in a large-scale video-ethnographic research project on mono- and multilingual courtroom interactions in relation to the introduction of videoconference systems. He has also made progress in extending EM/CA analysis to various forms of mediated interaction in order to understand the development of distinctive interactional sequences in relation to particular socio-technical ecologies and communicative affordances.

Michael Mair is a senior lecturer in sociology at the University of Liverpool. Michael is an ethnomethodologist whose research falls into two main areas: the methodology and philosophy of research; and politics, government, and the state. The focus of that work includes: the politics of evidence and accountability in different settings; and methodological practice in the social and natural sciences, including qualitative, quantitative, and digital methods as well as experimentation, machine learning, and artificial intelligence.

Lorenza Mondada is Professor of Linguistics at the University of Basel. Her research deals with social interaction in ordinary, professional, and institutional settings, from an ethnomethodological and conversation analytic perspective. Her focus is on video analysis and multimodality, researching how the situated and endogenous organization of social interaction draws on a diversity of multimodal resources such as, besides language, gesture, gaze, body posture, movements, object manipulation, as well as multisensorial practices such as touching, tasting, and seeing. She has extensively published in the *Journal of Pragmatics*, *Discourse Studies*, *Language in Society*, *Research on Language and Social Interaction*, and the *Journal of Sociolinguistics* and has co-edited several collected books.

Ricardo Moutinho is an associate professor of linguistics at the University of Macau. His research explores social phenomena within the fields of ethnomethodology and conversation analysis. His current research examines guided-tour interactions in astronomical observatories and he is a research fellow at the Institute of Advanced Studies in Humanities and Social Sciences, University of Macau.

Jessica Robles is a lecturer in the School of Social Sciences and Humanities and a member of the Discourse and Rhetoric Group at Loughborough University, UK. Jessica has a PhD from the University of Colorado at Boulder, and her research uses discourse and conversation analysis to examine the social organization of difference and its relevance to how people interactionally manage ordinary moral troubles in their everyday lives. This work has covered, for example, political disagreements, gift-exchange dilemmas, responses to racist talk, and complaints about social media and technology use.

Wes Sharrock is Emeritus Professor of Sociology at the University of Manchester. In a career spanning 50 years at Manchester, Wes has explored two central themes – the relevance of empirical data and an understanding of ordinary language for an understanding of social practice and the respecification of social theory – pursuing them across a huge variety of settings, from ordinary scenes of everyday social life through to complex domains of practical action and reasoning in various academic and industrial work situations. He has supervised more than 60 PhD students, authored 17 books, and established the Manchester School of Ethnomethodology as a major site of ethnomethodological and natural language studies. He received a lifetime achievement award from the American Sociological Association in 2011 and has written critically on, inter alia, moral philosophy, cognitive science, computational science, workplace studies, research methodology, interactionism, pragmatics, and social psychology, as well as sociology.

Robin James Smith is a senior lecturer in sociology at Cardiff University. He has studied interaction in public space, urban outreach work with rough sleepers, and the work of mountain rescue. These projects coalesce around an interest in the accomplishment of mobility, 'space', and perception, with a particular focus on members' categorisational practices. He has published on these matters in a number of leading journals and is the editor of *Urban Rhythms* (Wiley-Blackwell) and *The Lost Ethnographies* (Emerald). He has also published critical pieces on various issues in qualitative methodology, is an assistant editor of SAGE *Research Methods Foundations* and is current Editor-in-Chief of *Qualitative Research*.

Elizabeth Stokoe is Professor of Social Interaction and an associate pro vice-chancellor at Loughborough University. She uses conversation analysis to understand how talk works, from first dates to medical communication. Outside the university, she runs research-based communication training for practitioners. In addition to publishing more than 120 scientific papers, she is passionate about science communication and has spoken at TED, *New Scientist*, Google, Microsoft, the Royal Institution, and Cheltenham Science Festivals. Her book, *Talk: The Science of Conversation*, is published by Little, Brown (2018).

Rod Watson (Manchester University UK, Institut Marcel Mauss, and Télécom ParisTech Paris) is a distinguished researcher in the sociological field of ethnomethodology. He began his career during the early development of ethnomethodological and conversation analysis, and his work spans almost 50 years during which he contributed to and influenced a generation of researchers. While his work encompasses a broad range of sociological and ethnomethodological interests, he brings a particular focus to Harvey Sacks's work on membership categorisation.

Kevin A. Whitehead is an assistant professor in the Department of Sociology at the University of California, Santa Barbara. His primary research areas involve the use of ethnomethodological and conversation analytic approaches to study the interactional organization of membership categories, focusing on ways in which they are used, reproduced, and resisted in talk-in-interaction. His research also examines basic structures and practices of talk-in-interaction in ordinary conversational and institutional settings, and their intersections with social problems, including racism and violence.

1 On Sacks

Methodology, materials, and inspirations

Robin James Smith, Richard Fitzgerald, and William Housley

This book is devoted to the reintroduction of the remarkably original approach to sociological inquiry developed by Harvey Sacks. We intend the volume as an incitement to experts to return to Sacks's original lectures with fresh eyes, and a provocation for those not familiar to read Sacks for the first time. Sacks's remarkable analyses offer a means of doing sociology that provides for highly technical, detailed, and yet stunningly simple solutions to some of the most trenchant troubles for the social sciences relating to language, culture, meaning, knowledge, action, and social organisation. The influence of Sacks's work has not been widespread – something we aim to address with this collection. Yet certain areas of sociology, human geography, communication and media studies, psychology, and linguistics have been reoriented to the sorts of analyses that are made possible by starting with the lived details of action and language-in-interaction, details that are discoverable, rather than contrived or modelled in and through social scientific theory, as they are actually produced, used, and accomplished by members engaged in actual activities. In this collection, scholars working in a range of different fields and with a range of interests outline the ways in which their work has been inspired, influenced, and shaped by Sacks's approach, and how their current research is taking those insights forward in new directions. As such, it provides both an introduction to, and an exploration of, the work and influence of Harvey Sacks.

A mind at work

Sacks's insights and ground-breaking analyses are perhaps best expressed – if 'best' is taken to mean most accessibly – in the lectures delivered at UCLA Berkley and Irvine between 1964 and 1972. More than any other sociologist, Erving Goffman included, Sacks's analyses shone a light on seemingly trivial social phenomena hidden in plain sight. Yet, whereas Goffman is one of the most cited sociologists of the 20th century, Sacks's contribution remains relatively marginal outside ethnomethodology and conversation analysis. This is, perhaps, explainable through the relatively restricted availability of the *Lectures* and the relatively few formal works published before his untimely death. The limits of the influence of the ground-breaking ideas Sacks introduces in the

Lectures are, however, more likely attributable to the radical challenge that Sacks's work poses to the usual ways of doing sociology and social science and the recurrent problems found in those disciplines' 'peculiar' approach to the description of social world (Sacks, 1963: 1). The 'primitive natural science' of society (Lynch & Bogen, 1994) that Sacks proposes – that stays with the practices and resources that underpin the possibility of description employed by members, discoverable, and only discoverable, in the lived detail of ordinary actions – offers no easy way out and, in many ways, pulls the rug from under more accepted forms of doing social science.

Working with recorded and transcribed talk, ethnographic observations, and a range of other materials, Sacks demonstrated social organisation to be the work and product of a shared, finely tuned, extensive, and powerful 'machinery' (McHoul, 2005: 125). Social order, in keeping with Garfinkel's (1967) programme of respecification, was not a conceptual or theoretical matter or puzzle to be 'solved' by social scientists but, rather, a consequence of members' methodical and routine practices. Indeed, Sacks was quite explicit when he stated, in a seminar with Garfinkel in 1962, that he was not much interested in professional sociology and was more focused on members' means of doing sociology (Harvey Sacks Papers, 2017, Box 15 File, *New Version of the Problem of Order*).[1]

Sacks identified a panoply of methods and actions used and analysed by members in the course of interaction, including: turn-taking, forms of repair, 'adjacency pairs' and associated methods for sequential order, categorisational methods and maxims operational within membership categorisation devices, the membership inference-rich representational (MIR) device, practices relating to omni-relevancy, and partitioning, all of which are employed by members in their congregational and constitutive activities. Sacks rejected the recurrent problems of social science disciplines as formulated as problems *for* those disciplines. This was one of the key reasons that Sacks's analyses start from the position of 'another member'. Key in this discussion is *how* the 'things themselves' of social action and interaction are available for observation and, moreover, how 'observation' and 'witnessing' are unavoidably ubiquitous, ordinary practices that cannot be naively put to use by the social scientist (see Mair and Sharrock; Carlin, both this collection).

Treating social life both as a domain of inquiry *and* as an arena which yielded the methods for its study was ground-breaking. Importantly, Sacks was at pains to emphasise that it was with the *machinery* for that order that he was concerned, and that any discoverable order is a methodical accomplishment and also a by-product thereof; that is to say that members are not necessarily directly concerned with *producing* order (Liberman, 2019). It was in this way that Sacks both resolved the previously troublesome relation of production to recognition and radically undercut social scientific methodologies – both qualitative and quantitative – that operate, in different ways, with a sense that 'culture' is only apprehendable through aggregate or composite models (Schegloff, 1995: xlvi). There is, instead – as Sacks's analyses recurrently demonstrated, and as is unavoidably discoverable – order at all points.

Across Sacks's lectures, and certainly across the archived research and teaching materials, there are multiple threads teased out and others not followed up, analytic hunches developed and dropped, and an under-acknowledged, wide-ranging, creative, and what would now be called a markedly 'interdisciplinary', analytic creativity. Additionally, as those familiar with the published *Lectures* will recognise, Sacks regularly attended to diverse methodological concerns – from experiments, to statistical research, to fieldwork and ethnographic description. Indeed, although Sacks is perhaps best known for his later work that focused in the main on the analysis of transcribed audio recordings, the *Lectures*, both early and late, are characterised by an exacting attention to a whole manner of materials and topics. Any materials that were 'good enough' for the analysis of social action were submitted to scrutiny. Sacks's lectures are replete with inspirations for inquiries into the ordinary routine organisation and recognition of activities. A common feature of the *Lectures*, and the stark originality of Sacks's approach more generally, is the scientific treatment of the seemingly 'trivially obvious' details of social life (1995[I]: 200). In taking seriously trivial and 'disorganised' activities such as answering the phone, telling a story or a dirty joke, or playing games, Sacks further opened up the possibility of the sociological analysis of the 'seen but unnoticed' (Garfinkel, 1967) features of mundane social organisation and sociology.

The lectures, recorded and transcribed by his students and early collaborators, most notably by Gail Jefferson, were initially circulated internationally in mimeograph form between various clusters of researchers – a 'core group' – who were already working on resolving the various critiques of social science methodology present in the writings of the phenomenologists, Wittgenstein and others such as Stanley Cavell, Gilbert Ryle, and Peter Winch. The 'naturalistic' approach that Sacks was developing – influenced by and influencing Garfinkel's ethnomethodology – found fertile ground in Boston, Edinburgh, Manchester, and beyond (Watson, this collection). At the heart of this enterprise was a research community with a collaborative yet critical spirit. As Dusan Bjelić (2017) recently remarked, 'to have a method you have to have your own analytical "corporation" … To this end, Sacks had to erect his own tent in the wild and assemble a squad of loyal eyes and ears'. In the context of continued and important debates regarding directions of travel (see e.g. Lynch, 2017, 2019), it is gratifying to see this collaborative spirit remaining and, if anything, gathering strength among the contemporary global community of EM/CA practitioners. For better or worse, the tent is situated in less of a wilderness than it once was.

The circulation of Sacks's work increased when, in 1992, the *Lectures on Conversation* were published as two volumes and, later, as a single tome in 1995. The *Lectures* contain and represent, in pedagogic form, several key iterations of Sacks's approach. Some of the evolving analytic concerns present in Sacks's work are traced in the chapters of this collection, demonstrating both departure from and continuity between, for example, Sacks's reliance on 'self-reflexive' analyses in the early lectures and his increased focus on recorded transcripts and how participants themselves oriented to their and others' social actions in situ (Sacks, Schegloff, & Jefferson, 1974; and see Bilmes; Fitzgerald; Robles; Stokoe et al., this collection). Beyond the affordance of the tracing of an intellectual trajectory – if, indeed, that is the correct way to the read the *Lectures*[2] – the transcripts make clear, even to those who have never heard his voice, that Sacks was an undoubtedly brilliant lecturer (Lynch, 1999). He would often present ideas yet to be developed, or, at least, would give the impression to his students that he did not quite have something figured out and was letting them in on something special: as Schegloff (1995: xii) memorably remarks, the students must have hardly known what they were hearing. As evidenced by the chapters in this collection, the *Lectures* contain a panoply of themes, hunches, insights, topics, and analyses, many of which have received either little or no attention at all.

Although Sacks published relatively few papers, his publications with Garfinkel (1970) on formal structures of practical actions, with Schegloff and Jefferson (1974) on the simplest systematics of turn-taking, and his analysis of a child's story (Sacks, 1974) are each seen to reflect the essence of contemporary forms of ethnomethodology, conversation analysis, and membership categorisation analysis (MCA). These publications often formalised ideas that surfaced at different points in the *Lectures* and further demonstrated Sacks's remarkably penetrating understanding of social science, his early papers 'On Sociological Description' and 'Max Weber's Ancient Judaism' being key examples. Sacks's creativity and analytic attention to detail are also reflected in the Sacks archives, which, along with the lectures, document a magpie-like empirical curiosity containing all manner of materials, from initial hand-written annotations and analyses of adverts and posters to field-note vignettes and passing observations, as well as recordings and transcribed seminars with colleagues. It is worth reiterating, and continually restating, that Sacks's research was only 'incidentally' about conversation. Indeed, conversation served as a means to end, an aspect of social life through which one could begin to handle the 'details of something that actually happened' (1995[II]: 26).

We believe, then, that there are plentiful reasons to return to Sacks in his own words, and not least to continually recapture and reinvigorate that sense of innovation, creativity, and discovery that characterises his legacy. In our own reading, research, and discussions, we have found Sacks's work to be what he would himself describe as an 'inexhaustible' topic (Sacks, 1995: Lecture 8, 178–179).[3]

This collection

The impetus for this collection emerged from a conversation that took place in Cardiff. The topic was the first time we (the editors) could recall reading Sacks 'in his own words', rather than mediated by an intermediary or commentator such as Schegloff (1995[I & II]) or Silverman (1998), or in that difficult yet immensely rewarding paper co-authored with Garfinkel (1970). Subsequent correspondence followed where we recounted first readings of the *Lectures*, recalling analyses of 'The Baby Cried', the 'Bullock's Store' story, 'Exchanging

Glances', and the various treatments of the 'Group Therapy Sessions'. These lectures are also returned to by other contributors in this collection. Their recurrence points to just how many of Sacks's lectures are deeply memorable as texts. Certainly, reading the transcripts for the first time *is* a remarkable and memorable experience, as Mair and Sharrock (this collection) aptly put it:

> Any first-time reader of Sacks, and something similar could be said in relation to the work of Harold Garfinkel, will encounter the same 'shock of the new' … And it is a shock; a jolt indeed. Until you read it, it's difficult to imagine that sociology could be approached *that* way. After you read it, the idea you could approach it any *other* way becomes difficult to imagine.

For the first-time reader, perhaps the most striking of the many significant aspects of the *Lectures on Conversation* is the degree of insight Sacks was able to wring either from observations of small fragments of data or from observations that, at least initially, anyone could make. Pushing past such naïve readings and the use of natural language in analysis provided Sacks with a means of exposing *just how* it is that given actions are viewed as having the order that they do. In staying with the seemingly trivially obvious, Sacks's work – which, to repeat and emphasise, should be understood as an *approach for the doing of sociology*, rather than a 'method' to be deployed – offered a radical redress of accepted social scientific treatments and constructions of relationships between 'culture', 'structure', 'behaviour', and so on. As Sacks's analyses repeatedly demonstrated, such phenomena are not only 'given presence' in social interaction, but are irremediably and inextricably and at once members' accomplishments and resources for the production and recognition of the order that the social world observably has.

Although there exist authoritative introductions and guides to Sacks's work – from Schegloff's (1995[I],[II]) introductions to the *Lectures*, via David Silverman's (1998) methodological introduction, to more recent engagements with various aspects of Sacks's method and sensibility (Fitzgerald, 2019) – the corpus of secondary literature on Sacks remains relatively sparse.[4] In this collection, we do not aim to 'set the record straight' or provide a framing of how to 'read Sacks'. What we do aim for is a demonstration of the ways in which Sacks's work has inspired and influenced others. As Sacks himself is reported to have told Jeff Coulter (1976, in Fitzgerald, 2019: 206): 'once it's out there, it's anybody's'. Contributors in this volume reflect on what they and others have done with what Sacks bequeathed. In this sense, the collection is intended as something of a *re*introduction to what is inspirational and unique in those original materials and analyses. As a result, we intend this collection as a provocative reminder of the stark originality of Sacks's approach and the ways in which he himself continually resisted possibilities of his approach to sociology and social life (and, of course, the ways in which members themselves engage in sociology) settling in to methodological doxa. Indeed, Sacks's approach should not be reduced to techniques to be straightforwardly taught and applied, without the depth of the imagination, creativity, and wider sociological project in and through which they were developed. A central aim of this collection is, then, to re-emphasise, perhaps to a new community of researchers, just how many avenues of inquiry, topics, and curiosities are contained within the *Lectures* and other sources. We do not introduce the chapters at length here, turn by turn. The authors do a good enough job of introducing their work themselves. Still, this is the structurally preferred slot for this sort of work, so we can provide something of an outline for the patient reader.

The first chapters of the collection introduce the legacy of Harvey Sacks's ground-breaking work in various intellectual and analytic contexts.

The initial contribution, by Rod Watson, one of the foremost authorities on Sacks's work, describes how he first encountered Sacks's approach following a recommendation by Goffman to Garfinkel's soon to be published *Studies in Ethnomethodology* (1967) for which he had helped secure a publisher. Although Goffman had not mentioned Sacks in Manchester, despite being involved in his PhD, Garfinkel's acknowledgement of Sacks in *Studies* prompted Watson and many others to write to Sacks to request his lectures. As the archive documents, Sacks received many requests from all over the world, from people across the academic spectrum, with some confessing to be a closet fan, but also from outside academia, including from a state police force, and he would generously arrange for his lectures and papers to be sent (Harvey Sacks Papers, 2017, Box 6, *Correspondence*).[5] Although the mimeographed lectures influenced his own PhD, being one of the first to be based on Sacks's work, and a lifelong engagement with Sacks, for Watson and others, the early-circulated lectures provided a glimpse of the depth and breadth of Sacks's interests and the spirit of Sacks's approach to analysis that would be reignited with the publication of the two volume set of lectures in 1992.

Each of the next four chapters either provides something of an overview of a key aspect of Sacks's work or traces the influence of Sacks's approach within and through a particular domain. Mair and Sharrock kick this off with a focus on Sacks's radical approach to the study of society and social action through focusing on what people are doing, where seeing sociologically was a matter of observation rather than theory. Although 40 years separated their first encounters with Sacks, it is their common experience of this 'shock of the new' and the gestalt shift in thinking this brought about that transcends the time between their first readings. Tracing the way Sacks handles the relationship between action, meaning, and understanding, Mair and Sharrock remind us, even when we have read it a number of times, of the enduring analytic weight this seemingly simple observation contains. Andrew Carlin, in the next chapter, focuses on Sacks's contribution beyond conversation analysis and especially the 'ethnographic edge' of his studies as part of what he describes as Sacks's 'Plenum'. In his discussion, he highlights that throughout the different elements of Sacks work there is a keenly developed ethnographic sensibility that would be turned on any particular phenomenon of interest. For Carlin, it was not then any particular form of data or action that captured his attention, but that Sacks's ethnographic sensibility could be turned to any social action, such as his own work in the field of libraries and information science. For Bilmes, reading Sacks influenced the direction of his early work. In particular, Bilmes highlights how the contribution of Sacks's analysis of the child's story provided a unique way of approaching semantics as members' phenomena, central to the development of what has become known as occasioned semantics. The final chapter in this section, by Stokoe, Huma, and Edwards, also reflects on the way generations of researchers have been and continue to be influenced by Sacks. Tracing one of the earliest interests in discursive psychology (DP) on gender inequality as a situated activity, the authors discuss how Sacks's work inspired their own interest and the continuity that continues to inspire new research in the area of DP.

The next series of five chapters deals with the two key themes in Sacks's work and the ways in which they have been increasingly shown to be inextricably intertwined: categorisation practices and sequential analysis. Of course, recent work has demonstrated how category and sequence are interrelated aspects of the members' machinery for accomplishing, together, social order (Housley & Fitzgerald, 2002; Fitzgerald & Housley, 2015; Stokoe, 2012; Watson, 2015), and the chapters in this section trace different aspects of the ways in which those two pillars of Sacks's sociology have been taken forward in the work of scholars and analysts in different fields. The first three chapters discuss: the moral organisation of categories in talk and how members do the 'morality of ordinariness' via sequentially realised projections and recognition of problematic (racial) talk (Robles); how, over the series of lectures, Sacks builds a three-dimensional, layered analysis to show how a single action (a greeting) is oriented to as relevantly done for the participants through the 'omni-relevant' categorially ordered context of the group therapy session (Fitzgerald); and the local mobile organisation of sequence and category in the embodied activity of walking as part of a guided tour, and the challenges and contributions of MCA for the multimodal analysis of video materials (Mondada). The next two chapters focus specifically upon Sacks's attention to turns in different interactional ecologies as actions that have significance for the overall organisation of the structure of conversation – for example, in the organisation of multiple greetings that handle the contingencies of 'appearance events' in online interaction (Licoppe) and in the ways members produce and orient 'lapses' in doing 'self-deselection' through recruiting various available resources for disengagement and avoidance of taking a next turn at talk (Hoey).

The final six chapters trace and develop topics that Sacks develops in specific analyses, but also to different extents, across the *Lectures*. The authors here demonstrate both the influence of Sacks on their own research interests and careers, as well as the range of work that remains to be done. The first three chapters of this section might be read as a complementary set. They all discuss the implications and challenges of Sacks's methodological commitment to close observation in the context of research with children and draw from the respecification of formal sociology's 'developmental' treatment of children as 'proto-adults' who lack 'adult' skills for doing social interaction (Garfinkel, Girton, Livingston, & Sacks, 1982), as well as dominant and reified conceptions including the model of discourse format and, indeed, the seemingly central conceptual analytic binaries of 'macro' and 'micro' structures and the analysis thereof.

The first considers how that respecification is available through close observation of children's use of action sequences to produce simultaneous participation in 'imaginary' and 'reality-framed' projects (Danby); the second also displays the influence of Sacks's insistence on close observation to describe members' own uses of and orientations to the developmental lens as an occasioned 'developmental scheme' as an omni-relevant device embedded in and tied to particular sequential and categorial orders in child–parent interaction (Keel); the third describes the primary school classroom as a participant-produced social system in which relation pairs (dual in this case: 'teacher–pupil' and 'adult–child') and omni-relevant devices are produced, made relevant, and oriented to by members in second language learning interactions (Moutinho).

The next two chapters return to Sacks's seminal work on categorisation practices and the 'work' of categories for and within particular forms of talk. They also demonstrate a key point made across the collection – that Sacks's original materials and analyses (both chapters return to the 'Bullock's Store' analysis) serve as inspiration for analytic projects but can also be re-analysed in light of further developments of his work and interests. The first outlines Sacks's early analyses of the use of place and setting categories in interaction and, particularly, in storytelling, before going on to consider how such practices may also have an operational relevance for a diverse range of activities within and without talk-in-interaction (Smith). The second demonstrates how a conversation analytic treatment of racial 'categories-in-action' can demonstrate how 'race' – as a category system – is a 'by-product' of speakers' ordinary actions and how speakers employing racial categories can become subject to negative categorisations and sanctions (Whitehead).

The final chapter of the collection, fittingly enough, considers how the new frontier of 'routine, everyday mundane socio-technical interaction' provides new challenges and opportunities for ethnomethodology and the study of membership categorisation practices, while at the same time representing a contemporary form of social ordering that invites us to reflect on the continued relevance of Harvey Sacks's work and ideas (Housley).

Reading the chapters as a set, it is interesting to note some convergence between these fields in terms of 'what next' for the close study of social action and phenomena. Although there may be an element of recipient design between contributor and editor, contiguities emerge between the various discussions such as categorisational practices and relevancies beyond talk, embodied practices, the intertwined and inextricable reflexive organisation and sequence and categorisation, and what we might, perhaps tentatively, call the 'lived politics' of recognition and description (in the sense that it is perfectly possible to read a number of key analyses by Sacks as an effort to 'dismantle official reality' (Bjelić, 2017)). Indeed, something we are particularly pleased to see is a developed attention to members' treatments of the 'politics' and morality of category use and of description itself. Such a concern was in no way absent from Sacks's lectures, particularly the earlier sessions (although see Schegloff, 1995[I]: xx). Attention to the resources for constituting moral order can see the beginnings of a challenge to common-sense assumptions. As Robles (this collection) notes, 'recognition in itself can be incredibly radical'.

Despite the complementary nature of the collection, some tensions remain, and it is not our intention to resolve them. There remain discussions to be had, particularly around the matters of adequacy of description, the relationship between action and the locus of 'methods' and 'production', differing approaches and insistences upon single-case analyses as opposed to collections (and Sacks's own position on the matter), and the continued variance in the treatment of the relevancy and relationship of sequence and category (see, for preceding discussion: Housley & Fitzgerald, 2002; Fitzgerald & Housley, 2015; Watson, 2015). As we have already said, it is not our intention to resolve such tensions, but rather to consider how those tensions are productive for resolving remaining issues in the study of social life. The contributions, in different ways, also consider the influence that Sacks's ideas may make to the current intersection of new forms of data and materials (Housley, this collection). As a result, it is intended that researchers across the social sciences will find much in Sacks's ideas, insights, and analyses that will cast new light on the ways in which researchers are engaging with new forms and contexts for data capture and emergent phenomena and applying extant methods of analysis. Our methods and approaches need continual stress testing (Fitzgerald, 2019) to ensure they are apace with the methods employed by members when, for instance, interacting online or handling digital materials (Licoppe, this collection; also Housley et al., 2017). The collection is also intended to provoke new directions in the analysis of communication, interaction, and everyday life more generally. There remains much work to do in explicating the lived detail of, for example, visual order, mobilities, repeat interactions over time, embodied action, gaze, and gesture, and members' own handlings of objects, materials, and knowledge in the world.

This, then, is not a textbook 'about Sacks', but, rather, a collection of reflections 'on Sacks'. Each contribution looks back to a key lecture or theme in Sacks's work in discussing the influence that reading Sacks 'in his own words' had upon their own studies, while, at the same time, demonstrating the ways in which they are taking things forward and, sometimes, in new and challenging directions. The *Lectures*, as well as the rich resource of the Harvey Sacks archive at UCLA (Fitzgerald, 2019), reveal an actively curious mind and a sustained interest in a vast range of practices and contexts, materials and data. Something that this collection is intended to encourage is a return to those original workings and the many analytic threads that are teased out, or that are only mentioned in passing, the analytic hunches developed and dropped, and the often-under-acknowledged, wide-ranging creativity of what would now be called Harvey Sacks's markedly 'interdisciplinary' sociological imagination. In returning to Sacks in his own words, the collection aims to recall the creativity and multiple inspirations in Sacks's methodology and the broad and interdisciplinary character and reach that approach had and continues to have. In this manner, the collection is also intended as something of a rendezvous point for the sometimes disconnected and sometimes competing fields represented therein. In drawing together different perspectives and fields in which Sacks's work is central, between which there is often friction, the collection is proposed as an opportunity to generate light rather than heat.

As Rod Watson remarks in the opening contribution in this collection, this volume will hopefully come to serve as something of a catalyst for further considerations of the scope and breadth of Sacks's interests that, some 40 years after his passing, have only just begun to be pursued and developed. Adopting the collaborative, communal, and inclusive approach evidenced in Sacks's work might, as Watson suggests, provide for further dialogue and convergence between concerns traditionally held apart, with a hope that the collection will be read in line with this inclusive spirit.

We hope so too.

Notes

1 Harvey Sacks's archive (Collection 1678) is held at the Charles E. Young Research Library at UCLA and consists of 145 boxes containing multiple files, folders, books, drafts of papers and lectures, as well as other materials that were collected from his office following his death. Despite the archive's relation to Sacks, there is a large amount of material that is not his work, such as books, theses, reports, as well as writing and collaborative discussions and transcriptions where the speaker or speakers are not clear. To reflect this, and in consultation with UCLA archivists, documents are attributed to the 'Harvey Sacks Papers' rather than explicit authorship being attributed, except where this is clear. Also, the date cited is the date the material was obtained from the archives (i.e., 2017), as the boxes remain uncatalogued and largely unexplored at this time (Fitzgerald, 2019).

2 The early lectures prior to spring 1966 are perhaps difficult to read in this way owing to reported gaps (Schegloff, 1995: x). There are breaks and divergences, particularly in methodological approach, between the earlier and later lectures, but there are also continuities and returns – for instance, the lecture 'On dreams', which closed the Fall 1971 series, and the well-known lecture 'Doing being ordinary' retain something of the character of the early lectures.

3 Interestingly, in this lecture, Sacks's work goes on to suggest these topics may be sacred objects. We would argue that Sacks is an inexhaustible topic, not a sacred one.

4 Perhaps there is good reason for this: Sacks was himself focused on the doing of sociological analysis, rather than discussing sociology itself at length (although see, e.g., Sacks, 1963, 1995: 26–31). This is, of course, true for ethnomethodology more generally, which has long fuelled a range of misconceptions and false critiques (Peyrot, 1982).

5 The archive contains many of the letters and requests sent to Sacks, including from Rod Watson.

References

Bjelić, D.I. (2017). 'Hotrodder: A Revolutionary Category' – A genealogy of a Sacks' conversation(al) analytic method. Paper Presented at *IIEMCA 2017: A Half-Century of Studies International Institute for Ethnomethodology and Conversation Analysis*, Otterbein College, Westerville, OH, July 10–13, 2017, available at: https://radicalethno.org/documents/bjelichotrodder.pdf

Coulter, J. (1976). Harvey Sacks: A preliminary appreciation. *Sociology*, 10(3), 507–512.

Fitzgerald, R. (2019). The data and methodology of Harvey Sacks: Lessons from the archive. *Journal of Pragmatics*, 143, 205–214.

Fitzgerald, R. & Housley, W. (Eds.) (2015). *Advances in Membership Categorisation Analysis*. London: Sage.

Garfinkel, H. (1967[1991]). *Studies in Ethnomethodology*. Cambridge: Polity Press.

Garfinkel, H., Girton, G., Livingston, E., & Sacks, H. (1982). *Studies of Kids' Culture and Kids' Talk*, unpublished research project. Los Angeles: University of California.

Garfinkel, H. & Sacks, H. (1970). On Formal Structures of Practical Actions. In J.C. McKinney & E. Tiryakian (Eds.), *Theoretical Sociology* (pp. 338–366). New York, NY: Appleton Century Crofts.

Housley, W. & Fitzgerald, R. (2002). The reconsidered model of membership categorization analysis. *Qualitative Research*, 2(1), 59–83.

Housley, W., Webb, H., Edwards, A., Procter, R., & Jirotka, M. (2017). Digitizing Sacks? Approaching social media as data. *Qualitative Research*, 17(6), 627–644.

Liberman, K. (2019). A study at 30th street. *Language & Communication*, 65, 92–104.

Lynch, M. (1999). Silence in context: Ethnomethodology and social theory. *Human Studies*, 22, 211–233.

Lynch, M. (2017). Garfinkel, Sacks and formal structures: Collaborative origins, divergences and the vexed unity of ethnomethodology and conversation analysis. Keynote Address, *IIEMCA 2017: A Half-Century of Studies International Institute for Ethnomethodology and Conversation Analysis*, Otterbein College, Westerville, OH, July 10–13, 2017, available at: https://radicalethno.org/documents/lynchbanquet.pdf

Lynch, M. (2019). Garfinkel, Sacks and formal structures: Collaborative origins, divergences and the history of ethnomethodology and conversation analysis. *Human Studies*, 1–16. DOI: https://doi.org/10.1007/s10746-019-09510-w.

Lynch, M. & Bogen, D. (1994). Harvey Sacks's primitive natural science. *Theory, Culture & Society*, 11(4), 65–104.

McHoul, A. (2005). Aspects of aspects: On Harvey Sacks's 'Missing' book, Aspects of the sequential organization of conversation (1970). *Human Studies*, 28(2), 113–128.

Peyrot, M. (1982). Understanding ethnomethodology: A remedy for some common misconceptions. *Human Studies*, 5(1), 261–283.

Sacks, H. (1963). Sociological description. *Berkeley Journal of Sociology*, 8(1), 1–16.

Sacks, H. (1974). On the analysability of stories by children. In R. Turner (Ed.), *Ethnomethodology: Selected Readings* (pp. 216–232). Harmondsworth: Penguin Education.

Sacks, H. (1995 I & II). *Lectures on Conversation (Volumes I and II)*. Edited by G. Jefferson with introduction by E. A. Schegloff. Oxford: Blackwell.

Sacks, H., Schegloff, E.A., & Jefferson, G. (1974). A simplest systematics for the organization of turn-taking for conversation. *Language*, 50(4), 696–735.

Schegloff, E.A. (1995). Introduction. In H. Sacks (Ed.), *Lectures on Conversation, Volume 1* (pp. ix–lxii). Oxford: Blackwell.

Silverman, D. (1998). *Harvey Sacks: Social Science and Conversation Analysis*. Oxford: Oxford University Press.

Stokoe, E. (2012). Moving forward with membership categorization analysis: Methods for systematic analysis. *Discourse Studies*, 14(3), 277–303. DOI: 10.1177/14614456124415342012.

Watson, D.R. (2015). De-reifying categories. In R. Fitzgerald & W. Housley (Eds.), *Advances in Membership Categorisation Analysis* (pp. 23–50). London: Sage.

2 Discovering Sacks

Rod Watson

In September 1967, I came down from the University of Leicester, England, with a BA and MA in Sociology and took up an academic post in the Department of Sociology at Didsbury College of Education, Manchester. Leicester was a, perhaps the, leading university in Europe for sociology; still, I had an uneasy feeling that much of the sociology I had learned in Leicester was on the verge of obsolescence. Change was in the air, or seemed to be.

I looked around for new bearings in the discipline. Things were happening. In Britain, there were developments in sociology that supposedly espoused the radical politics of the time. Many of these developments were false starts – the 1960s were redolent with false starts – and did not last long. For instance, one of the most fashionable was the York (later the National) Deviancy Symposium, which in general tried to force together a vulgar interactionism with a vulgar Marxism in the analysis of crime. What this produced, in fact, was an apparently political radicalism but an obvious methodological conservatism. To me, this was the 'same old, same old', and this pattern was repeatedly found as I rummaged around in the discipline.

However, Didsbury College degrees were officially ratified by the University of Manchester, and the sociology degrees were overseen by the Department of Social Anthropology and Sociology there. This necessarily brought me into a relationship with that department. Unbeknownst to me at the time, that relationship was to set the scene for the new bearings that I sought. For a start, the anthropological 'side' of the department had a profound influence on the sociology 'side'. There was something of an emphasis on observation-based fieldwork, whereas sociology in sociology departments was usually 'top–down' or even theoreticist. In Manchester, the 'ground-floor-up' approach meant that the Chicago ethnographies, especially the 'interactionist' ones, were both understood and valorised. A couple of brilliant young sociologists there, John Lee and Wes Sharrock, espoused and sought to advance this naturalistic approach, and their other interests – Schutz's phenomenology, a bit of Garfinkel, Goffman, linguistic or 'analytic' philosophy (John Lee had been a student of the philosopher Alan White) – directed them towards that naturalistic orientation. I happened to know much of that material too (e.g. Peter Winch's philosophy), and so John and Wes's interests made a lot of sense to me and served as an essential background for our collective acquisition of ethnomethodology and conversation analysis.

In spring 1966, Erving Goffman came to the University of Manchester as Visiting Simon Professor, invited by the Department of Social Anthropology and Sociology. He presented an early version of his 'frame analysis' which, inter alia, was meant as an attack on Schutz's notion of the paramountcy of the natural attitude over 'tensions' such as dreams, fantasies, ludic experiences and the like. Wes later produced a critique of Goffman's argument (Sharrock, 1976). In Wes and John's debates with Goffman, the name of Garfinkel came up; of course, Garfinkel was on the 'Schutzian side' of the debate, but Goffman did say that Garfinkel was to publish a book, *Studies in Ethnomethodology*, in the following year. In fact, the book had proved difficult to get accepted by any publisher, and it was only through Goffman's good offices that his own publisher, Prentice-Hall, agreed to publish it at all.

When it appeared, *Studies* created an enormous stir and, predictably, some very hostile reactions. Although some parts of the book were lucidly, wittily, even beautifully, written, much of Garfinkel's writing was dense and obscure. Too often, the style was *obscurum per obscurius*. If one knew some phenomenology – Schutz, Scheler and so on – Garfinkel's concepts were somewhat less challenging, but his text could still be fiendishly difficult in parts. Anyway, phenomenology was not a major part of sociological training: in fact, sociologists were often 'trained out' of it. Garfinkel's prose was often highly compressed, leading Wes to suggest that most sociologists could only express the content of a single paragraph of Garfinkel's by writing a full article or even a monograph. The compression and outlandish vocabulary meant one had to grind through the book very slowly, often re-reading whole sections more than once. It was a Sisyphean task. However, for Wes, John and I, the book had a huge impact.

In the Preface to *Studies in Ethnomethodology*, in making his acknowledgements, Garfinkel (1967) said, 'Harvey Sacks must be mentioned particularly because his extraordinary writings and lectures have served as critical resources' (p. viii). Who was this Harvey Sacks? Although Sacks had studied with him, Goffman had not mentioned Sacks, his graduate student, to John and Wes. They, and I when I arrived, began over the next couple of years to write to Garfinkel and many of his associates – Sacks, Edward Rose and others – and in return we received very many manuscripts. In 1969, Wes received a first batch of Sacks's lectures, cyclostyled or mimeographed, and the package was posted by airmail – the first of many over the ensuing years.

The lectures were indeed extraordinary, unprecedented. Sacks's few published writings seemed to be as almost as obdurate in style as Garfinkel's, but the lectures were more accessible. That is not to say they were highly accessible, for they preserved the way that Sacks actually spoke (with the exception of the uncomfortably long pauses that characterised his speech): what we had in the lectures was Sacks, with his extraordinary mind, thinking aloud. The lectures seemed to be delivered 'on the hoof' and tracked Sacks's mental meanderings. In the end, however, one found that he had noticed things that others (we) had not. Sacks had come up with analytic insights that really came from 'left field', insights that seemed unimaginable. This was sociology, but not as we had ever known it. It was the new bearing I had been looking for.

The particularly useful thing about what Sacks sent us is that they were *lectures*, teaching devices, and that made them somewhat easier to learn from. There was no such 'ladder' in Sacks's publications. Indeed, the design features of the lectures for pedagogy deserve far more attention than they have been accorded: for instance, Schegloff's (1992a, 1992b) otherwise excellent 'Introduction' to Sacks's published lectures accords only a couple of pages plus a few comments to the pedagogic nature of the lectures. An often-found feature of even the content of lectures is to raise to visibility phenomena that we take so much for granted, to argue that they were important objects of study and to show how we might analyse them. The lectures are clearly designed for students who know very little about such things, but also for those who would read the mimeoed print-outs later. They covered a truly extraordinary wide range of matters, and those critics such as Hammersley who accuse Sacks's CA of narrowness should consider whether it is the narrowness of their own reading that is the real issue.

Given Garfinkel's tribute to Sacks, and Sacks's fulsome acknowledgement to Garfinkel, I felt that it made sense to attempt to find links between Garfinkel's and Sacks's approaches. On the surface, their analytic styles seemed so different, as did the substantive topics they addressed. Garfinkel's extraordinary study of an intersexed person, 'Agnes', seemed on the face of it so different from Sacks's allusions to gender in terms of 'membership categorisation' practices.

Naturally, I subjected Garfinkel's *Studies* and Sacks's lectures to prolonged and intense reading. In doing so, I was able to dismiss some of the simplistic or reductive conceptions that prevailed at the time about the relation between Garfinkel's and Sacks's work. One of these reductions was that Garfinkel provided the theory of ethnomethodology and that Sacks provided the empirical application to a particular phenomenon, conversation. One set of sociologists in particular, at Goldsmith's College, conceived of Garfinkel as a new direction in sociological theory.

Of course, in conceptual terms, Garfinkel did effectuate a seismic shift conceptually speaking, but throughout his entire career he explicitly eschewed purely theory-driven concerns such as theory-derived, theory-formed descriptions of phenomena. Moreover, his *Studies* consist of an impressive set of empirical exhibitings of his conceptual shift – of coroners' work, jurors' work, the work of compiling and reading clinic records, and so on. In particular, we have the sustained, trailblazing empirical case study of the achievement of accountable sex status in an intersexed person; this study was from the 1950s, before such phenomena were seen by many as even comprising the proper stuff of sociology. The particular study is, of course, deeply conceptual in very many ways, such as in its consideration of game theory and its critique of the episodic nature of Goffman's treatment of self-presentation.

Similarly, Sacks, with his tenacious focus on conversation in his lectures, was involved in a sustained conceptual exercise. From the very beginning, he showed a concern for conversational practices – membership categorization and utterance sequencing – and he taught that these practices were methodic, reproducible: they were ethnomethods. Speaking in turns was a case in point. In doing so, Sacks made available for sociology and beyond a phenomenon, conversational interaction, that few social scientists had recognised or taken up in a sustained way (some social psychologists, small group sociologists and some anthropologists such as Goffman, Ethel Albert and Dell Hymes constituted partial exceptions). Consequently, the 'theory' and 'application' binary did not describe the division of labour between the two: the fact was that, by virtue of devising methodologically radical new concepts, Garfinkel and Sacks submitted those concepts to empirical constraints. These constraints included any eschewed methodological irony, the refusal to set up an analytic frame of reference that was in competition with, or that downgraded or relativized, ordinary members' own common-sense reasoning concerning the phenomenon under examination.

Nowhere was the non-ironic cast of Garfinkel and Sacks's work more evident than in their concern for 'sociological description'. Garfinkel's espousal of Schutz's phenomenology sets the scene, here. Both Schutz and Garfinkel argued that the social world the professional sociologist purports to describe 'for the first time' has in fact already been described, and in a competent, sophisticated way, by ordinary society members themselves. Whether they recognise it, whether they deny it, this is the ineluctable fact of the matter. Indeed, the issue of sociological description is, for Garfinkel, an absolutely generic feature of sociology, one that is, too often, passed over. Both Garfinkel and Sacks focused on the generic features of sociology, a 'back to basics' approach to sociology across its *entire* extent – so much for narrowness.

For Sacks, too, description is a basic issue. His first article (Sacks, 1963), from its title onwards, was clearly intended to show the importance of description for members and analysts alike. Subsequently, and particularly in his early lectures, the fundamental importance of description is to be found in his extensive concern for the describing of persons as a methodic practice, a practice with a 'systematics' of its own. The observations in his lectures on membership categorization, as one form of person description, stand as a reminder of the importance Sacks attached to the issue of description – descriptions of persons, events, action and settings in society. He did not exempt sociologists from his consideration of description as culturally methodic practice (Sacks, 1999; Schegloff, 1999), one that, willy-nilly, is grounded in the descriptive practices of ordinary members. Indeed, no matter how rigorous her/his formal socialization into professional sociology, the professional sociologist always perforce encounters her/his object of study in the first instance as an ordinary society member, an ordinary describer of her/his social object, an ordinary practical reasoner, an ordinary speaker-hearer; this is Schutz's and Garfinkel's point about the primacy of the natural attitude, the attitude of everyday life. For most mainstream sociologies, this is an awkward fact, one to be buried, denied or, at least, trivialized (recall Durkheim's dismissive comments concerning 'popular conceptions'). For an ethnomethodologist or conversation analyst, the sociologist as ordinary member is something to be acknowledged, to be mined for the resources it yields. Garfinkel and Sacks agree that, whatever we know about society, we know it in the first instance in common-sense terms. This had a huge effect on how I set up my own sociological projects.

However, when it comes to mainstream sociologies, there is a certain divergence of Garfinkel's and Sacks's positions. As Richard Fitzgerald (2018a) points out, Garfinkel sets up his ethnomethodology as an irreconcilable alternative to orthodox, 'formal analytic' sociologies, but he defined ethnomethodology by contrasting it with orthodox ones. In this sense, he treated orthodox sociologies as, sort of, 'having a place' in ethnomethodological study; indeed, he alludes to an ethnomethodology–formal analysis 'pair', related if only through a gestalt switch. By contrast, Sacks's position is that orthodox sociologies should be, by and large, ignored, and that we should start again in the discipline. Of course, this distinction is not an absolute one. For instance, Sacks valorised the Chicago ethnographies as just about the only thing in (orthodox) sociologies that are even worthy of criticism. For Sacks, almost all sociology was to be ignored. Sacks, for good reason, would not compromise on this – rather like his early hero, the sociological outlander C. Wright Mills. In Sacks's lectures, after his graduate work (Sacks, 1999), one certainly does not find any dialogue with orthodox sociologies, and, as time goes on, we find him subjecting his sociology more and more to interdisciplinary concerns. By contrast, Garfinkel's work can be read as an uncompromising dialogue with orthodox sociology.

Despite this difference in orientation towards orthodox sociologies, both Garfinkel and Sacks, in their different ways, address the most primitive terms of sociology. They both have a 'back to basics' approach, such as sociology's use of descriptive practices, the conception of sociological theory as practice. I learned much from this. Garfinkel initially set me on the radical praxeology trail, but it was Sacks, in his lectures rather than his publications, who showed me the huge range of conceptual and empirical issues that could be addressed through taking this turn and, even more importantly, showed me a great range of ways of doing so – ways of thinking, ways of handling data. He was an astonishing 'lateral thinker' about all kinds of things – the diagnosis of depression, utterances such as 'how are you?' and so on. It was C. Wright Mills who coined the term 'the sociological imagination'. Seldom can there have been a better characterisation of Sacks's 'take' on phenomena such as sociological description (see Sacks, 1999, and also his many analyses of membership categorization as a set of common-sense descriptive practices). As it evolves, his approach facilitates a rigorously anti-cognitivistic approach (see, e.g., his observations on 'understanding'), a resolutely non-ironic approach and, with Garfinkel, a radical approach to context that linguists and discourse analysts, even the revisionist ones, have not yet properly taken on board – for example, Garfinkel's notion of 'gestalt contexture' does not feature at all in a famous collection on 'context' by Duranti and Goodwin (1992) and has hardly appeared since then outside ethnomethodology.

All of these orientations helped me greatly in writing my own work, starting with my PhD. I had gathered data from calls to a 'crisis intervention centre' and decided to re-study Sacks's famous 'New Year's Eve' analysis in which he analysed such calls. I wondered if I would find similar phenomena to those Sacks found: I was geared up for a possible critique of his work. However, I found myself confronting Sacks's own dictum about analysing natural data as 'they happen to fall'. He said that, in such data, you 'find order at all points'. I did, and I discovered that the order I found had dimensions and characteristics that – to the best of my knowledge – even Sacks had not described: this order was far from unidimensional. I found myself pursuing these new-found dimensions and, in my doctoral thesis, I largely moved on from my critique of Sacks into considerations of 'moral profiles', organizational relevancies and the like (Watson, 1975). But I never abandoned Sacks's 'analytic mentality'. So far as I am aware, mine was the first PhD thesis in Britain (and maybe even Europe) to be largely conversation analytic, largely Sacksian, in orientation.

Continuing to discover Sacks

Unlike many collections, the current volume represents an unusually wide range of the interests and concerns that animated Sacks's work. As we learn more and more from Sacks's lectures and archives about these concerns, we may hope that this is the first of many collections and other productions with that ambition. The contributors to this volume come from several disciplines; this illustrates the fact that, over the decades, people in many disciplines have found inspiration in Sacks's thought. This being the case, it is worth noting that, although Sacks never ceased to espouse a resolutely sociological approach (in his own new sense of the discipline), his work, along with that of his frequent co-authors Emanuel Schegloff and Gail Jefferson, came to be increasingly explicitly directed towards an interdisciplinary readership. This is discernible from, among other things, the journals in which he or they placed their later papers.

As Fitzgerald (2018b) has shown, these submissions to both sociological and non-sociological journals encountered many impediments presented by editors who were applying frames of reference deriving from the then current frames of those disciplines. This is evident from much of the early work being published in edited volumes as well as the difficulties getting published in academic journals, not least in the publication of the 'Simplest Systematics' paper.

It is to be hoped, then, that this collection will act as a catalyst for the further exploration of the scope and penetration of Sacks's concerns – not to 'curate' Sacks's work, to preserve it in aspic, but, importantly, to derive pointers for future analyses. This is not, of course, to detract from those studies that focalise in depth one aspect of Sacks's work, but to complement them, to balance and fill out the picture.

One possible outcome of this inclusive approach is that those involved in what Edward Rose termed 'ethno-inquiries' might work towards a convergence and, indeed, unification of areas of Sacks's work that are currently often treated separately – say, the sequential analysis of utterances and membership categorisation analysis in talk-in-interaction. There would seem to be clear benefits to be gained from the synergies deriving from this – for example, in the consideration of how a unified treatment of sequential and membership categorisation analysis might afford us a new 'take' on Sacks's generic concerns such as those of ordinary sociological description in natural language use. I hope that this collection will be considered in that inclusive spirit.

References

Duranti, C. and Goodwin, C. (Eds.) (1992). *Rethinking Context: Language as an Interactive Phenomenon*. Cambridge: Cambridge University Press.

Fitzgerald, R. (2018a). *1962 Seminar. Sacks and Garfinkel: On Ethnomethodology and Sociological Inquiry*. Presentation to the Hong Kong Macau Ethnomethodology and Conversation Analysis data group. University of Hong Kong, October 2018.

Fitzgerald, R. (2018b). *Drafting the Simplest Systematics*. Paper presented at the Australian Institute of Ethnomethodology and Conversation Analysis (AIEMCA) November 2018. University of Macau.

Garfinkel, H. (1967). *Studies in Ethnomethodology*. New Jersey: Prentice Hall.

Sacks, H. (1963). Sociological description. *Berkeley Journal of Sociology*, 8(1): 1–16.

Sacks, H. (1999). Max Weber's Ancient Judaism. *Theory, Culture & Society*, 16(1): 31–39.

Schegloff, E.A. (1992a). Introduction. In H. Sacks (Ed.), *Lectures on Conversation, Volume 1* (pp. ix–lxii). Oxford: Blackwell.

Schegloff, E.A. (1992b). Introduction. In H. Sacks (Ed.), *Lectures on Conversation, Volume 2* (pp. ix–lii). Oxford: Blackwell.

Schegloff, E.A. (1999). On Sacks on Weber on *Ancient Judaism*: Introductory notes and interpretive resources. *Theory, Culture and Society*, 16(1): 1–29.

Sharrock, W.W. (1976). Review of *Frame Analysis*. *Sociology*, 10: 332–334.

Watson, D.R. (1975). *Calls for Help: A Sociological Analysis of Telephoned Communication to a 'Crisis Intervention Centre'*. PhD thesis, Department of Sociology, University of Warwick, Coventry, England.

3 Action, meaning and understanding

Seeing sociologically with Harvey Sacks

Michael Mair and Wes Sharrock

Harvey Sacks suffers no want of authoritative interpreters, and reading, for example, the likes of Coulter (1976), Schegloff (1992a, 1992b), Lynch and Bogen (1994), Watson's commentaries (1994, 2009) or Silverman's introductions (1998) certainly deepens our understanding by revealing layers in Sacks's work we might otherwise miss. Nonetheless, although these guides are invaluable, the real "joy of Sacks", as Fitzgerald (2012) memorably puts it, lies in reading and engaging with his work for ourselves, as anyone who has begun to delve into *Lectures in Conversation*, his transcribed lectures, quickly comes to see. The ground Sacks covers, his breadth of interests and the diverse range of examples and materials he focuses on mean his work affords all manner of opportunities for engagement – returning to it, there is always something else to be discovered in it and taken away (also see Bjelić 2017; Lynch 2017; Fitzgerald 2019, for just some of the more recent returns). Rather than try to anticipate a variety of possible engagements, however, this chapter attempts something much more limited: it charts just one line through Sacks's wider body of work, concentrating on the distinctive way Sacks handles and helps us to handle the relationship between action, meaning and understanding. Although that relationship has long been treated as a problem in and for the social sciences, based on his detailed analyses of our everyday practices, Sacks refused to follow suit and treat it as a problem for the sociologist at all. For Sacks, to understand the meaning of someone's actions is just to grasp what they're doing, and that is not a theoretical but a practical matter, one internal to and resolved in social life. Although Sacks did not dwell on this insight, but put it to work in developing a new way of practising sociology, tracing its bases and what it shows about the value of his approach to doing sociology is salutary in several respects. Drawing from material across his lectures and published writings, the aim of this chapter is, therefore, to do just that and highlight one of the ways in which Sacks shows us how to see sociologically.

In that, this chapter is also an attempt to excavate the grounds of and thus communicate something about our own first engagements with Sacks. Reading Sacks for the first time is an intellectually revelatory experience in many ways. It is something we did some 40 years apart, with one (Sharrock), along with other colleagues at Manchester, making his way through mimeographed copies of the transcribed lectures distributed shortly after they had been delivered by Sacks (a group that also had the benefit of meeting and discussing Sacks's work with Sacks himself; see Carlin, this volume), but with the other (Mair) making his way through the print version of the collected lectures as a postgraduate student in discussion with the first-generation Manchester ethnomethodologists who, like Sharrock, originally got them hot off the press. That 40-year gap is not negligible, of course, but nor does it overdetermine a reading of Sacks's work. Any first-time reader of Sacks, and something similar could be said in relation to the work of Harold Garfinkel, will encounter the same "shock of the new" (Hughes 1980). And it is a shock; a jolt indeed. Until you read Sacks's work, it's difficult to imagine that sociology could be approached *that* way. After you read it, the idea you could approach it any *other* way becomes difficult to imagine. In light of that before and after contrast, we want to draw out something that connected us as first readers. That is, we both read Sacks on the understanding that Sacks intended his work to be read *as* sociology. Sacks was ambivalent about sociology (1963), and conversation analysis has drifted away from it as it has developed. However, as part of what we might term a local "anthropology of reading" (Livingston 1995), here our own, we want to stress the value of preserving that connection by engaging in an explicitly sociological reading of Sacks. For all the flaws he diagnosed in it, sociology provided Sacks and, hence, his readers with problems for thinking with and pushing against, and it is an aspect of that critical dialogue with sociology that we seek to foreground here.

Language, perception and social activities

One of Harvey Sacks's most significant and enduring intellectual contributions, attested to in various ways by all the contributors to this volume, was to show through fine-grained empirical analyses that our language comprises heterogeneous collections of methods of practical action and reasoning whose coherence, orderliness and stability are grounded in their use by us, as members of society, on actual occasions. Rather than focusing on what "language" was in itself, whatever that might mean, as if "it" somehow stood apart from our practices, Sacks demonstrated time and again, particularly in his lectures, that to talk of language was to talk not just of what we do with language, but of how we go about doing it, typically with others, in all manner of situations. Considerations of recorded talk thus became a central focus for a respecification of the "problem of language", with ordinary conversations providing a primary site for studying "the [variety of] methods persons use in doing social life" (Sacks 1984a: 21), that is, how they "do … whatever they do, in the ways that they do it." (Sacks 1992: V1 416).

Sacks's influence on how we might revisit (mis)conceptions of language by attending to its ordinary use is profound; however, his work also raised a range of other concerns, some fleeting, some recurrent. One of the recurrent concerns, conventionally framed, was perception. Sacks was interested, for example, in explicating how parties to a conversation come to see, to borrow from Austin, what others are doing with words – not least because that might involve something being done to them (e.g., Sacks 1992: V1 350–351; 417–426) – but extended his examination of seeing as understanding beyond communicative exchanges to how we ordinarily and routinely get the measure of scenes of social life and what can relevantly be said to be happening within them – a concern explicitly topicalised in a study of the methods the police employ to assess "moral character" (Sacks 1972) and found more generally throughout his work. For Sacks, and this shall provide our point of departure, part of "seeing sociologically" (Garfinkel 2015) involved explicating how any and all "activities … are done, and done recognizably" (Sacks 1992: V1 245).

Just as the phenomena of language, when approached via Sacks's characteristic ways of working, decomposed into assemblies of locally organised social activities (Lynch & Bogen 1994), so perception did too. Undermining the very idea of a unified theory of perception as he went, social, scientific or otherwise, Sacks provided a series of vivid examples of ways of seeing and their ordinary social grounds – that is, of "praxiologies of perception" as they have subsequently come to be called (Coulter & Parsons 1990). The observability of social action – that is, the connections between action and its recognition and the "possibility" of both (Sacks 1992: V1 422; see also Livingston 1987: 59–64; Wieder & Pratt 1990) – was a major focus in this. As Sacks puts it, "social activities are observable; you can see them all around you, and you can write them down … If you think you can see it, that means we can build an observational study, and we can build a natural study" (Sacks 1992: V1 28). Moreover, because social activities are "routinely observable" (Sacks 1992: V1 31) – that is, available to members of society's (or, more simply, members') ordinary ways of looking "as anyone can easily find" (Sacks 1992: V1 40) – sociology does not need to "await developments in … genetics or analyses of the light spectra [i.e. the presumed 'scientific' bases of perception] to gain a secure position from which members' knowledge, and the activities for which it is relevant, might be investigated" (see also here Lynch 1993; Lynch & Bogen 1994). Instead, given social activities *are* observable, sociology can instead proceed with the work of describing "how it is that any activities … which members do [are done] in such a way as to be recognizable as such *to members*" (Sacks 1992: V1 245; emphasis added). For Sacks, the question thus becomes: "For anybody … to do … an activity, what makes it recognizable as whatever it happens to be?" (Sacks 1992: V1 422). From there,

> [what] we want to do then … is to provide for how it is that something that's done is recognized for what it is, where the big thing is that some action is recognized as a something, as a case of some activity.
>
> (Sacks 1992: V1 236–237)

Armed with these insights, Sacks got on with his observational studies rather than setting out lengthy programmatics as a prelude to them. We want to return to these issues and some of the better-known sections of the *Lectures*, however, because we think there are things worth emphasising in the explicitly sociological bases of what Sacks was seeking to do. It can be easy to forget the enterprise's starting points and the manner in which Sacks both responded to but also departed from conventional social science (mis)treatments of the phenomena he concentrated his analytical attention on. Recovering those starting points may strike some as unnecessary. However, there are dangers in forgetfulness: confusions and misunderstandings can proliferate, for instance, if we lose sight of the care Sacks took in setting out the grounds of his observational social science, dangers we will expand on next.

Starting with not arriving at "the action"

It is easy to be deceived by Sacks's apparently "naive" stance on what would count as sociologically relevant phenomena or an adequate treatment of them. He did indeed emphasise "unmotivated looking" and worked with "found" objects conventional social science by and large rejected as too "small" or "uninteresting" to take up and systematically study (Sacks 1984a). Yet, as his various papers and off-hand references in the *Lectures* indicate, that naivety was deeply informed; Sacks was steeped in the theoretical, methodological and empirical literatures of the social and indeed natural sciences, but remarked that he found social science "strange" and sought to develop his approach to sociological description independently of the standard presuppositions that characterised the bulk of work conducted in it (Sacks 1963). In working through an alternative approach to the study of social life, Sacks thus paid close attention to the kinds of work it was to be an alternative to. Missing that can have consequences; cultivated naivety is one thing, genuine naivety quite another. One area in particular where those consequences can be particularly pronounced connects to the classical sociological problem concerning the relationship between action, meaning and understanding.

As Wittgenstein (whose work Sacks admired) once noted, the "*general* notion of … meaning … [is] a haze which makes clear vision impossible" (1953: §5; emphasis added), and, from their discipline's inception, sociologists have found themselves lost in the conceptual "fog" surrounding it. Although committed to the study of social life, sociologists have had great trouble specifying what would constitute an adequate account of what people do and do routinely. The typical solution has been to devise external criteria by which the sociologist could independently arrive at a determination of the meaningful character of social action, but it is a solution which creates its own problems. Even Max Weber's attempt (e.g., 1962) to found an interpretive sociology that would overcome these problems ended up following the same unstable twin track others had laid before him, separating out action and meaning by treating their relations as an observer's problem – that is, as something to be decided outside the social activities under examination and resolved through analytical means (Sacks 1963, 1999). Sociology has thus been caught in the grip of the view that, unless the discipline's investigators secured meaning, meaning couldn't be secured. Despairing at the difficulties associated with that task, many social scientists simply sought to do without meaning altogether, offering instead various reductive schemes in which action would be accounted for in more "basic" terms. The 20th century thus saw a raft of reductionist projects that aimed to achieve that goal, but with no more success than their "integrationist" precursors. In seeking to do away with the meaningful bases of our ordinary practices in favour of something putatively more elementary, these projects effectively did away with the sense of those practices, making them systematically *un*recognisable. They had not been accounted for; they had simply been blocked from analytical view, and pretending something is not there has never been a particularly satisfactory way of dealing with it, whether among ostriches or sociologists.

As Sacks saw clearly, it is their starting point that generates the intractable analytical problems as well as the need for increasingly extreme measures to "resolve" them. Once we have accepted there is something called "action" and something else called "meaning" that somehow stands separately from it or is layered on top it, and an analytical reconciliation is required if the two are to be brought back together again, we are already lost. It is not that people do things and then find meaning in them as part of a separate process. It is, instead, that action is something that is done recognisably and in ordinary, routine and unproblematic ways – something Sacks reminds us of time and again in his work. That is, we do not see some doing and then work out what it is that has been done as if that were an addition to the action.[1] Instead, we see what was done in its doing; action and meaning are, as we might say, "internally related" (Read, Hutchinson & Sharrock 2009: 96). Moreover, and this was Sacks's central insight and one he developed in conjunction with Harold Garfinkel, "understanding that relation" isn't and could not be the analyst's problem in any primary sense. Insofar as it is a problem (and it generally isn't, as Wittgenstein reminds us), it is one that is encountered and dealt with by members of society on specific occasions in the course of their ongoing dealings with one another. It is a practical matter, not a theoretical one. In starting with the ordinary recognisability of social action in its contexts, taking action and its displayed meaning together, Sacks short-circuits the analytical problems that have continued to waylay conventional social science: we cannot advance down the twin track when we begin where Sacks begins.

Unfortunately, the picture of action and meaning as separate retains its grip on the sociological imagination. In setting out to undertake an "observational study", it is all too easy to imagine that the best way to develop an understanding of what is going on in any social scene is first to watch the doings and then arrive at an account of what has been done – but then, to repeat what we said above, we have simply reinstated the same insoluble problem. As Sacks notes, that is precisely *not* how members of the society either act or recognise actions in the doing. Yet the misconception persists, often in research that invokes Sacks as a precursor. We therefore want to show next how a return to Sacks can help dispel that misconception.

Natural observational studies

"Natural observational studies" as conceived and practised by Sacks have a particular character. Some elements of what Sacks was proposing and doing can seem relatively transparent. For example, according to Sacks, "what we want to watch for is the kind of components that complex activities have, and the ways that sets of complex activities can be put together" (1992: V1 425). Proceeding in this way, "it may be that we can come up with findings of some considerable generality by looking at very singular, particular things. By asking what it takes for those things to have come off" (1992: V1 298). The question is, however, what things? How are they to be identified? This is important, because it can sometimes appear as if Sacks is advocating a sociologically inflected version of something like the work of Eadweard Muybridge, the Victorian photographer who undertook some of the first photographic studies of bodies in motion, capturing, for example, the "component parts" of the "complex" physical movements involved in such things as walking, climbing stairs or throwing a discus. In Muybridge's photo studies, a specific human body (often his own) was made to stand for *any* body by the instantiation of what were treated as typical forms (see Figure 3.1), something that could be and was extended to equivalent studies of how non-human animals typically move too. In its pursuit of generality via specifics, then, Muybridge's project may seem to have affinities with the analytical "aesthetic" Sacks outlines (1992: V1 113).

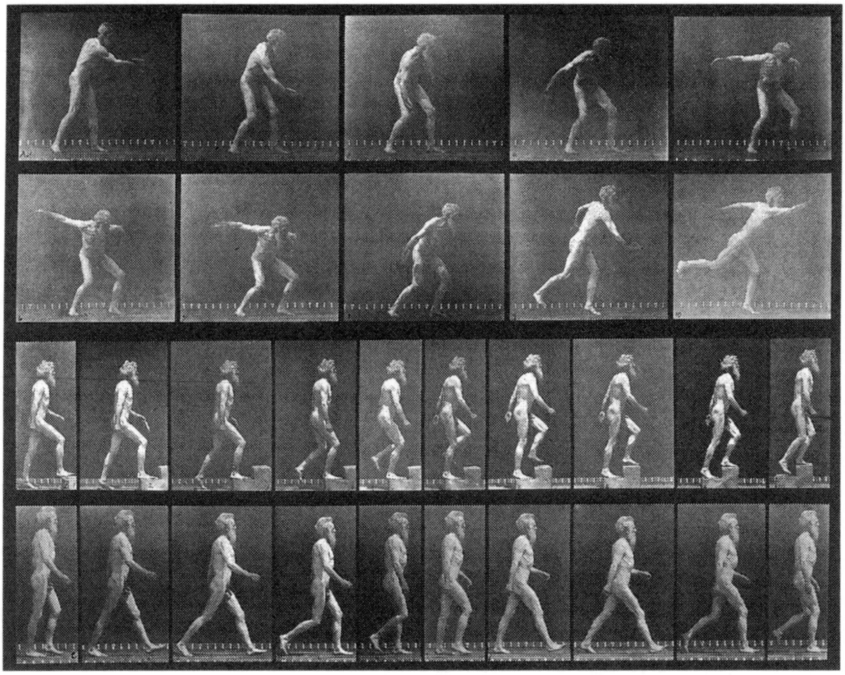

Figure 3.1 Eadweard Muybridge's studies of bodies in motion[2]

The parallels in approach may seem clear: pick some quotidian activity, meticulously record how it "comes off" in detail and then construct an account of the components it is built up out of based upon, ideally, a mechanically recovered and "replayable" record. However, the idea that Sacks's observational sociology is akin to stop-motion photography is misleading in several respects. Part of the problem derives from the idea that we could come to an understanding of social activities just by inspecting them (Sacks 1963: 15). Although we might be able to begin a study of the biomechanical organisation of typical human movements based on Muybridge-style pictures – that is, flexing joints, twisting ligaments, progressively tensed and relaxed muscles and so on – this is not a sociological account. Nor does it provide materials that might be used in developing one. This is primarily because observational studies, at least in Sacks's hands, proceed from the recognition that "observation" is something that those being studied engage in as well. What is more, their ways of looking are analytically primitive, the sociological observer's derivative. That is, observation is already a feature of the social world and, because it is, it has to be accounted for; it cannot be naively employed in accounts of its organisation, as this would presuppose its availability to and for description, the very aim of the exercise (Sacks 1963, 1992: V1 295, 1999). There is in Sacks's work, therefore, "no room in the world" (Garfinkel & Sacks 1970: 176; Sacks 1992: V1 516) for "just looking" – that is, for observing, scrutinising, eyeballing or otherwise sizing up what members of society are doing (Sacks 1992: V1 258; cf. Foucault 1973: ix). Witnessing is already part of the action and has to be dealt with on that basis. As Sacks himself put it,

> [What] I have been proposing could be restated as follows: For members, activities are observables. They see activities. They see persons doing intimacy, they see persons lying, etc. ... And that poses for us the task of being behaviorists in this sense: Finding how it is that people can produce sets of actions that provide that others can see such things.
>
> (1992: V1 119)

That characterisation is important; if this is a form of naturalistic behavioural study, it is so in a highly qualified way. Such studies are behaviouristic only in the sense that they focus on how *members* go about making use of "procedures to find the sense of some set of observables" (Sacks 1992: V1 120). Contra behaviourism, however, Sacks's "observational studies" treat observation as part of the phenomenon and not a privileged means for accessing it. Those studies unavoidably start where members start, with the witnessed and witnessable scenes of social life and the sense those scenes demonstrably have for those within them. As Schegloff neatly puts it,

> This way of working, then, mixes a *kind* of naturalism (in its insistence on noticing and crediting the potential seriousness of particulars of the natural occurrences of conduct) with the ethnomethodological concern for Members'

> methods for the production of a mundane world and commonsense understandings of it.
>
> (1992a: xxx; emphasis added)

Seeing sociologically, for Sacks, turns on just these considerations. This comes across very strongly in Lecture 11 of Sacks's Fall 1964–Spring 1965 lecture series, "On Exchanging Glances" (1992: V1 81–94). In the lecture, Sacks discusses an assignment he had set the class in which they had to report back on observations they had made of people exchanging glances. In a much-quoted passage, Sacks has the following to say:

> Let me make a couple of remarks about the problem of "feigning ignorance". I found in these papers that people will occasionally say things like, "I didn't really know what was going on, but I made the inference that he was looking at her because she's an attractive girl". So one claims to not really know. And here's a first thought I have. I can fully well understand how you come to say that. It's part of the way in which what's called your education here gets in the way of your doing what you in fact know how to do. And you begin to call things "concepts" and acts "inferences", when nothing of the sort is involved. And that nothing of the sort is involved, is perfectly clear in that if it were the case that you didn't know what was going on – if you were the usual made up observer, the man from Mars – then the question of what you would see would be a far more obscure matter than that she was an attractive girl, perhaps. How would you go about seeing in the first place that one was looking at the other, seeing what they were looking at, and locating those features which are perhaps relevant?
>
> (1992: V1 83)

He continues,

> And that's why it's sort of a pain to intellectualize this stuff such that you already talk about it as though, "I see a blob, and then I infer that it's my mother because she's a blob like that", when what you see is not that … You may find that some philosopher has convinced you of this. But "inference" has another kind of use.
>
> (1992: V1 86)

In "On Doing Being Ordinary", Sacks underlines his non-inferential, non-interpretive point again:

> [People] are not [from their perspective] arguing anything, they are not imagining anything … [All] they are doing is scanning a scene to see what is happening.
>
> (Sacks 1984b: 420–421; adapted)

The sorts of issue involved in conducting studies that would not (pseudo)intellectualise the recognisability of social activities are illustrated in "The Navy Pilot" (1992: V1 205–222). There, Sacks begins with a piece of "found data", a newspaper article, a typically brilliant examination of which leads him to the following point:

> Knowing thyself does not mean knowing something very private, it means knowing oneself as a member of a community, knowing, that is, the things that obtain for one, which obtain for persons commonly … [It does] not involve knowing something about one[self] which … [is] distinctive, or special, or private.
>
> (1992: V1 221)

Sacks, ever attendant to the need for analytical consistency, understood that these considerations apply equally to researchers as these are the local conditions of possibility for their work too. Insofar as social activities are available to overlooking analysts, it is because they are available in the first instance to members of society, where an "equally extraordinary part of this … [is] that they [typically also] know what it is that you saw, that they saw the same thing, … and they make the same assessment" (1992: V1 93). If this was not the case, then we would be in the position of the observers from Mars. This comes across in an exchange with a student at the end of the lecture on exchanging glances:

> *Q*: It seems like that was the basic assumption of the assignment; that we could notice them doing it [i.e., exchanging glances].
>
> *HS*: Right. It was the basic assumption, which could have been wrong. But of course it's not like I came into this world the day before I gave that assignment. I know that people can do this, I've watched it many times, and I take it that you've seen it also. However, people who get this far in their education are very prone to intellectualize the whole operation and not see it. And so you don't see [it] … you figure it's a philosophical impossibility, or you'd have to go through four years of analysis, etc.
>
> (1992: V1 94)

The lesson, as we see it, is straightforward: to proceed as if we came into the world the day before yesterday, to operate on the basis that we don't know what we're dealing with, is to deny the very bases of our whole enterprise. We may seek to offer procedural accounts that show how people go about producing actions recognised as such by others in the doing, but the action is where we begin. Where that is obscured, the whole edifice becomes unstable. On this last point, and as part of reaching a conclusion, we want to offer a brief comment on the ways in which a *natural* observational study, specifically, might address – by refusing to accept – the separation of action, meaning and understanding. We think Wittgenstein is again helpful here. As he puts it in the *Philosophical Investigations*,

> Commanding, questioning, recounting, chatting, are as much a part of our natural history as walking, eating, drinking, playing.
>
> (Wittgenstein 1953: §25)

He later adds,

> What we are supplying are really remarks on the natural history of human beings; we are not contributing curiosities however, but observations which no one has doubted, but which have escaped remark only because they are always before our eyes.
>
> (Wittgenstein 1953: §415)

Sacks's advocacy of "naturalism" seems to us to follow from similar insights. One of the initial missteps that led sociologists into trouble was to divide actions and meaning from the outset. The components of action were primitive and first on the scene, meanings secondary and arrived at after-the-fact, and one, it seemed, had to be dealt with independently of the other. This, in effect, created a special realm of activities involved in determining meaning that were supervenient on other apparently "more basic" forms of activity, a substrate of bodily movements, physical gestures and the like. Sacks, like Wittgenstein, wanted to collapse that artificial partition. Our tutored sensibilities, shaped by "what's called … [our] education" (Sacks ibid.), leave us blind to what is "before our eyes" (Wittgenstein ibid.), namely, the fact that meaningful activities are as much in the world as anything else. Equally plainly, however, Sacks, like Wittgenstein, knew we have to tailor our inquiries to the available particularities of the activities we are attempting to make sense of, such as exchanging glances. All activities require an approach suited to their particular character, and Sacks's great contribution was to open new vistas in that regard, whether by attending to the particularities of language-in-use or "how we see" on actual occasions (Sacks 1992: V1 488).

Conclusion

In this short, "alternative" sociological reading of Sacks's work, we have attempted to draw out aspects of his way of working through a consideration of his response to the problem of meaning in the social sciences. Based on that, we have argued that Sacks began his studies, in the first instance, from the position of "another member" (Garfinkel & Sacks 1970: 175; Sacks 1992: V1 486–488). That is, Sacks's starting point was the unproblematic recognisability of action in context, its "routine observability" for members of society on particular occasions. From there, Sacks would investigate its production procedurally, seeking to find ways members could have arrived at those "products" together. This, for Sacks, was the basis of "natural observational studies", studies in which observability would be treated as a phenomenon in its own right. What we have argued, drawing on passages from Sacks's lectures and writings, is that Sacks always understood such considerations to apply equally to the analyst's task in producing accounts of social action. That is, if "observation" is part of the phenomenon, social scientists can't hope to naively make use of it to study social life. Seeing sociologically with Harvey Sacks involves, then, attempts to come to terms with the sense witnessed scenes and witnessed activities have for members in the ways they routinely do.

This may strike many as yesterday's news, but we feel it is worth repeating. As social scientists, and ethnomethodologists and conversation analysts among them, increasingly make use of video in their studies of social life, for example, there is a danger that such studies collapse back into the sociology of the spectator. Muybridgean collages, under such conditions, can come to be seen as adequate sociological analyses. Such collages, however, resurrect the very problems Sacks's observational studies – that is, his studies of observability as an accomplished feature of contexts of practical (inter)action – worked to dissolve. Treating "meaningful actions", for instance, as amalgams of non-meaningful movements, gestures and other "more basic" elements of conduct puts the componential cart before the analytical horse. Ethnomethodology and conversation analysis may now be following different paths, but neither can afford to forget Sacks's starting points: both seek to treat common-sense knowledge of social structures, in all the ways it is observably displayed, as their fundamental phenomenon, but, even though they do, both still start from a social world whose features are known and knowable by virtue of it. Proceeding otherwise leads to a re-entanglement in "the problem of meaning". As Sacks shows us, the relationship between action, meaning and understanding is not ordinarily a problem at all; it is only when social activities are approached in a particular way that it becomes problematic – the problem of meaning is, thus, methodogenic, a conceptual oubliette of the social scientist's own devising. The only way of avoiding this self-constructed trap is to ensure the "methods persons use in doing social life" are recognised as the practical grounds of our inquiries too. We can watch or film people going about their affairs as much as we like, but it does not resolve the crucial prior problem: if we don't know what we are looking at, what the action properly speaking is, we cannot arrive at an account of how it was done. This because what was specifically done won't be available to us, leaving us to offer descriptions to a sociological void. That lesson remains as important as it was when Sacks first began his demonstrations of its salience in, to and for our everyday practices and, by extension, studies that might seek to get *their* measure. It is also an insight that remains as striking for us now as it did upon our first reading.

Notes

1 Indeed, if we did have to begin with doings, if that was all we had, we'd never be able to specify "where the action is" (Ebersole 2001). This is because an account of action in "brute" terms *fails* to specify the action at all (Ebersole 2001: 379; Read, Hutchinson & Sharrock 2009: 98–100; Hutchinson 2012; Lavin 2013; Sidnell 2017; Fish 2018: para 21).

2 Image courtesy of Wikimedia Commons:

https://commons.wikimedia.org/wiki/Eadweard_Muybridge#/media/File:Muybridge_disk_step_walk.jpg

References

Bjelić, D.I. (2017) "'Hotrodder: A Revolutionary Category' – A Genealogy of a Sacks' Conversation(al) Analytic Method", Paper presented at *IIEMCA 2017: A Half-Century of Studies International Institute for Ethnomethodology and Conversation Analysis*, Otterbein College, Westerville, OH, July 10–13, 2017, available at: https://radicalethno.org/documents/bjelichotrodder.pdf

Coulter, J. (1976) "Harvey Sacks: A Preliminary Appreciation", *Sociology*, 10(3): 507–512.

Coulter, J. & Parsons, E.D. (1990) "The Praxiology of Perception: Visual Orientations and Practical Action", *Inquiry*, 33(3): 251–272.

Ebersole, F. (2001) "Where the Action Is", pp. 356–381, in Ebersole, F. (Ed.) *Things We Know: Fifteen Essays in the Problem of Knowledge*, Philadelphia, PA: Xlibris.

Fish, S. (2018) "The Interpretive Poverty of Data", online article, available at: https://balkin.blogspot.com/2018/03/the-interpretive-poverty-of-data.html

Fitzgerald, R. (2012) "Membership Categorization Analysis: Wild and Promiscuous or Simply the Joy of Sacks?", *Discourse Studies*, 14(3): 305–311.

Fitzgerald, R. (2019) "The Data and Methodology of Harvey Sacks: Lessons from the Archive", *Journal of Pragmatics*, DOI: 10.1016/j.pragma.2018.04.005

Foucault, M. (1973) *The Birth of the Clinic: An Archaeology of Medical Perception*, London: Tavistock.

Garfinkel, H. (2015) *Seeing Sociologically: The Routine Grounds of Social Action*, London: Routledge.

Garfinkel, H. & Sacks, H. (1970) "On Formal Structures of Practical Actions", pp. 338–366, in McKinney, J.C. & Tiryakian, E. (Eds.) *Theoretical Sociology*, New York, NY: Appleton Century Crofts.

Hughes, R. (1980) *The Shock of the New*, London: BBC.

Hutchinson, P. (2012) "Two Worlds of Action: Social Science, Social Theory and Systems of Sociological Refraction", *Russian Sociological Review*, 11(2): 75–99.

Lavin, D. (2013) "Must There Be Basic Action?", *Noûs*, 47(2): 273–301.

Livingston, E. (1987) *Making Sense of Ethnomethodology*, London: Routledge.

Livingston, E. (1995) *An Anthropology of Reading*, Bloomington, IN: Indiana University Press.

Lynch, M. (1993) *Scientific Practice and Ordinary Action: Ethnomethodology and Social Studies of Science*, Cambridge: Cambridge University Press.

Lynch, M. (2017) "Garfinkel, Sacks and Formal Structures: Collaborative Origins, Divergences and the Vexed Unity of Ethnomethodology and Conversation Analysis", Keynote Address, *IIEMCA 2017: A Half-Century of Studies International Institute for Ethnomethodology and Conversation Analysis*, Otterbein College, Westerville, OH, July 10–13, 2017, available at: https://radicalethno.org/documents/lynchbanquet.pdf

Lynch, M. & Bogen, D. (1994) "Harvey Sacks's Primitive Natural Science", *Theory, Culture & Society*, 11(4): 65–104.

Read, R., Hutchinson, P., & Sharrock, W.W. (2009) *There Is No Such Thing as a Social Science: In Defence of Peter Winch*, Farnham: Ashgate Press.

Sacks, H. (1963) "Sociological Description", *Berkeley Journal of Sociology*, 8(1): 1–16.

Sacks, H. (1972) "Notes on Police Assessment of Moral Character", pp. 280–293, in Sudnow, D. (Ed.) *Studies in Social Interaction*, Glencoe, IL: The Free Press.

Sacks, H. (1984a) "Notes on Methodology", pp. 21–27, in Atkinson, J.M. & Heritage, J. (Eds.) *Structures of Social Action: Studies in Conversation Analysis*, Cambridge: Cambridge University Press.

Sacks, H. (1984b) "On Doing 'Being Ordinary'", pp. 413–429, in Atkinson, J.M. & Heritage, J. (Eds.) *Structures of Social Action: Studies in Conversation Analysis*, Cambridge: Cambridge University Press.

Sacks, H. (1992) Jefferson, G. (Ed.) *Lectures on Conversation: Volumes 1 & 2*, Oxford: Blackwell.

Sacks, H. (1999) "Max Weber's Ancient Judaism", *Theory, Culture & Society*, 16(1): 31–39.

Schegloff, E.A. (1992a) "Introduction", pp. ix–lxii, in Sacks, H. (Ed.) *Lectures on Conversation, Volume 1*, Oxford: Blackwell.

Schegloff, E.A. (1992b) "Introduction", pp. ix–lii, in Sacks, H. (Ed.) *Lectures on Conversation, Volume 2*, Oxford: Blackwell.

Sidnell, J. (2017) "Action in Interaction Is Conduct under a Description", *Language in Society*, 46(3): 313–337.

Silverman, D. (1998) *Harvey Sacks: Social Science and Conversation Analysis*, New York, NY: Oxford University Press.

Watson, R. (1994) "Harvey Sacks's Sociology of Mind in Action", *Theory, Culture & Society*, 11(4): 169–186.

Watson, R. (2009) "Harvey Sacks", pp. 206–214, in D'hondt, S., Östman, J.O., & Verschueren, J. (Eds.) *The Pragmatics of Interaction: Handbook of Pragmatics Highlights Volume 4*, Amsterdam: John Benjamins.

Weber, M. (1962) *Basic Concepts in Sociology*, London: Peter Owen.

Wieder, D.L. & Pratt, S. (1990) "On Being a Recognizable Indian among Indians", pp. 45–64, in Carbaugh, D. (Ed.) *Cultural Communication and Intercultural Contact*, Hillsdale, NJ: Lawrence Erlbaum.

Wittgenstein, L.W. (1953) *Philosophical Investigations*, Oxford: Blackwell.

4 Sacks's plenum

The inscription of social orders

Andrew P. Carlin

Schuessler: The generation of these findings does not differ from what any other investigator might do. I mean going up to the point where the results are available.

Garfinkel: The investigator might count; put it that way.

Schuessler: Yes, in getting these findings, the procedure will be very similar to what I might do. Is that correct? It is objective.

Garfinkel: There seems to be a criticism of Goffman that goes like this; "It is all very well, but you have to be Goffman to do what he's doing." It seems that a similar kind of thing is coming up here. I think it is all very well to be talking this way but you are not Sacks.

(Hill and Crittenden 1968, p. 49)

In this chapter,[1] I shall outline "Sacks's plenum" – an inclusive approach to Sacks's work that moves beyond conversation analysis – and how this is manifest in my own research. My take on Sacks has been influenced by my sociological apprenticeship at the University of Manchester, where students received generous coaching from John Lee, Wes Sharrock, and Rod Watson, who conjointly initiated and consolidated an unrivalled research culture for the reproduction of future ethnomethodologists.

Visiting Didsbury College of Education, Manchester, in 1973, Harvey Sacks encouraged a group of ethnomethodologists to move beyond the form of "conversation analysis" emerging in the US. In advice reminiscent of his suggestion to Gene Lerner (Lerner 2004), to devise his own transcription system for the phenomena of interest, Sacks enjoined the Didsbury cohort to make distinctive contributions to interaction analysis by developing their own approaches to the study of social order.

Rod Watson organized the "Didsbury Seminars" series, and he followed through on Sacks's injunction. In addressing deficits in Sacks's positions as well as extending Sacks's analyses, Watson's respecification of Sacks left a particularly lasting impression on my own research. Watson brought Sacks's analyses to fieldwork data (Lee and Watson 1993). These data would afford Watson the empirical basis for his percipient and sophisticated arguments advancing membership categorization analysis as he advocated for a recombining of ethnomethodology and conversation analysis (Watson 1997a, 1997b, 2009a, 2009b; Wowk and Carlin 2004). Watson's practice, to bring the technologies of data collection and analysis to the classroom – and, de facto, introducing these as technologies of teaching and learning – furthered students' interest in ethnography, and in Sacks. Retrievable data (in the forms of video-recordings and transcripts) enabled students to participate, in a genuine manner, in ongoing research and allowed us to appreciate how course materials related to the lived work of people's moving through urban settings.

In moving a student cohort from the analysis of talk for the practical purposes of reading a degree to a lifelong fascination with Sacksian forms of inquiry, Watson challenged the received view within different forms of sociology that studying Sacks was limited to studying talk and challenged the hegemonic (turn-taking) approach to talk (Watson 1994a). Accordingly, our engagement with Sacks's work was not defined by turn-taking or sequentially organized conversational phenomena, and our orientation to Sacks was never "reducible" to conversation analysis. As students, we were recipients of an "ethnomethodological conversation analysis". This meant more than examining conversation analysis and membership categorization. It involved consideration of how Sacks's work – as constituted by sequential and categorial forms of analysis and his sophisticated switching between specific cases and general implications of specifics – provided for radical, real-world sociology.

Sacks's plenum

In itemizing a range of book titles that Harvey Sacks recommended to his students, Michael Moerman (1992, p. 28) intimates that the "mutual resonances" those disparate works may have had is apparent to those with a serious interest in the study of language use. Throughout my career, some of the most important resources – for different reasons – have been *The Sociological Eye* (Hughes 1971), the constituent reports in *Public Space as an Interactional Order* (Lee and Watson 1993), and *Lectures on Conversation* (Sacks 1992). In outlining what I shall call "*Sacks's plenum*", the "mutual resonances" of these resources will hopefully become apparent. More importantly, however, describing Sacks's work as a plenum suggests that Sacks's contributions to sociology are not just defined by his development of conversation analysis.

In one of several inscriptions of "the Plenum paper", Harold Garfinkel (1991) outlines the terms indicated by a plenum. A dictionary defines "plenum" by contrast with "vacuum": plenum is to matter what vacuum is to absence of matter. Garfinkel was less interested in its precise definition, as a "full assembly", than in its use. Crucially, Garfinkel was concerned how the use of a particular plenum – opening up a gap between the orderliness of society and the explanation of its orderliness, an explanation that could only be derived through sociological theorizing – became the impetus for ethnomethodology's programme. In this chapter, I shall take on the "full assembly" definition of plenum to gloss and account for a range of approaches, developed by Sacks, that afford the inscription of social order.

"*Sacks's plenum*" is constituted by a panoply of interrelated, coherent features. First, there is attention to members' work, and its constituent detail, that members are competent users of natural language and are concerned with the recognizability of ordered, natural language activities (Garfinkel and Sacks 1970). Second, there are the methodological policies regarding data and data analysis (Sacks 1972a, 1984), which afford analysts' demonstrations of social order through competent natural language use, in contrast to invented reconstructions, and "plain ordinary theorizing" (Garfinkel, in Carlin 2007, p. 99). Through these methodological strategies with which to make natural language practices available for detailed study, Sacks enabled sociology to take a "linguistic turn" (Watson 2009c).

Third, there is the development of analytic procedures explicating how members' use of natural language practices produces order in situ, including membership categorization, sequential organization, and turn-taking. Fourth, there is the identification of "formal structures of practical action" (e.g. formulations, openings and closings, recipient design, topic), which has since been refined (Carlin 2010a; Wowk and Carlin 2004) and taken up as an agenda for research (Lerner 2004). Fifth, there is the "*ethnographic Sacks*" (Watson 2009c; Watson and Carlin 2012). Sacks exhibits a "profound ethnographic sensibility" (Watson 2009c, p. 209), which could be mistaken within his *Lectures* as background to analysis, but it is hard-earned, obtaining high standards according to criteria he himself sets for the recognizable description of phenomena (Sacks 1989). Sixth, there are *formal* versus *quiddity-based* analyses. Sacks moved seamlessly between the provision of general contours of interactional settings – which he discerned from various sources of data, including observation, recorded talk, and texts – and analyses of specific stretches of recorded talk.

These reticulated features of what I call Sacks's plenum suggest that a full description of Sacks's *Lectures* is not captured by the term "conversation", which "can mislead in a way that loses the phenomenon it seeks to illuminate" (Katz 2012, p. 27). Moreover, as this enumeration suggests, Sacks's plenum, as documented within the *Lectures*, is beyond the scope of what Sacks (in Fitzgerald 2019, p. 208) called "Conversational Activities" – Sacks's *Lectures* far exceed membership categorization and turn-taking in conversation.

Sacks's plenum: perspicuous settings

In terms of radical criteria for rigorous sociological description, Harold Garfinkel once claimed that,

> The studies by Sacks, Schegloff and their colleagues have demonstrated and settled the matter that where technical order-production phenomena are concerned, no issues of the work of conversational orderliness can be adequately identified by an analysis of reportage, and none can be formulated or solved.
>
> (Garfinkel, quoted in Carlin 2007, p. 100)

Sacks's development of conversation analysis, to which Garfinkel refers, was an expression of the study of members' methods (or ethnomethods). Garfinkel's attention moved from the unsettling of social order for propaedeutic purposes to the analysis of "normal, natural" instantiations of "hidden" phenomena that his disruptive exercises had made visible to sociologists (Carlin 2016a). Social orders would become inscribed as "instructably observable as the work of a population that staffs its production" (Garfinkel 2002, p. 92), where Garfinkel refers to "endogenous" populations as the cohort of members engaged as parties in the reflexive production and recognition "from within" a particular activity or setting – for example, getting stuck in a traffic jam, joining a queue, engaging in conversation. Sacks's development of conversation analysis cohered with Garfinkel's concern for "normal, natural" environments in which social order was visibly and accountably produced and reproduced: "Sacks' discovery of what was going on in conversation is the discovery of persons engaged in analysis" (Garfinkel, in Wiley 2019, p. 179). Conversation was a "perspicuous setting" in that it provided access to a work site through which members' methods were available for inspection without disrupting the social orders that members were engaged in producing.

Members' methods are not limited to talk in interaction, for which Garfinkel celebrated Sacks's achievements, and Garfinkel's "studies of work programme" can be approached as being addressed to problems of rigorous description that are unavailable to conversation-analytic inquiries. This moves beyond foundationalist disputes between micro/macro contexts (Sharrock and Watson 1988), or between talk and social structure (Schegloff 1991). The studies of work programme recognizes that "work-site" contexts – laboratories, libraries, martial arts classes, pavements – are constituted by their endogenous populations – that is, the cohort of members engaged in the reflexive production and recognition of a particular activity – with relevant materials to hand. This collaborative production is accomplished through talk – "shop talk" – as well as through the assemblage of members' activities that provide for the identifying details of an activity, which may or may not be accomplished through talk – such as the recognition of a car as an abandoned car (Garfinkel 2002, pp. 181–182; Sacks 1992, pp. 385, 607) or the realization of anomalies on an oscilloscope as a particular category of object (Garfinkel et al. 1981) – formulated as the "shop floor problem". Indeed, the shop floor problem addresses the indexicality of utterances within the gestalt contextures of their production:

> meaning was relative to such contextual matters as (a) who as saying it (i.e. that it was a resident); (b) to whom it was being said (e.g. to a staff member or, e.g. myself being treated as an auxiliary of the staff; (c) where it was being said (e.g. in the halfway house); (d) on what kind of occasion it was being said (e.g. in a meeting attended by both staff and residents); (e) the social relationship between teller and hearer (e.g. a parolee speaking to his parole agent); and so forth.
>
> (Wieder 1974, p. 187)

The study of perspicuous settings is informed by Sacks's distinctions between topics, and how topics are organized by conversationalists, and is an analytic complement to what are often taken to be Sacks's legacies. The quiddities of activities and settings may not be available to conversation-analytic study – for example, "You know I can't organize a pool tournament" (Wieder 1974, p. 170); rather, they require inquiry "from within". Howard Schwartz (2002) provides such an example, highlighting queues (in waiting rooms, for instance) in which there may not be a visible service turn order, but turn order is transparent to the cohort who constitute the queue. The "characterization problem" of work-site activities, such as queuing, enjoins a Sacksian orientation to prioritize "parties to the setting" and their definitions of "context",

> not as an undifferentiated background resource from which selected features are extracted for a particular analysis, but as the witnessable structuring of an activity through which and in which the identifying details of that activity are recognizable.
>
> (Livingston 2008, p. 841)

We happen upon the characterization problem elsewhere, such as in the explication of the identifying details of alchemy as a specific occult science (Eglin 1986) and in the detailed observation of the teaching of Kung Fu to students by a master (Girton 1986). It is not only that accounts of Kung Fu are necessarily distorted (e.g. fictional materials) or incomplete accounts (e.g. instructional materials); it is competence in the activity that enables members to recognize how materials are distortions or incomplete accounts of an activity. In their own ways, the work-site studies by Eglin, Girton, and Schwartz bring the tension between generalities and particularities into sharp relief.

Sacks's plenum: formal and quiddity-based analysis

The ethnographic edge that Sacks brought to the study of in situ language use deserves to be celebrated also, as well as his identification of membership categorization activities and bringing into visibility the sequential organization of talk (Watson 2009c). This neglected aspect of his work was discernible when following Sacks's logic first hand within seminars (Watson 1994b) and became available to readers of Sacks's transcribed *Lectures*, though it has yet to be exploited. The "ethnographic Sacks" (to use Watson's term) is to be distinguished from the erroneous description of membership categorization as "ethnographic conversational analysis" (Hustler and Payne 1985), which is an unfortunate misdirection: Sacks's work contains a great deal of "ethnographic" analyses, but these are not coterminous with membership categorization. This misnomer obscures the acuity of Sacks's "*sociological eye*".

A comprehensive listing of topics considered by Sacks, based on copies of his mimeographed lectures, appeared in Coulter (1976, pp. 508–509). When Sacks's lectures were eventually collected together and edited by Gail Jefferson,

Watson observed that, "the title *Lectures on Conversation* might be taken as an inadequate representation of the range of Sacks' considerations and of their implicativeness for the discipline of sociology" (Watson 1994b, p. 185). Coulter agreed with this trivializing and delimiting of Sacks's oeuvre whereby "'lectures' seems somehow too commonplace a term with which to characterize them" (Coulter 1995, p. 327). Sacks brought us far more than the analysis of talk. One of his students, Gene Lerner, argues that,

> one of his most important legacies can be found in the ways he worked up empirical materials – ways of working that other researchers could adopt and adapt. It is this clarity of purpose and method – embodied in Sacks' investigations of conversation more than offered up as explicit research policies – that was necessary for a new discipline to emerge.
>
> (Lerner 2004, p. 1)

Lerner's observation, that for conversation analysis to become a field in its own right required a move from individual cases to classes of cases, which Sacks credits to Schegloff (Lerner 2004), is echoic of Garfinkel's remark to Karl Schuessler, quoted at the beginning of this chapter. It was not only that "the canons of scientific objectivity" (Bittner 1973, p. 114) would accommodate a field – and it took decades before there was such begrudging acceptance – that conferred its observations with the credibility of multiple instances and comparative analysis (Watson 2008). Rather, Schegloff's intervention in multiple instances was also a recognition that Sacks stood alone in his ability to draw general implications for social order from individual cases of interaction.

It is this aspect of Sacks's work to which I shall now turn, for Sacks's influence upon my work extends beyond the methodology of sociology, and beyond sequential and categorial forms of analysis. Sacks provides sociology with organizing devices for sociological research of action: Sacks's work is thoroughly praxeological. This means that the implications of Sacks's work are not limited to talk, but apply to texts also and afford technical respecification of work-site details.

When I read Everett Cherrington Hughes (1971), there is a striking array of suggestive (or "sensitizing") concepts that have generalizing, or at least formal, potential – careers, dirty work, master status traits, mistakes, social drama – and productive contrasts – "good" people, old versus new. Hughes's organizing devices as useful figurations for analysis are rightly celebrated (Becker 1986).[2] My engagement with Sacks's corpus recognizes his writings to be redolent with organizing devices also, though these are descriptions of members' methods – sociological reconstruction, listing items in series, making inferences, recognizing normal appearances, acknowledging noticeable absences – as well as analytic pairs such as possessables and possessitives, preservation and transformation.

Unlike Hughes, Sacks's organizing devices are not dependent upon perspectives by incongruity for their explicative power. Indeed, Sacks (1972b) identified members' use of perspectives by incongruity as a constituent feature of their routine work, which I took up in my own research (see below), but this is different from using it as an analytically ironic rubric. Further, as these are occasioned by the study of members' methods, they are not the product of "plain ordinary theorizing". Importantly, also, Sacks's organizing devices are bespoke; they are fitted to settings and occasioned actions within settings.

Another crucial difference, for me, is how Sacks's work may be used as organizing devices. In an analogous manner to Hughes' writings, Sacks's corpus is suffused with sensitizing concepts that, as descriptions of members' methods, may be termed *sensitizing practices* (Carlin 2003a, p. 18). Using Sacks's corpus, documenting members' methods, provides for the scaffolding of explanatory devices within methodologically non-ironic approaches to study – for example, ethno-inquiry, ethnomethodology, ethnomethodological conversation analysis, and membership categorization analysis. Hence, Sacks's organizing devices are coherent rather than disjunctive with the phenomena of investigation. As such, using Sacks's corpus affords descriptive precision and analytic purchase on setting-specific phenomena, without the creation of (what Gilbert Ryle called) category errors.

An "ethnographic" base can be observed in Sacks's formal and quiddity-oriented discussions. In raising quiddity issues, the significance of talk in situ was not limited to conversation analysis. Indeed, the corpus of Sacks's lectures exhibits eclecticism towards talk and its occasions, what members achieve through talking, and Sacks's "disquisitions" (to use Coulter's term) on language use within settings. Sacks's generalities/particularities orientations are exhibited throughout the "Therapy Sessions", in which a group who define themselves as "hotrodders" talk to a therapist. Sacks describes "hotrodder" as a "revolutionary" form of membership category in contrast to the membership categories we all use in order to make sense of the world and those around us. Sacks argued that the category "hotrodder" is revolutionary because categorial incumbents own and determinate its application. How categories are used is indicative of category membership, whereby "if [such a category] is used, [it] would be recognized to be used as a nonmember" (Sacks 1979, p. 9).

In making a novel and sophisticated analysis accessible, Sacks cites the biblical reference "Abraham the Hebrew", where the use of this category at that time suggests to biblical scholars that this was not written by a Jew (Sacks 1979, p. 8). The articulation of categories is thus seen to formulate the position of the referrer apropos the articulated category. The "revolution" of the category "hotrodder" is apparent when category members themselves, rather than nonmembers, determine who is to be recognized or seen as a member of that category. This is not a process of initiation, but rather an assessment of a candidate member's credentials or bona fides by category incumbents.

The pivotal aspects of the hotrodder category, according to Sacks, are the identifying characteristics of hotrodders. We can see here how Sacks's analysis complements Garfinkel's notion of quiddities (later, haecceities). The categorial work done – that is, iterated by category incumbents – reveals the quiddities or identifying characteristics of the category: the categorial features that define a hotrodder according to co-incumbents of that category, and how category incumbents define and recognize other hotrodders as hotrodders, rather than categorizing them as other teenagers.

I am, therefore, presenting a difference in emphasis in Sacks's work, involving two styles of analysis or "analytic alternatives". Sacks used recordings of group therapy sessions as occasions to discuss generic procedures that members use to structure talk, as well as orienting to the local ecology of the sessions themselves. These two styles of analysis may be referred to as formal and quiddity-based analyses. The therapy sessions data allow Sacks to draw out formal properties of talk, such as the ratified administration of membership categories (Sacks 1979) or the sequential organization of jokes (Sacks 1974, 1978), and afford opportunities to explicate the social-organizational quiddities of specific interactions between the teenagers and the therapist.

The rigour and viability of Sacks's work on the analysis of texts (Eglin and Hester 1999; Lee 1984; Watson 1997a) provided me with a warrant to bring Sacks to my own research on textual orders, including journal articles and their attendant reference sections, specifically bibliographies as formal accounts of discipline-specific entailments.

Bringing Sacks's plenum to phenomena of order*[3]

Bibliographies, information*, information work*

Following an examination of the linguistic organization of sociological methods and taking mundane requirements of scholarly work as members' methodic achievements, I moved into library and information science for a project on the social organization of bibliographies. A series of parenthetical remarks (Sacks 1989) alerted me to "intersubjectively problematic"[4] criteria used to assess scholarly work. Then, Garfinkel's (1996) paper provided me with analytically productive organizing principles on approaching texts and, in particular, a *deliberate misreading* of Garfinkel's work by looking at bibliographies as "formal accounts". Bibliographies are phenomena of order* – as such, described ethnomethodologically as bibliographies*. Sacks's "Max Weber's *Ancient Judaism*" paper was contemporaneous with "On sociological description" (Sacks 1963), and Schegloff (1999) points up, in miniature, some of the contiguities between these analyses. Sacks's treatments of Durkheim (Sacks 1963) and Weber (Sacks 1999) displayed "elective affinities", which are not reducible to the timescale of their production. Schegloff details how Sacks's (1963) paper trades upon "Max Weber's *Ancient Judaism*" but, whether or not we see this as a more limited paper than "On sociological description", I certainly read – or *read into* – Sacks's (1999) paper as being more immediately relevant to the concerns of the bibliography project.

Treating bibliographies* as formal accounts of topic-specific and discipline-specific contingencies cohered with members' practices of reading monographs and journal articles (Carlin 2003b). This research was facilitated by the generalizing potential of Sacks's work (Sacks 1972b, 1985). Within the project, I was able to observe how practitioners of disciplines and journal personnel – for example, authors, editors, and reviewers – oriented to scholarly communications as having "normal appearances", according to disciplinary priorities. Also, readers oriented to attendant bibliographies* as organized statements of a paper's location within topic-/discipline-specific literatures; as such, they were able to discern "noticeable absences" from bibliographies* and to provide accounts relating to the "inference-richness" of particular noticeable absences within these.

While the elective affinities between Garfinkel and Sacks are given full expression elsewhere (Watson 2016), their papers (Garfinkel 1996; Sacks 1999) established a coherent, ethnomethodological approach to textual analysis that, used together, afforded my analytic extension of the bibliographies* project into considerations of resources for teaching and learning as a practical matter (Carlin 2010b). I tried to move beyond the inscription of "this novel is relevant for that concept" approach found in teaching sociology resources (e.g. anomie/ *Lord of the Flies*), towards a lecture-specific scaffolding of sociological concepts for inclusive learning through which the lecturer reconstructs the relevance of a non-sociological source with which a learner may be familiar. This problematized the teaching and learning practices involved in selecting sources from outside a discipline-specific context and "reading into relevance", to use Macbeth's (2011, p. 73) term, through the work of sociological reconstruction, as outlined by Sacks (1999).

I was alerted to the use of standardized rule systems through a phenomenologically inclined examination of librarians' workplace practices (Ikeya 1997); during periods of fieldwork in libraries and "information agencies", I witnessed the outcomes of such rule-following with the discrepant classification of Sacks's *Lectures* in various libraries (Carlin 2003c). The more I moved towards a uniquely adequate position for studying library-specific information organizations and practices, the more practitioner-recognizable Ikeya's identification of phenomena of order* became.

Sacks's plenum enabled my library inquiries (e.g. Carlin 2007; Watson and Carlin 2012) to respecify abstractions as concrete practices, such as members' organization and uses of "information" within routinely available, routinely identifiable formal types – for example, stories, openings, and so on. Crucially, the attention to information as an interactional accomplishment enables a "party-administered" approach to information, rather than the external imposition of a particular definition of information qua "theoretical imperialism" (Schegloff 1997), which is an identifying detail of information science (Carlin 2009a).

Sacks's work (Garfinkel and Sacks 1970) also provides leverage on the institutional aspects of information organization. Information is an "outcome of disciplined practices" (Macbeth 2011, p. 88), organized according to standardized systems, and local adaptations. The procedural rules and routine practices involved in "core competencies" (e.g. cataloguing, classification, collection management) of information professionals, at the library-specific level, account for how information – the ideal-typical organizations represented in procedural rules – "should" be organized, and how information already is organized as a workplace contingency. Respecified as a members' phenomenon, library-specific and discipline-specific orders are endorsed on a case-by-case basis to organize information*.

Public space: the ordinary as extraordinary

Public Space as an Interactional Order (Lee and Watson 1993) provided me with a career interest in public space. As a categorial respecification of sequential contours of pedestrian locomotion (Ryave and Schenkein 1974), this collection of studies documents a source of "ultra-rich" instructional materials that are available for inspection, and subsequent analysis, by student cohorts. The local specificities described therein cohere with the generalizing potential of Sacks's plenum to inform, qua Everett Hughes, street scenes – including observable phenomena that are suspicious according to the normal appearances of pedestrian locomotion (Carlin 2003d) and constitute busking and other street-level performances. A "broad reading" of Sacks's work (Housley et al. 2017), taking Sacks's work as providing analytic devices for the observation of street scenes, affords the recognition of how street performers use location-specific "members' measurement systems" (Sacks 1988/1989) in doing waiting – waiting accountably for an "audience" before commencing their act (Carlin 2014).

Various projects have been informed by Sacks's plenum, such as how mundane security sweeps and the recognition of suspicious devices *in extremis* are amenable to generalizing operations, wherein emergency services personnel exhibit ordinary, members' use of incongruity procedures (Carlin 2009b, 2016b), cohering with Sacks's ethnographic version, not Hughes' imposition, of perspectives by incongruity; also how members orient to the reflexivity of categorial and sequential aspects of public space (Carlin 2017a, 2017b) and such "pavement cultures" that pedestrian cohorts concertedly produce.

Conclusion

Sacks's corpus has analytic depth and is wide-ranging, and the strands of his work are mutually elaborating. The most visible contours of his work are sequentially organized conversation analysis, and membership categorization. In this chapter, I have suggested that an important aspect of his work is attention to developing formalized descriptions, generated from single cases – that is, Sacks's plenum glosses sequential and categorial analyses, and formal and quiddity-based analyses. Sacks's plenum encompasses and extends beyond a broad range of "Sacksian principles" (Housley et al. 2017), which can be used to address analyses of text and talk; Sacks's plenum constitutes a gestalt contexture, which may be conceptualized using the example of searching for a place for a piece in a jigsaw puzzle:

> The puzzle-specific relevance of a puzzle piece's features is found only in the discoverable relationships of the pieces with each other.
>
> (Livingston 2008, p. 845)

My sociological apprenticeship treated conversation analysis (Sacks) and ethnomethodology (Garfinkel) as mutually elaborating, with complementary concerns with natural language use and members' methods. The "Manchester" approach was not "tied" to Sacks-as-sequential-conversation-analysis, but disclosed a range of sociologically perspicuous approaches to social order phenomena via Sacks, as problems for research:

> In its entirety Sacks' work constitutes an alternate methodology which is an integral feature of an ethnomethodological respecification of foundational matters in the human sciences.
>
> (Button 1991, p. 8)

Students of ethnomethodological inquiries at Manchester found the analytic attitudes of Garfinkel and Sacks as mutually informing, presenting praxeological alternatives to stipulative sociology. This approach was particularly attuned to avoiding category errors, such as the mixing of ethnography and conversation analysis – an internal debate that has animated EMCA work (see Watson and Seiler 1992) but is finding a new form of expression in multimodal analysis.

Rod Watson's studies of public space are informed by Garfinkel's and Livingston's approaches to phenomena such as queues (Livingston 1987) and are characterized by his realigning emphases within Sacks's work that were becoming distal concerns to each other. Watson's studies of public spaces accessed the range of complementary ethnomethodological and Sacksian approaches, producing empirically based analyses that accounted for the sequential and categorial features of members' methods in public spaces as reflexively constituted aspects of settings and their population cohorts. Watson's approach to Sacks has, in turn, informed my own ethnographic studies of urban settings.

We are only touching the surface of how implicative Sacks's plenum could be for various research programmes. For example, in my own research, I recognize that members' real-world orientations to information organization as gestalt contextures, and members' particularization procedures – how members design information for particular recipients – fall outside the remit of information science. The challenge is to initiate research programmes that explicate how people "see" information (Carlin 2003a; Macbeth 2011); that praxeologize information in the concrete, rather than theorize information in the abstract. The scope for Sacksian inquiries within specific disciplinary domains is yet to be realized.

Notes

1 My readings of Sacks have been mediated by my teachers – friends of both Garfinkel and Sacks – to whom I shall always be grateful: Kenneth L. Brown, John R.E. Lee, Edward L. Rose, and, in particular, Rod Watson. They are not responsible for errors in this chapter – but they are wholly responsible for my continued engagement with Sacks's work. My thanks to K. Neil Jenkings for extremely helpful suggestions in organizing this chapter. This work was supported by the Macau Science and Technology Development Fund, award number 0054/2019/A1.

2 Another similarity is the indicative contents of *The Sociological Eye*, produced by Hughes, and *Lectures on Conversation*, which are posthumous glosses (Gail Jefferson, personal communication, 8 September 1999).
3 On the significance of asterisks in drawing attention to ethnomethodological properties, see Garfinkel (1991, 2002).
4 This term, found in Lee and Watson (1993), is scaffolded from Lee's "subjectively problematic" teaching device, which discloses how interactional matters are problems for individual persons.

References

Becker, Howard S. 1986. *Writing for Social Scientists*. Chicago and London: University of Chicago Press.

Bittner, Egon 1973. Objectivity and realism in sociology. In George Psathas, editor, *Phenomenological Sociology: Issues and Applications*. New York: John Wiley, pp. 109–125.

Button, Graham 1991. Ethnomethodology and the foundational respecification of the human sciences. In Graham Button, editor, *Ethnomethodology and the Human Sciences*. Cambridge: Cambridge University Press, pp. 1–9.

Carlin, Andrew P. 2003a. Pro forma arrangements: The visual availability of textual artefacts. *Visual Studies*. 18 (1), pp. 6–20.

Carlin, Andrew P. 2003b. Some bibliographic practices in interdisciplinary work: Accounting for citations in Library and Information Science. *Accountability in Research*. 10 (1), pp. 27–45.

Carlin, Andrew P. 2003c. Aspects of spatial arrangements in public and academic libraries. In Tomke Lask, editor, *Constructions Sociales de l'Espace: Les Territoires de l'Anthropologie de la Communication*. Liège: University of Liège Press, pp. 87–99.

Carlin, Andrew P. 2003d. Observation and membership categorization: Recognizing "normal appearances" in public space. *Journal of Mundane Behavior*. 4 (1), pp. 77–91.

Carlin, Andrew P. 2007. Auspices of corpus status: Bibliography* as a phenomenon of repecification. In S. Hester and D. Francis, editors, *Orders of Ordinary Action: Respecifying Sociological Knowledge*. London: Ashgate, pp. 91–103.

Carlin, Andrew P. 2009a. Segmented professions: Further considerations of theory and practice in LIS and librarianship. *Library Philosophy and Practice*. October, pp. 1–9.

Carlin, Andrew P. 2009b. Edward Rose and linguistic ethnography: An ethno-inquiries approach to interviewing. *Qualitative Research*. 9 (3), pp. 331–354.

Carlin, Andrew P. 2010a. Reading "A tutorial on membership categorization" by Emanuel Schegloff. *Journal of Pragmatics*. 42 (1), pp. 257–261.

Carlin, Andrew P. 2010b. The corpus status of literature in teaching sociology: Novels as "sociological reconstruction". *The American Sociologist*. 41 (3), pp. 211–231.

Carlin, Andrew P. 2014. Working the crowds. Features of street performance in public space. In Tara Brabazon, editor, *City Imaging: Regeneration, Renewal, and Decay*. Dordrecht: Springer, pp. 157–169.

Carlin, Andrew P. 2016a. On some limits of interdisciplinarity. *Social Epistemology*. 30 (5–6), pp. 624–642.

Carlin, Andrew P. 2016b. A bomba de Manchester, 1996: Serviços de emergência, evacuação e etnométodos. *SILVA: Humanidades em Ciências Militares*. 1 (1), pp. 66–86.

Carlin, Andrew P. 2017a. Navigating the walkways: Radical inquiries and mental maps. *Ethnographic Studies*. 14, pp. 24–48.

Carlin, Andrew P. 2017b. Visibility and street ethnography: A lesson in "pavement culture". *Etnografia e Ricerca Qualitativa*. 10 (2), pp. 287–302.

Coulter, Jeff 1976. Harvey Sacks: A preliminary appreciation. *Sociology*. 10 (3), pp. 507–512.

Coulter, Jeff 1995. The Sacks Lectures. *Human Studies*. 18 (2/3), pp. 327–336.

Eglin, Peter and Hester, Stephen 1999. "You're all a bunch of feminists": Categorization and the politics of terror in the Montreal Massacre. *Human Studies*. 22 (2–4), pp. 253–272.

Eglin, Trent 1986. Introduction to a hermeneutics of the occult: Alchemy. In Harold Garfinkel, editor, *Ethnomethodological Studies of Work*. Abingdon, UK: Routledge, pp. 123–159.

Fitzgerald, Richard 2019. The data and methodology of Harvey Sacks: Lessons from the archive. *Journal of Pragmatics*. 143, pp. 205–214.

Garfinkel, Harold 1991. Respecification: Evidence for locally produced, naturally accountable phenomena of order*, logic, reason, meaning, method, etc., in and as of the essential haecceity of immortal ordinary society, (I) – An announcement of studies. In Graham Button, editor, *Ethnomethodology and the Human Sciences*. Cambridge: Cambridge University Press, pp. 10–19.

Garfinkel, Harold 1996. Ethnomethodology's program. *Social Psychology Quarterly*. 59 (1), pp. 5–21.

Garfinkel, Harold 2002. *Ethnomethodology's Program: Working Out Durkheim's Aphorism*. Lanham, MD: Rowman & Littlefield.

Garfinkel, Harold, Lynch, Michael and Livingston, Eric 1981. The work of a discovering science construed with materials from the optically discovered pulsar. *Philosophy of the Social Sciences*. 11 (2), pp. 131–158.

Garfinkel, Harold and Sacks, Harvey 1970. On formal structures of practical actions. In John C. McKinney and Edward A. Tiryakian, editors, *Theoretical Sociology: Perspectives and Developments*. New York, NY: Appleton-Century-Crofts, pp. 337–366.

Girton, George 1986. Kung Fu: Toward a praxiological hermeneutic of the martial arts. In Harold Garfinkel, editor, *Ethnomethodological Studies of Work*. Abingdon, UK: Routledge, pp. 60–91.

Hill, Richard J. and Crittenden, Kathleen S 1968. *Proceedings of the Purdue Symposium on Ethnomethodology*. Lafayette, IN: Institute for the Study of Social Change, Department of Sociology, Purdue University.

Housley, William, Webb, Helena, Edwards, Adam, Procter, Rob and Jirotka, Marina 2017. Digitizing Sacks? Approaching social media as data. *Qualitative Research*. 17 (6), pp. 627–644.

Hughes, Everett C. 1971. *The Sociological Eye*. Chicago and New York: Aldine Atherton.

Hustler, David E. and Payne, George C.F. 1985. Ethnographic conversational analysis: An approach to classroom talk. In Robert G. Burgess, editor, *Strategies of Educational Research: Qualitative Methods*. London: Falmer Press, pp. 265–287.

Ikeya, Nozomi 1997. *The Practical Management of the Social Stock of Knowledge: The Case of an Information Giving Service*. Unpublished PhD thesis, University of Manchester.

Katz, Jack 2012. Emotion's crucible. In Dale Spencer, Kevin Walby and Alan Hunt, editors, *Emotions Matter: A Relational Approach to Emotions*. Toronto: University of Toronto Press, pp. 15–39.

Lee, John R.E. 1984. Innocent victims and evil-doers. *Women's Studies International Forum*. 7 (1), pp. 69–83.

Lee, John R.E. and Watson, D. Rod 1993. *Final report to the Plan Urbain: Public space as an interactional order*. University of Manchester: Department of Sociology.

Lerner, Gene 2004. *Conversation Analysis: Studies from the First Generation*. Amsterdam: John Benjamins.

Livingston, Eric 1987. *Making Sense of Ethnomethodology*. London: Routledge & Kegan Paul.

Livingston, Eric 2008. Context and detail in studies of the witnessable social order: Puzzles, maps, checkers, and geometry. *Journal of Pragmatics*. 40 (5), pp. 840–862.

Macbeth, Douglas 2011. A commentary on incommensurate programs. In Timothy Koschmann, editor, *Theories of Learning and Studies of Instructional Practice*. New York: Springer, pp. 73–103.

Moerman, Michael 1992. Life after CA: An ethnographer's autobiography. In Graham Watson and Robert M. Seiler, editors, *Text in Context*. Newbury Park, CA: Sage, pp. 20–34.

Ryave, Alan L. and Schenkein, James N. 1974. Notes on the art of walking. In Roy Turner, editor, *Ethnomethodology: Selected Readings*. Harmondsworth, UK: Penguin, pp. 265–274.

Sacks, Harvey 1963. Sociological description. *Berkeley Journal of Sociology*. 8, pp. 1–16.

Sacks, Harvey 1972a. An initial investigation of the usability of conversational data for doing sociology. In David Sudnow, editor, *Studies in Social Interaction*. New York: The Free Press, pp. 31–74.

Sacks, Harvey 1972b. Notes on police assessment of moral character. In David Sudnow, editor, *Studies in Social Interaction*. New York: The Free Press, pp. 280–293.

Sacks, Harvey 1974. An analysis of the course of a joke's telling in conversation. In Richard Bauman and Joel Scherzer, editors, *Explorations in the Ethnography of Speaking*. Cambridge: Cambridge University Press, pp. 337–353.

Sacks, Harvey 1978. Some technical considerations of a dirty joke. In Jim Schenkein, editor, *Studies in the Organization of Conversational Interaction*. New York: Academic Press, pp. 249–269.

Sacks, Harvey 1979. Hotrodder: A revolutionary category. In George Psathas, editor, *Everyday Language: Studies in Ethnomethodology*. New York, NY: Irvington, pp. 7–21.

Sacks, Harvey 1984. Notes on methodology. In J. Maxwell Atkinson and John Heritage, editors, *Structures of Social Action. Studies in Conversation Analysis*. Cambridge: Cambridge University Press, pp. 21–27.

Sacks, Harvey 1985. The inference-making machine: Notes on observability. In Teun Van Dijk, editor, *Handbook of Discourse Analysis Volume 3: Discourse and Dialogue*. London: Academic Press, pp. 13–23.

Sacks, Harvey 1988/1989. On members' measurement systems. *Research on Language and Social Interaction*. 22 (1–4), pp. 45–60.

Sacks, Harvey 1989. An impromptu survey of the literature. *Human Studies*. 12 (3/4), pp. 253–359.

Sacks, Harvey 1992. *Lectures on Conversation* (2 vols.). Oxford: Basil Blackwell.

Sacks, Harvey 1999. Max Weber's *Ancient Judaism*. *Theory, Culture and Society*. 16 (1), pp. 31–39.

Schegloff, Emanuel A. 1991. Reflections on talk and social structure. In Deirdre Boden and Don H. Zimmerman, editors, *Talk and Social Structure: Studies in Ethnomethodology and Conversation Analysis*. Cambridge: Polity Press, pp. 44–70.

Schegloff, Emanuel A. 1997. Whose text? Whose context? *Discourse & Society*. 8 (2), pp. 165–187.

Schegloff, Emanuel A. 1999. On Sacks on Weber on *Ancient Judaism*: Introductory notes and interpretive resources. *Theory, Culture and Society.* 16 (1), pp. 1–29.
Schwartz, Howard 2002. Data: Who needs it? Describing normal environments – examples and methods. *Ethnographic Studies.* 7, pp. 7–32.
Sharrock, Wes and Watson, Rod 1988. Autonomy among social theories. The incarnation of social structures. In Nigel G. Fielding, editor, *Actions and Structure: Research Methods and Social Theory.* London: Sage, pp. 56–77.
Watson, Graham and Seiler, Robert M. 1992. *Text in Context: Contributions to Ethnomethodology.* Newbury Park, CA: Sage.
Watson, Rod 1994a. Catégorization, séquentialité et ordre social: Un nouveau regard sur l'oeuvre de Sacks. In Louis Quéré and Jean Widmer, editors, *L'Enquête sur les Catégories de Durkheim à Sacks.* Paris: Éditions de l'École des Hautes Études en Sciences Sociales, pp. 151–184.
Watson, Rod 1994b. Harvey Sacks' sociology of mind in action. *Theory, Culture & Society.* 11 (4), pp. 169–186.
Watson, Rod 1997a. Ethnomethodology and textual analysis. In David Silverman, editor, *Qualitative Research: Theory, Method and Practice.* London: Sage, pp. 80–98.
Watson, Rod 1997b. Some general reflections on "categorization" and "sequence" in the analysis of conversation. In Stephen Hester and Peter Eglin, editors, *Culture in Action: Studies in Membership Categorization Analysis.* Washington, DC: University Press of America, pp. 49–75.
Watson, Rod 2008. Comparative sociology, laic and analytic: Some critical remarks on comparison in conversation analysis. *Cahiers de Praxématique.* 50, pp. 197–238.
Watson, Rod 2009a. Constitutive practices and Garfinkel's notion of trust: Revisited. *Journal of Classical Sociology.* 9 (4), pp. 475–499.
Watson, Rod 2009b. *Analysing Practical and Professional Texts: A Naturalistic Approach.* Farnham, UK: Ashgate.
Watson, Rod 2009c. Harvey Sacks. In Sigurd D'hondt, Jan-Ola Östman and Jef Verschueren, editors, *The Pragmatics of Interaction.* Amsterdam: John Benjamins, pp. 206–214.
Watson, Rod 2016. Harold Garfinkel and pragmatics. In Jan-Ola Östman and Jef Verschueren, editors, *Handbook of Pragmatics: Volume 20, 2016 Instalment.* Amsterdam: John Benjamins, pp. 1–64. https://doi.org/10.1075/hop.20.gar1
Watson, Rod and Carlin, Andrew P. 2012. "Information": Praxeological considerations. *Human Studies.* 35 (2), pp. 327–345.
Wieder, D. Lawrence 1974. *Language and Social Reality.* The Hague: Mouton.
Wiley, Norbert 2019. Interview with Harold Garfinkel. *Human Studies.* 42 (2), pp. 165–181.
Wowk, Maria T. and Carlin, Andrew P. 2004. Depicting a liminal position in ethnomethodology, conversation analysis, and membership categorization analysis: The work of Rod Watson. *Human Studies.* 27 (1), pp. 69–89.

5 From ethnosemantics to occasioned semantics

The transformative influence of Harvey Sacks

Jack Bilmes

When I was a graduate student in anthropology, before what might be called "the indexical revolution" had fully set in, the major preoccupation seemed to be to reduce culture and social behavior to relatively simple structures. One manifestation was Levi-Straussian structuralism. A more dominant approach in my university, and one to which I felt an affinity, was "ethnographic semantics" or "ethnosemantics."[1]

The technique of ethnosemantics that is most relevant to my current purposes is taxonomic analysis. The main type of structure examined was what was commonly called "inclusion taxonomies." These taxonomies represented "kind of" relations between levels and contrast within levels. (See Frake 1962; Kay 1971 for formal definitions.)

For example, see Figure 5.1. This taxonomy tells us, among other things, that a loblolly is a kind of pine, which is, in turn, a kind of tree (and thus a loblolly is also a kind of tree).

An inclusion taxonomy is one type of taxonomy. Another type, called a "partonomy" (or, sometimes, "meronomy"), represents "part of" relations (see Brown 1976; Brown et al. 1976). In Figure 5.2, I use arrows to represent part-of relations.

The logic of partonomies is quite different from the logic of inclusion taxon omies, but both are structures of inclusion/subsumption.[2] The students of ethnosemantics saw inclusion taxonomies and partonomies as representing native cognitive and linguistic/cultural structures.

The structural approach of ethnosemantics lost currency with the emergence of the Wittgensteinian critique of philosophy and the ethnomethodological critique (or "respecification") of standard social science.[3] Wittgenstein's notion of family resemblances dissolved componential approaches to meaning. For Wittgenstein, with his concepts of "language games" and grammars, there were multiple, perhaps innumerable, kinds of social order, with different constellations of meanings, and reductive exercises, such as taxonomic and componential analysis, were futile.

For Harold Garfinkel, the founder of ethnomethodology, the central notion was *indexicality*. The meaning of any linguistic expression is inherently unstable, because it must be understood in its unique context of occurrence on each occasion that it is used. The goal of social science – to reduce the description of social life to

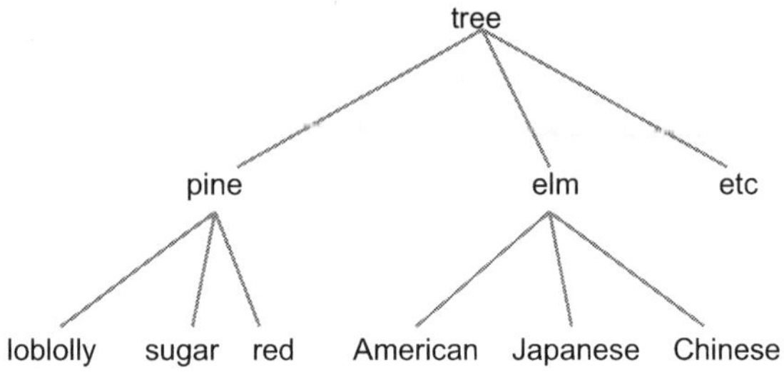

Figure 5.1 Inclusion taxonomy

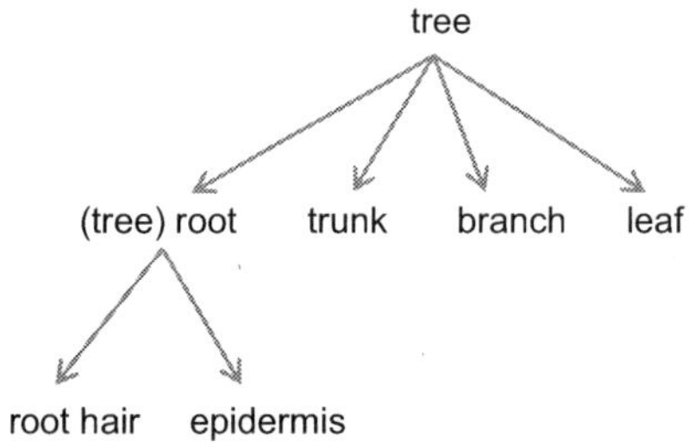

Figure 5.2 Partonomy

"objective expressions" and general rules – is unreachable, because all such formulations are themselves indexical. The ethnomethodological approach is saved from sociological nihilism by the notion of *methodic procedures* or *ethnomethods*. Perhaps we cannot generalize directly about the actual content, shape, and rules of social order, but we can describe the methods that members use to produce the sense and appearance of order.

In contrast to the goals and procedures of ethnosemantics, both Wittgenstein and Garfinkel favored a non-cognitive understanding of language as it is actually used, rather than as an abstract structure of meaning located in native minds or idealized linguistic systems and elicited through formal techniques. And both attended to speakers' agency and the creative aspects of members' language use.

This brings us to Harvey Sacks. My interest here is in Sacks's work on categories, rather than his seminal work in sequential analysis. Sacks, I will argue, offered a kind of ethnomethodological take on taxonomic analysis.[4] His notions of "apparatus" and "machinery" resemble ethnosemantic ideas of structure. However, as we shall see, he deals with three signal weaknesses of taxonomic analysis: (1.) Taxonomic analysis tended to ignore the fact that categories can be created on the spot for current circumstances or for any purpose. (2.) It failed to adequately recognize that the same item may be variously categorized. (3.) Most importantly, in contrast to ethnosemantic approaches, Sacks always focused on the ways that categories are deployed and organized on specific occasions of verbal interaction.[5]

Sacks saw categories as members of "collections," belonging to a "device." For example, doctors and lawyers are collected in the device "occupation."[6] Moreover, as Watson (1978) pointed out, devices could themselves belong to higher-order devices. This apparatus is identical to the ethnosemanticists' taxonomy. (Sacks included in his notion of device "rules of application." These rules of application, in my understanding, consist of various rules [such as the consistency rule] and hearers' and viewers' maxims that Sacks proposed [e.g., Sacks 1992: 243–260]. Since these rules and maxims apply across devices, as general rules and maxims guiding production and interpretation, I don't think that they are properly part of the definition of device.)

An arguable weakness of Sacks's concept of device is that he does not distinguish between "kind of" and "part of" relations. So, in his famous analysis of "The baby cried. The mommy picked it up," he posits a *stage-of-life device*, consisting of *baby*, *child*, *adult*, and so on, and a *family device*, consisting of such categories as *mother*, *father*, and so on. But the relations in the first device are "kind of," in the second "part of." He makes the important observation that some devices are "duplicatively organized," that is, they have the character of teams. If he had made the kind-of/part-of distinction, he would have noticed that duplicative organization is characteristic of the latter. In fact, it seems that duplicative organization is definitive of partonomy – a higher-level parton entails a set of lower-level parts.

There was one ethnosemanticist, in particular, whose work could be seen as a bridge to Sacksian category analysis. Charles Frake, in "The Diagnosis of Disease among the Subanun of Mindanao" (1961), connected taxonomy to purposeful talk: He recognized that taxonomic hierarchies gave individual speakers choices in regard to how they might categorize particular phenomena, and that these choices were strategic resources that could be used in conversational environments. Noting that skin disease terms may enter into situations such as bride-price negotiation, competitive joking, and maligning, Frake observes that, "in many of these situations it is imperative to speak at just the level of generality that specifies the pertinent information but leaves other, possibly embarrassing, information ambiguous" (122).

For Frake, categorization subtracts information. When we generalize from *yaws* to *skin disease*, or *elm* to *tree*, we omit certain information.[7] Sacks emphasized a contrary point: For Sacks, categorization *added* information. For Sacks, it was crucial that we have choices as to how to categorize items and terms. We might say, truthfully, that "John is a soldier" or "John is a Catholic." We might characterize rats as rodents or vermin. The choice we make carries information. It may tell us something about the subject that we didn't know, and the choice of category says something about the situation of speech and the speaker's relevancies and purposes. It tells us, as Edwards (1998) put it, "the relevant thing about [the subject]." Of course, Frake is talking about a situation where one might say, for instance, "I saw a rodent" instead of "I saw a rat." But this, too, would convey information about the situation and the speaker's purposes and perhaps the speaker's knowledge and interests, even as it concealed the specific nature of the rodent.[8] Categories are, in Sacks's phrase, "inference rich."

A point which clearly follows from the preceding discussion is that, when we categorize, we are doing something consequential. As Sacks writes:

> Members can't do pure formulating. That is to say, you can't be engaged in "merely" – non-consequentially, non-methodically, non-alternatively – saying "This is, after all, a group therapy session". To do that – even though you're merely invoking one thing that's true about this – is to do other things as well, e.g., put somebody down for something they said, propose special relevancies, propose that some topic ought to be discussed or not be discussed, invoke a status hierarchy, etc. At any rate, in each case that a formulation of a setting, or an identity, is done, that's something that has some line of consequences, and some analyzable bases, for participants, which can be one differentiated from another possible formulation, and also from not doing it at all.
>
> (1992, Vol. 1: 516)

Of course, categorizing is a major type of formulating, and so it follows that we can't do pure categorizing – we are always doing something else as well. Not only must we attend to the actual usage of categories, but we must treat them as forms of social action rather than manifestations of linguistic or cognitive structure.

One aspect of the inferential richness of categories is expressed in Sacks's notion of *category-bound activities*. Crying, for example, is an activity that is bound to the category *baby*. Each category of living thing would seem to have characteristic activities. Mention of the activity may lead us to infer the presence of the category. And, by choosing one applicable category (say, soldier) over another (say, Catholic), we invoke a certain set of category-bound activities. Sacks's successors expanded the notion of category-bound activity. Sharrock (1974) adds category-associated knowledge, and Watson (1978) proposes "category predicates," which include rights and obligations associated with particular categories. Jayyusi (1984), who elaborates extensively on Sacks's original notions, expands the concept to "category-bound features," which includes category-associated activities, knowledge, rights and obligations, and "properties, habits, beliefs, etc." (35). This expanded concept goes a long way in accounting for the fact that categories are inference-rich.

At this point, I would like to introduce a distinction between two types of category-bound features. Type 1: the category implies the feature. So, to use Sacks's classic example, the category "baby" is bound to the activity "crying," in the sense that all babies cry. If we observe that someone is a baby, we can deduce that that person cries. But, when we observe that someone is crying, we cannot necessarily infer that that person is a baby. Older children and adults sometimes cry as well.[9] Type 2: The feature implies the category. For example, not all women give birth, but, if you are a human and you give birth, you are a woman. So, to simply say that activity X is bound to category Y is to make a seriously imprecise statement.[10]

One aspect of Sacks's analysis of categories seems to depart somewhat from certain strains of both ethnomethodology and sequential conversation analysis, as it has developed under the influence of Emanuel Schegloff. Sacks draws, explicitly, on preexisting cultural understandings. The reason that categories are inference-rich is that they are cultural entities. Consider Sacks's analysis of the following segment: A man ("B" below) has been instructed to call a social agency because of some marital problems he is having. Sacks provides us with an excerpt from B's discussion with the social worker ("A"). Here is the excerpt, in Sacks original format:

Segment 1

1. *A*: Yeah, then what happened?
2. *B*: Okay, in the meantime she [wife of B] says, "'Don't ask the child nothing.'" Well, she stepped between me and the child, and I got up to walk out the door. When she stepped between me and the child, I went to move her out of the way. And then about that time her sister had called the police. I don't know how she … what she …
3. *A*: Didn't you smack her one?
4. *B*: No.
5. *A*: You're not telling me the story, Mr B.
6. *B*: Well, you see when you say smack you mean hit.
7. *A*: Yeah, you shoved her. Is that it?
8. *B*: Yeah, I shoved her.

(Sacks 1992, Vol. 1: 113)

Sacks notes that A, not being a party to the events in question, is nevertheless able to see that B is not telling "the story," and B can recognize A's grounds for doing so. They are able to do this because both realize that B's story has not provided an adequate warrant for B's sister-in-law calling the police. We might say that the category "calling the police" is bound to a set of actions, such that one of those actions (e.g., smacking) or more, but not necessarily all, must occur with that category.[11] This analysis requires that A and B share certain cultural knowledge about what is a proper warrant for calling the police. It requires as well that Sacks be a party to this knowledge, in order to see the source of A's objection. Culture is part of, rather than an unnoticed or unacknowledged condition of, Sacks's analyses. In this respect, there is some continuity with the emic studies of the ethnosemanticists.

Unlike the ethnosemanticists, however, Sacks recognized that categories were not always entries in a fixed cultural inventory. They could be created on the spot for the purposes of the moment. This is beautifully demonstrated in Sacks's Lecture 14 from 1971 (1992, Vol. 2: 499–503). Bob is quoting his mother complaining about the sorts of gifts that her husband gets her: "When's that guy gonna learn that I don't want an electric skillet, I wanna coat, or I wanna sweater" (499). Sacks notes that, if she had said, "I want a coat," it would be understood that that one particular item is what she wanted; by mentioning two things, *coat* and *sweater*, it may be that she is suggesting the *sort* of thing she wants. That is, she is indicating a category of things that includes coats, sweaters, and other things, a category that contrasts with the category of things that includes electric skillets. When it is pointed out later in the exchange that her husband had gotten her a "little Zippo" lighter for Christmas, Ted, one of the participants, comments, "At least it was for her use." This seems to evidence an analysis by Ted of what the mother was getting at with *coat* and *sweater*. Bob goes on to say: "So we went out and bought her a bracelet." Again, this exhibits an analysis of his mother's desires: Although they didn't get her either of the things she mentioned, they got the *sort* of thing she apparently wants, a personal thing.

The presently relevant point, again, is that we can create categories as we need them. We can do it explicitly with a phrase such as "things that are meant for personal use," or we can suggest them by more indirect means – for example, with lists that contain or imply "etcetera." A cultural analysis of the ethnosemantic sort is incapable of revealing, let alone analyzing, such categorial creations.

In all the various ways that I have mentioned, Sacks leads one from a cultural/cognitive conception of categories to an approach that treats categories and categorization as embedded in and constructive of everyday interaction.

The Sacksian tradition of category analysis has been further developed by various scholars, many of them contributors to the present volume. In what follows, I will describe *occasioned semantics* (OS), an approach that I have been developing over the last 12 years (Bilmes 2008, 2009a, 2009b, 2010, 2011, 2015, 2019, 2020; also Bilmes 1993).[12] OS is the study of the emergence and nature of structures of meaning in discourse. In practice, it has focused mainly on interactive talk. Like Sacks, it is concerned with co-categorization and contrast. But, I have attempted to expand Sacksian analysis in several ways. First, whereas Sacks was primarily (although not, as we have seen, exclusively) concerned with membership categorization and built his "apparatus" to deal with that, OS deals with all types of categorization and with formulations that are not, strictly speaking, categories.

Second, although, as I mentioned above, devices can be nested within devices, neither Sacks nor his successors have developed this hierarchical perspective on categories. Perhaps because I had some training in the analysis of folk taxonomies, this became the opening that led to the development of OS. Processes of generalization and specification were the primary concern of my first OS papers.

Along with co-categorization, contrast, and inclusion/subsumption, there was a further fundamental structural element to be considered – scaling. This was not a central concern for Sacks, certainly not one for which he tried to develop a general, formal apparatus, but there are points in his work where one can see an interest in scale-like phenomena. There is, for example, Sacks's notion of "positioned categories" (1992, Vol. 1: 585), where one member can be said to be higher or lower than another (as with baby–adolescent–adult). Another example from Sacks is the ordered invocation of different categories of persons, as described in "The Search for Help" (Sacks 1967), although I find it difficult to put a name to the scale involved, as it involves not only intimacy (family, friends), but also professional expertise. Scaling is also implicit in the notions of upgrading and downgrading and extreme case formulation, both introduced into the CA literature by Pomerantz (1978, 1984, 1986).[13] OS tries to examine scales in a more explicit and formal way. One finding has been that a great deal of verbal interaction can be seen as scaling actions – identifying and negotiating scale types and position – and understanding scaling choices is a key to understanding implicature and implication and, in general, how utterances function (see especially Hauser and Prior 2019).

In addition, I have tried to augment Sacks's rules and maxims. Sacks's earliest treatment of what he called *preference* led to my development of the notion of response priority and priority mention (Bilmes 1993):[14] *If X is the first priority response (or first priority mention), then any response (or mention) other than X, including no response (or mention), implicates (when it does not explicitly assert) that X is not available or is not in effect, unless there is reason to suppose that it has been withheld.* The notion of response priority resulted from (or perhaps led into) my interest in scaling. Moreover, as I worked with structures of inclusion, I "discovered" a number of maxims. So, for example: *When item A is contrasted with a more inclusive item B, this may suggest a categorization of item A.* When a party in a mediation session said, "I didn't come here … just to give a phone number and put something down in writing … I come in here for substantial reasons," he was implicitly categorizing the two specific actions that he mentioned as trivial reasons (see Bilmes [2015: 98–100] for a more detailed discussion of this utterance). Or, to take another example: *To maximize communicated information, make your contrast at the highest taxonomic level that maintains the contrast.* One can say that poodles bark and Herefords moo, but it is more informative to say that dogs bark and cows moo.

I have space for only two brief examples of OS analysis. The first deals with taxonomic concerns – co-categorization, contrast, hierarchy. The segment is from a radio interview of a brothel manager first presented by Lawrence (1996) and reanalyzed in Chapters 3 and 4 of Bilmes (2015):

Segment 2: radio interview

1. IE: … I can remember
2. picking up the socialhh section of the newspaper, and seeing
3. young men that I knew as customers, .hh that married nice
4. gir:ls .hh uh but while they were courting, .h um while
5. they were (0.4) into u:h .hh u:h the relationship, .h they

6. didn't want they didn't want to go out on these girls.
7. (1.1) They used (.7) the house and its facilities. (2.3)
8. IR: Rather than:: (0.5) wwhat is the saying violate:
9. the one that they love. (.7)
10. IE: Y:es. (.) or as opposed to going to a bar and maybe
11. getting mixed up with a bar gir:l. .h o:r u::h (1.1) .hh
12. (0.6) u::h there is a difference .h between a house
13. girl and a street girl an' anything .hh we- u- let me
14. define what street means that means any (.) .hh girl that
15. works on the street .h or in a ta:vern (0.2) or- (.4) a
16. massage parlor, (.4) .h where uh: (1) she doesn't
17. have a place to live right along with it (.) those are
18. street girls.

(Lawrence 1996)

Looking at this extract, we can see that IE has built a structure of taxonomic relations, as shown in Figure 5.3.

In my analysis of this interview (in Bilmes 2015: Chapter 3), a good deal of the discussion is focused on this taxonomy. Because of space limitations, I will deal only with a single point. This multilayered structure has two occurrences of what Horn (1984) terms "autohyponymy." Both "girls" and "street" (girls) appear at two taxonomic levels. (I have differentiated these homophonic usages with subscripted numbers.) The first of these is of particular interest. When IE says "any girl" in line 14, she clearly does not literally mean any girl. There are, for instance, girls who work in taverns who are not "bar girls." So, whereas "girls$_1$" refers generically to (sexually mature) females, "girls$_2$" (as in "any girls") refers to some subset – to wit, prostitutes. (Apparently, it is common practice within the trade to refer to prostitutes as "girls," regardless of age.)

To come at this from a different direction, the co-categorization of house girls and street girls as prostitutes is locally implied in two ways. First, the "as

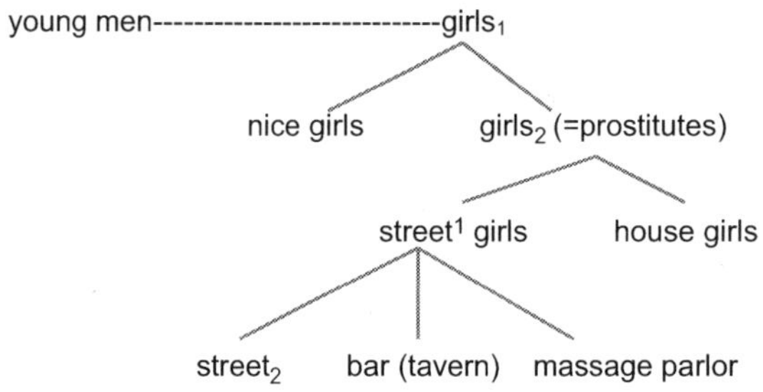

Figure 5.3 The madam's taxonomy

opposed to" juxtaposition of house girls and street girls suggests that they are members of a common category. That is, contrastive oppositions imply common categorial membership. Sacks makes a related point: "If two or more categories are used to categorize two or more Members to some population, and those categories can be heard as categories from the same collection, hear them that way" (1992, Vol. 1: 247). In some contexts, "house girl" might be understood as meaning housemaid. The juxtaposition with "street girl" indicates (redundantly, in this case) how *house girl* is to be understood in this context. *House girl* and *street girl* can be heard as "categories from the same collection," that collection being *prostitute*, and so we hear them that way.

Second, IE says that, "there is a difference between a house girl and a street girl." The fact that she finds it necessary to mention this suggests that some people might not know the difference – that is, they might see them as essentially the same. So, we are directed to the feature that they share: namely, that they are prostitutes.

My point is simply to suggest that the representation and contemplation of participants' categorial formulations in taxonomic form can lead to insights that might otherwise not occur to the analyst. But it is apparent that something important is missing from the analysis of structures of meaning from a purely taxonomic perspective. That is valuation, or, more generally, scaling. (In the interview from which Segment 2 is drawn, house girls are valued differently from street girls.) Politeness, marking, and a variety of other conversational phenomena are encompassed in the study of scales. Just as Sacks's work provided the bridge connecting ethnosemantics to the treatment of taxonomic relations in OS, it connected the linguistic pragmatic approach to scalar relations to the treatment of scales in OS. The essence of that transformation is the discovery of scalar processes in actual occasions of talk, including how participants create, develop, and modify scales in the course of that talk.

The scales constructed and negotiated in actual talk can be highly articulated and may interact with one another. Again, I can offer as illustration only a small bit of analysis. (For the full analysis, see Bilmes 2010, 2019.) The data are part of a series of interviews that Matthew Prior did with a man who had immigrated to Canada as a youth.[15]

Segment 3: prior interview

64 M: But- (0.9) what about that one time you-(.) you s(h)aid (.) you
65 threatened=
66 E: =to kill them=
67 M: =That-(.) °that one cook°
68 (1.1)
69 E: Huh?
70 M: The one who took your shoes?
71 E: Oh yeah. (.) t' kill them (.) yeah.

72 M: What is it you said (.) I'm gonna kill you or=
73 E: Yeah
74 M: I'm gonna [cut you?
75 E: [yeah
76 M: What did you say?
77 E: No I said [(I wanna I'm gonna) punch you (0.9)
78 M: [punch you
79 E: But punch you not (.) I think it's not too bad.
80 But when I said I'm gonna kill you because (0.6) that time
81 because I really::-.hh (1.8) see (0.4) those anger (0.3) that
82 anger unh-I have a lot of anger inside of me::.
83 (0.9)
84 I knew I (ha') a lot of anger inside of me sometime.
85 (1.1)
86 This anger one day might explode like a-(.) uh (.) that's why
87 I-(.) the only thing I see myself (.) that's why I try to
88 seek counseling the best I-(.) I try to make time to seek
89 counseling to talk about my anger (.) all the time.
90 (0.9)
91 .hh but my anger toward to someone that (1.3) I think (.)
92 mistreating me.
93 (1.4)
94 I don't go pick a fight w-with people y'see? ((slaps hand on leg))
95 I don't go bullying people I don't ((slaps hand on leg))
96 Because (.) since I wa' a child (.) m-because mostly my
97 father (0.7) or people bully me all the time. An' this anger
98 s-s-keep carry on in me-in-inside of me (1.1) °You see?° (.8)
99 And then suddenly when I (.4) even now till today, if someone
100 arrogant (1.0) arrogant people(.)obnoxious pe-(.) o-o-obnoxious?
101 M: (0.6) ((nods head))
102 E: And (.) anywhere
103 (.05)
104 If someone come to me and say (1.8) You an asshole (.) example.
105 (1.4)
106 I either (0.3) punch him or s-sp-fight back with him.
107 (1.3)
108 M: Have you punched somebody?
109 E: Not yet=
110 M: H-hh ((soft laugh))
111 (.4)
112 E: Almost (.) ((smiles)) (1.8) HHH. ((laughing exhale))
113 (1.1)
114 M: Have you yelled at somebody?
115 E: Ye::s, (.5) All the time.
116 M: ALL the time? ((laughing))

117 E: >Not all the time but sometime I-< (.2) a s'few time in
118 Toronto. A few time. (.6) A few time (.)specially wit' the
119 car. ((E continues with a story about dangerous drivers))

Prior 2016b: 229–230

I suggested that the primary scale here is *yell<—>punch<—>cut<—>kill*. I can ground this scale, except for the placement of *cut*, in the data, although, again, because of space limitations, I must confine myself here to one point. E speaks about his anger and violent disposition, but, when M asks him, in line 108, if he has punched someone, he admits that he hasn't. (Note, though, that he qualifies this with "not yet" and "almost." It seems that there are degrees of *never*.) At this point, M moves down the scale, asking if he has yelled at someone. (Again, note how E "supercharges" his affirmative answer with "all the time.") I would suggest, subject to further research, that, when someone says, in answer to a specific question, that he did not do something of extremity X, it is then in order for the questioner to ask about X-minus-1; on the other hand, if the answer is that he did indeed do something of extremity X, this may lead to a question about X-plus-1. We see here how scales may have sequential implications.

When we deal with the structure of meaning in conversation, we are not dealing with A's conceptual structure, or B's, or a combination of the two, or a representation of their shared knowledge, even if we take that knowledge to be specifically-for-this-occasion. Rather, the taxonomy or scale represents the emergent structure of meaning of the conversation itself, a semantic skeleton, an abstract set of terminological–conceptual relations as manifested in a culturally contexted discourse. *It is a field of meaning, co-constructed in and for the moment.* These structures are not usually created in a linear fashion. Rather, the structure is cobbled together by the participants bit by bit, from every direction. The ultimate coherence of the structure arises from the participants' sensitivity to the parts that are already in place. A conversational structure is a product of sequential operations. But the structure of concepts represented by the taxonomy is suprasequential. Once the structure is created, it is there as a condition of further talk. Some structural relations that are evident in interactive talk are "relations in the language" – that is, they are conventional. But there are also "occasioned relations" (see also Jayyusi 1984: 81ff.). And even the in-the-language relations are occasioned in the sense that they are locally invoked for purposes of the current exchange.

Presumably, other broad dimensions of meaning structure, besides the taxonomic and scalar, will eventually be incorporated into OS. The essential character of the endeavor, though, will remain unchanged, rooted in the seminal work of Harvey Sacks. The key to OS, the thing that makes it a kind of Sacksian/ethnomethodological analysis, is the attention to the local construction and invocation of meaning. The question is, how have the participants constructed a structure of meaning on *this* occasion, and what is the nature of that structure? The *how* question is largely to be answered through the use of sequential analysis as it has been developed by Sacks, Schegloff, Jefferson, and their successors. But elucidation of the nature of the structure, as well as the overall orientation of the endeavor, draws primarily on the approach to categories and formulation developed by Sacks.

Notes

1 Also known as *ethnoscience*, *cognitive anthropology*, and *the new ethnography*. For a fairly comprehensive introduction, see Tyler (1969). Also, Sturtevant (1964) and Wallace (1962), among many others.
2 See Bilmes (2015: Chapter 2). For a different take on the logic of inclusion taxonomy vs. partonomy, see McClure (1975).
3 See Eglin (1980) for an application of the ethnomethodological perspective to taxonomic analysis and Wieder (1970) for an ethnomethodological critique of componential analysis, another ethnosemantic technique.
4 This is my view. I don't know if Sacks was cognizant of such an analogy. He may have been familiar with ethnosemantics; he mentions ethnoscience (another designation for ethnosemantics) briefly (1992: 26), so it is possible that it in some way influenced his development of membership categorization analysis.
5 "[Anthropologists are] studying the categories that members use [by asking questions of informants], except at this point they are not investigating their categories by attempting to find them in the activities in which they're employed" (Sacks 1992, Vol. 1: 27).
6 Although Sacks created this "apparatus" to deal with human social membership categories, clearly it has a more general application. For example, rats and squirrels belong to a collection including gerbils, beavers, porcupines, etc., collected in the device "rodent."
7 However, when we generalize a negative (e.g., "not elm" to "not tree"), we add information (Bilmes 2009).
8 E.g., maybe he said this because he saw a rat and he knows that I hate rats.
9 A variation of type 1 is that the category entails the occurrence of one or more, but not necessarily all, activities from a set. And, of course, there are *possible predicates*, that is, actions that are made possible, but not necessary, as a consequence of the category.
10 For another elaboration of Sacks's notion of category-bound activities, see Reynolds and Fitzgerald (2015).
11 This is an extended application of Sacks's system. It suggests that, for analytical purposes, any action may be treated as representing a category or as a predicate of a category. In this case, for example, I have treated "calling the police" as a category and "smack" as a possible predicate of that category. Sacks seem to be doing as much by suggesting that calling the police entails at least one of a (culturally known) set of activities that constitute "good grounds" for making such a call.
12 Others who have contributed to the development of occasioned semantics include Deppermann (2005, 2011), Hauser (2011, in press), Hauser and Prior (2019), Hayashi (2016, 2019), Izumi (2017, 2019), Lee (2019), Matsutani (2019), and Prior (2016a, 2016b, 2019).
13 Of course, much of the inspiration for OS work on scaling comes from linguistic pragmatic work on implicature (Grice 1975; Horn 1972; Levinson 2000).
14 Paul Drew's (1985, 1992) related notion of *maximization* should also be mentioned in this context, although I was not aware of his work on this matter when I developed the concept of response priority.
15 Prior (2016b) offers his own analysis of this segment.

References

Bilmes, Jack. 1993. Ethnomethodology, culture, and implicature: Toward an empirical pragmatics. *Pragmatics* 3, 387–409.

Bilmes, Jack. 2008. Generally speaking: Formulating an argument in the U.S. Federal Trade Commission. *Text & Talk* 28, 193–217.

Bilmes, Jack. 2009a. Taxonomies are for talking: A reanalysis of a Sacks classic. *Journal of Pragmatics* 41, 1600–1610.

Bilmes, Jack. 2009b. Kinship categories in a Northern Thai narrative. In: Kasper, G. and Nguyen, H. (eds.), *Talk-in-Interaction: Multilingual Perspectives*. Honolulu: University of Hawaii National Foreign Language Resource Center, pp. 29–56.

Bilmes, Jack. 2010. Scaling as an aspect of formulation in verbal interaction. In: *Language learning and socialization through conversations*. Conference proceedings. Center for Human Activity Theory. Kansai University, Osaka, Japan, pp. 3–9.

Bilmes, Jack. 2011. Occasioned semantics: A systematic approach to meaning in talk. *Human Studies* 34, 129–153.

Bilmes, Jack. 2015. *The Structure of Meaning in Talk: Explorations in Category Analysis. Volume I: Co-categorization, Contrast, and Hierarchy.* Internet document available on EMCA-legacy, academia.edu, researchgate.net

Bilmes, Jack. 2019. Regrading as a conversational practice. *Journal of Pragmatics* 150 *(Special Issue on Topicalizing Regrading in Interaction*, Prior, M. T. and Hauser, E. [eds.]), 80–91.

Bilmes, Jack. 2020. The discussion of abortion in U.S political debates: A study in occasioned semantics. *Discourse Studies* 22(3), 291–318.

Brown, Cecil H. 1976. General principles of human anatomical partonomy and speculations on the growth of partonomic nomenclature. *American Ethnologist* 3(3), 400–424.

Brown, Cecil H., Kolar, John, Torrey, Barbara J., and Truong-Quang, Tipawan. 1976. Some general principles of biological and non-biological folk classification. *American Ethnologist* 3, 73–85.

Deppermann, Arnulf. 2005. Conversational interpretation of lexical items and conversational contrasting. In: Hakulinen, A. and Selting, M. (eds.), *Syntax and Lexis in Conversation: Studies on the Use of Linguistic Resources in Talk-in-Interaction*. Amsterdam: John Benjamins, pp. 289–306.

Deppermann, Arnulf. 2011. The study of formulations as a key to an interactional semantics. *Human Studies* 34, 115–128.

Drew, Paul. 1985. Analyzing the use of language in courtroom interaction. In: van Dijk, T. A. (ed.), *Handbook of Discourse Analysis 3*. London: Academic Press, pp. 133–147.

Drew, Paul. 1992. Contested evidence in courtroom cross-examination: The case of a trial for rape. In: Drew, P. and Heritage, J. (eds.), *Talk at Work: Interaction in Institutional Settings*. Cambridge: Cambridge University Press, pp. 470–520.

Edwards, Derek. 1998. The relevant thing about her: Social identity categories in use. In: Antaki, C. and Widdicombe, S. (eds.), *Identities in Talk*. London: Sage, pp. 15–33

Eglin, Peter. 1980. *Talk and Taxonomy: A Methodological Comparision of Ethnosemantics and Ethnomethodology with Reference to Terms for Canadian Doctors*. Amsterdam: John Benjamins.

Frake, Charles O. 1961. The diagnosis of disease among the Subanun of Mindanao. *American Anthropologist* 63, 113–132.

Frake, Charles O. 1962. The ethnographic study of cognitive systems. In: Gladwin, T. and Sturtevent, W. C. (eds.), *Anthropology and Human Behavior*. Washington: Anthropological Society of Washington, pp. 72–85.

Grice, H. Paul. 1975. Logic and conversation. In: Cole, P. and Morgan, J. L. (eds.), *Syntax and Semantics 3: Speech Acts*. New York: Academic Press, pp. 41–58.

Hauser, Eric. 2011. Generalization: A practice of situated categorization in talk. *Human Studies* 34, 183–198.

Hauser, Eric. In press. Construction of an evaluative taxonomy within a story. *Text and Talk*.

Hauser, Eric and Prior, Matthew. 2019. Introduction to the special issue: Topicalizing regrading in interaction. *Journal of Pragmatics*. doi: 10.1016/j.pragma.2019.07.001.

Hauser, Eric and Prior, Matthew T. 2019. Introduction to *Journal of Pragmatics* 150 *(Special Issue on Topicalizing Regrading in Interaction*, Prior, M. T. and Hauser, E. [eds.]), 75–79.

Hayashi, Reiko. 2016. Categorization in talk: A case study of taxonomies and social meaning. *Pragmatics* 26(2), 197–219.

Hayashi, Reiko. 2019. Categorization for occasioned semantics: Reanalysis of a Japanese Yamagata 119 emergency call. *Discourse Studies* 21(5), 495–521.

Horn, Lawrence R. 1972. *On the semantic properties of logical operators in English*. PhD thesis, University of University of California, Los Angeles.

Horn, Lawrence R. 1984. In defense of privative ambiguity. *Proceedings of the Tenth Annual Meeting of the Berkeley Linguistics Society* 141–156.

Izumi, Hiroaki. 2017. A technical analysis of scaling in rehabilitation team talk. *Journal of Pragmatics* 121, 1–24.

Izumi, Hiroaki. 2019. Regrading and implicature: Sequential structures of mobility scales in Japanese rehabilitation team interaction. *Journal of Pragmatics* 150 *(Special Issue on Topicalizing Regrading in Interaction*, Prior, M. T. and Hauser, E. [eds.]), 111–132.

Jayyusi, Lena. 1984. *Categorization and the Moral Order*. New York: Routledge & Kegan Paul.

Kay, Paul. 1971. Taxonomy and semantic contrast. *Language* 47, 866–887.

Lawrence, Samuel G. 1996. Normalizing stigmatized practices: Achieving co-membership by doing being ordinary. *Research on Language & Social Interaction* 29, 181–218.

Lee, Josephine. 2019. Scaling as an argumentative resource in television talk shows. *Journal of Pragmatics* 150 *(Special Issue on Topicalizing Regrading in Interaction*, Prior, M. T. and Hauser, E. [eds.]), 133–149.

Levinson, Stephen C. 2000. *Presumptive Meanings: The Theory of Generalized Conversational Implicature*. Cambridge, MA: MIT Press.

Matsutani, Yuka. 2019. Regrading on and through timescales. *Journal of Pragmatics* 150 *(Special Issue on Topicalizing Regrading in Interaction*, Prior, M. T. and Hauser, E. [eds.]), 150–166.

McClure, Erica F. 1975. Ethnoanatomy: The structure of the domain. *Anthropological Linguistics* 17(2), 78–88.

Pomerantz, Anita. 1978. Compliment responses: Notes on the co-operation of multiple constraints. In: Schenkein, J. (ed.), *Studies in the Organization of Conversational Interaction*. New York: Academic Press, pp. 79–112.

Pomerantz, Anita. 1984. Agreeing and disagreeing with assessments: Some features of preferred/dispreferred turn shapes. In: Atkinson, J. M. and Heritage, J. (eds.), *Structures of*

Social Action: Studies in Conversation Analysis. Cambridge: Cambridge University Press, pp. 57–101.

Pomerantz, Anita. 1986. Extreme case formulations: Way of legitimizing claims. *Human Studies* 9, 219–229.

Prior, Matthew T. 2016a. *Emotion and Discourse in L2 Narrative Research*. Tonawanda: Multilingual Matters.

Prior, Matthew T. 2016b. Formulating and scaling emotionality in L2 qualitative research interviews. In: Prior, M. T. and Kasper, G. (eds.), *Emotion in Multilingual Interaction*. Amsterdam: John Benjamins, pp. 203–236.

Prior, Matthew T. 2019. The interactional dynamics of scaling and contrast in accounts. *Journal of Pragmatics* 150 (*Special Issue on Topicalizing Regrading in Interaction*, Prior, M. T. and Hauser, E. [eds.]), 92–110.

Reynolds, Edward and Fitzgerald, Richard. 2015. Challenging normativity: Re-appraising category, bound, tied and predicated features. In: Fitzgerald, R. and Housley, W. (eds.), *Advances in Membership Categorization Analysis*. London: Sage, pp. 99–122.

Sacks, Harvey. 1967. The search for help: No one to turn to. In: Shneidman, E. S. (ed.), *Essays in Self Destruction*. New York: Science House, pp. 203–223.

Sacks, Harvey. 1992. *Lectures on Conversation* (edited by Jefferson, G.). Oxford: Blackwell.

Sharrock, W. W. 1974. On owning knowledge. In: Turner, R. (ed.), *Ethnomethodology: Selected Readings*. Middlesex, England: Penguin, pp. 45–53.

Sturtevant, William C. 1964. Studies in ethnoscience. In: Romney, A. K. and D'Andrade, R. G. (Eds.), *Transcultural Studies in Cognition. American Anthropologist* 66(3), pt. 2: 99–131.

Tyler, Stephen. 1969. Introduction. In: Tyler, S. (ed.), *Cognitive Anthropology*. New York: Holt, Rinehart & Winston, pp. 1–23.

Wallace, Anthony F. C. 1962. Culture and cognition. *Science* 135(3501), 351–357.

Watson, D. R. 1978. Categorization, authorization and blame: Negotiation in conversation. *Sociology* 12, 105–113.

Wieder, D. Lawrence. 1970. On meaning by rule. In: Douglas, J. D. (ed.), *Understanding Everyday Life: Toward the Reconstruction of Sociological Knowledge*. Chicago: Aldine Publishing, pp. 107–135.

6 Sacks, categories, language, and gender

Elizabeth Stokoe, Bogdana Huma, and Derek Edwards

How does one study topics such as 'language' and 'gender'? Both terms open seams of empirical and theoretical work that stretch across the social sciences and humanities. Many academic disciplines claim ownership of 'language' – or 'communication', 'social interaction', and other cognizant formulations – and 'gender', making the landscape hard to navigate. In this chapter, we chart our journey from reading Harvey Sacks's work on conversation analysis and membership categories to applying it in research on gender and language. As a co-authored chapter, we tell our interconnected story. I (Elizabeth Stokoe) will narrate our research journey in the first person, referring to Bogdana Huma and Derek Edwards as the chapter unfolds. We are three generations of PhD supervisors and students working in discursive psychology, as formulated by Edwards and Potter (1992). Discursive psychology's core aim, aligned to conversation analysis and ethnomethodology, is the *respecification* of psychology's topics (e.g., cognition, attitudes, memory, prejudice, identity) as members' orientations; as members', rather than analysts', topics. This chapter will describe how we were inspired by Sacks to interrogate *identity* through the sequential analysis of membership categories. We show how researchers can 'capture' gender as it is made relevant for the doing of some action in sequences of conversation, and how we might 'scale up' from a single case to working with larger datasets.

'The relevant thing about her'

I started out in the language and gender field during the early 1990s as a psychology PhD student. My topic was 'gender differences in university tutorial talk', and I was reading constructivist studies of cognitive development and interaction in school classrooms (e.g., Vygotsky, 1978). A basic premise of this work was that talking in small peer groups facilitates learning. However, a parallel literature was claiming to find that 'access' to this valuable resource of talk was unequal, and, in particular, that, because boys dominate mixed-sex groupwork, girls were not getting their fair share (e.g., Holden, 1993).

My initial interest, then, was in whether such a pattern would also be found in post-compulsory education settings (Stokoe, 1995). The limited evidence indeed suggested that, like boys in classrooms, adult male students dominated classroom proceedings, by, for example, taking more, and longer, turns at talk than female students (e.g., Kelly, 1991). However, analyses of my own data were throwing up problems. I had video-recorded 30 hours of small-group interactions in university tutorials, but was not finding evidence for women 'losing out' to men either in terms of variables such as number of turns, turn length, interruptions, and unilateral topic shifts, or in terms of the sociolinguistic features of talk routinely identified as gendered (e.g., hedges, tag questions). I began to rethink the 'gender differences' agenda, with its imposition of 'gender' on to data that did not appear to be 'gendered' either in a quantifiable way or from the perspective of the participants themselves (Stokoe, 1997). And then, one of my supervisors – Derek Edwards – recommended that I read Sacks.

In the mid-1990s, Derek published a series of papers (e.g., 1994, 1995a) in which he used conversation analysis to examine marriage guidance counselling interaction and began to respecify core social psychological phenomena such as schemas and scripts. He also published a review essay (1995b) of Sacks's (1992) lectures, arguing for their relevance to psychologists. A key focus of that essay was to draw attention to Sacks's work on people's deployment of membership categories: how social identity categories – as a core interest of social psychologists – are handled in use. Derek described Sacks's concern with how participants use descriptive categories and apply membership criteria as a way of performing various kinds of discursive action.

In 1998, Derek published a chapter entitled, 'The relevant thing about her'. He described the following episode from a group therapy session, analysed by Sacks in his lectures. Dan is the therapist; Ken is a client.

Transcript 6.1

Extract 1: From Sacks, 1992, p. 597 (line numbers added)

Ken: So did Louise call or anything this morning?
Dan: Why, didju expect her t'call?
Ken: No, I was just kinda hoping that she might be able to figure
out some way t-to come to the meetings and still be able
t'work. C'z she did seem like she d-wanted to come back, but
uh she didn't think she could.
Dan: D'you miss her?
Ken: Well in some ways yes, it's- it was uh nice having- having
the opposite sex in-in the room, you know, havin' a chick in
here.

In the *Lectures*, Sacks focuses on Ken's switch from a named person ('Louise') to a generalized gender category (line 09: 'the opposite sex … a chick') to account for his concern for her absence and to specify in what restricted sense he might 'miss her' (lines 07–08). 'Chick' is one of a variety of colloquial gender categorizations available to this group (1960s California teenagers), such that its choice signals something further about what the speaker is doing than merely his choice of a gender category. In his article, Derek notes that Sacks does not pursue that issue and its possibly sexist implications; indeed, he understands the remark as, locally and for them, part of a compliment. The feature that Sacks highlights is that, by using the generalized gender categories 'opposite sex' and 'chick', Ken effectively forestalls any inference that his concern might have been personal.

Approaching categories as something people themselves attend to contrasted starkly with how they figure in other kinds of social science, and particularly psychology, as analysts' categories of people, according to which the analyst offers explanations of what people do, what they say, and how they think. Derek encouraged me to apply this approach to my own data, and so I began to trawl my recordings for places where gender became the relevant thing about a speaker or the action underway. Transcript 6.2 is the extract that changed the way I began to approach the study of language and gender. It comes from small-group work inside a university tutorial, in which four psychology students are analysing an image in a magazine. They have been instructed to produce a collaborative written report about the materials they are discussing. Bob reminds them of this task.

Transcript 6.2

UT-23 University Tutorial (Stokoe, 1998; 2018)

```
01  Bob:   Is somebody scribing. who's writin' it.=
02  Ned:   =Oh yhe:ah.
03               (0.8)
04  Matt:  Well you can't [ r e a d        m y    ] writin' once I've=
05  Ned:                  [She wants to do it.    ]
06  Matt:  =[wri:tten it.]
07  Klara:  [.hehhhh     ]
08  Ned:   We:ll secretary an' female.
```

```
09               (0.3)
10  Klara: .Hh heh heh heh
11               (0.4)
12  Matt:  It's uh::,
13  Klara: Yeah: I'm wearing glasses I must be the secretary.=
14  Bob:   =I think- (.) we're all agreed she's physical.
```

To meet the tutor-imposed task demands, one member of the group must write down their ideas. Bob's question at the start of the sequence 'Is somebody scribing.' is taken up after a reformulation: 'who's writin' it.'. Note that, through a variety of strategies, members of the group manage their responses such that they do not have to take on the role of scribe. At line 02, Ned's 'Oh yeah:.' treats Bob's turn as a proposal to be agreed with, rather than a request for action, and his subsequent nomination of Klara directs the role away from himself. Matt offers an account of why he cannot act as scribe: 'Well you can't read my writin'' (lines 04 and 06). By taking the opening turn and issuing the first pair part of an adjacency pair, Bob positions himself as someone requiring an answer or offer concerning who will 'scribe', rather than as someone who will take up the role. At line 05, Ned nominates Klara, his pointing gesture working in aggregate with the talk ('She wants to do it.') to accomplish the action, while also attributing agency to Klara for taking up the role. Her response at line 07, which overlaps with Matt's account, is to laugh rather than align with his suggestion.

At line 08, Ned nominates Klara for a second time, suggesting 'We:ll secretary an' female.', offering the category 'secretary' as a replacement for 'scribe'. Further, he juxtaposes 'female' with 'secretary'. Ned's second nomination accounts for the prior one, and is formulated so as to display his reasoning that coupling 'occupational' and 'gender' categories is or should be obvious and recognizable. A gloss might be 'secretaries in general are female, you're female, and so you can be our secretary'. Thus, Ned's turn achieves two things: it provides for a categorial identity for the person who will write for the group, and renders him (and the other group members) excluded from possible incumbency in that position.

Klara's response to Ned's second nomination is interesting. She picks up her paper and pen, thus aligning with the role nomination and carrying out its preliminary activities, but she does not join in with his formulation of 'secretary' as 'female'. Instead, she produces a different characterological imputation for 'secretary': 'Yeah: I'm wearing glasses I must be the secretary' (line 13). This may demonstrate some resistance towards Ned's categorical references. Alternatively, it may offer further category-bound reasons for why Klara should occupy the role. We do not have access to more than this; neither do the participants. Klara's response is ambiguous, and language is her resource for this ambiguity.

In Transcript 6.2, then, one participant invokes the notion that secretaries are women at a particular point to make something happen. And Klara becomes the secretary. Her participation in the discussion is reduced to note taker. The extract shows that, and how, one can solve the problem of 'capturing' gender as an endogenous feature of social interaction, without requiring an analyst to impose their interpretation or presume a priori things about women and men. For much of my PhD, I pursued this approach, discovering a handful of instances in which gender became the 'relevant thing' for the sequential organization of interaction. However, although my instances were all about gender, the category was not necessarily embedded in the same kind of turn, delivering the same kind of action, in the same kind of sequence. My problem later became how to 'scale up' my categorial analysis to identify practices across sequences of interaction.

From gender difference, to gender construction, to gender relevance

While I was grappling with my PhD, and Derek was working with other colleagues at Loughborough University to bring Sacks, and conversation analysis, into psychology, research on language and gender was going through multiple transformations. In the mid-1990s, across feminist social science, humanities, and linguistics, it was becoming commonplace to write about gender as a construction rather than as an essential and unchanging 'fact' of individuals, mapped to sex. This shift was in response to dissatisfaction, both conceptual and methodological, with work on gender differences in language (see Speer & Stokoe, 2011, for an overview).

'Difference' studies were criticized for committing what Cameron (1997) called the correlational fallacy, whereby particular linguistic features are attributed unproblematically to one sex/gender or the other. For example, the idea that men grab power by interrupting women (more than women interrupt men) is based on a methodological flaw in the analysis of 'interruption'. Consider Transcript 6.3.

Transcript 6.3

From Beattie (1983)

```
01  A:   … so he (.) he gives the impression that he
02       wasn't able to train them up. [Now
03  B:                                 [He didn't try hard
04       enough heh heh heh
```

The original analyst of this example claimed that 'Speaker B clearly interrupts Speaker A'. However, Kitzinger (2008) points out that, in fact, Speaker B starts talking *precisely* at the point when Speaker A reaches the end of their sentence – in technical terms, the end of a 'turn constructional unit', which constitutes a 'transition relevance place'. As conversation analysts have shown since CA's inception (Sacks et al., 1974), the placement and operation of turn-taking is entirely routine; in Transcript 6.3, B does not interrupt A.

For many feminists and other critically oriented researchers, 'difference' studies are both theoretically and methodologically circular, and politically unproductive. Difference studies, which prioritize the analyst's taken-for-granted assumptions about gender-/sex-based differences, prevented researchers from 'finding' anything other than a reified, dualistic category. The examples below show how this might work in practice. Transcript 6.4 is from the start of a telephone call from a prospective client to a double-glazing company, and Transcript 6.5 is from the start of a call from a pet owner to their vet.

Transcript 6.4

Buying double glazing
01 Sales: G'd afternoon, ↑Fine Bar ↑Wi:ndows,
02 (0.6)
03 Cust: .shih (.) .hh >hi< w'd it be ↑po:ssible f'somebody t'come an'
04 give me a quote on uh: a window an: some doors please.

Transcript 6.5

Calling the vet
01 Vet: Dunnetts Vets.=Highuptown, Maggie speaking, how can I ↓he:lp.
02 (0.4)
03 Cust: Hello there:.=um: I need t'make an appointment t'bring the
04 cat in t'get its um: updated ↓vaccina:tions.

In both cases, the callers are making a request. They design their requests differently. For some 'difference' researchers, the customer calling about windows uses stereotypically female language (e.g., Lakoff, 1973), with hedges and modal verbs ('Would it be possible'), hesitations ('.shih (.) .hh'), and politeness markers ('please'). The pet owner is stereotypically male, with a direct request ('I need ...') which is less 'polite'. However, the caller in Transcript 6.4 is a man; in Transcript 6.5, it is a woman. Perhaps these are just atypical cases – obviously not all men and women speak like their stereotype! But, if we start and stop with gender as the only lens through which to interpret the data, we identify only exceptions that prove the rule.

Following Sacks, and as articulated strongly by Schegloff (e.g., 1991), conversation analysts typically examine the action being done, rather than the speaker doing the action, and have shown that the design of requests is oriented to other kinds of contingency such as how urgent the request is, how entitled one is to make it, or how familiar one is with the grantability of it (Curl & Drew, 2008). These kinds of contingency better account for differences in request design than the presumption of gender difference. Järviluoma et al. (2003: 2) suggest that, 'gender should be understood as a concept requiring analysis, rather than as something that is *already* known about' (emphasis in original).

In the field of language and gender studies, the focus on 'difference', and its underpinning essentialism began to be replaced in the late 1990s by 'construction' and 'performance'; research was 'engulfed in a wave of social constructionism' as researchers resisted simple binaries (Holmes, 2007: 52). However, studies about the 'construction' of gender often tacitly maintained essentialism, particularly those that collected the talk of women or men, in interviews or natural settings, and then looked at how women perform femininities and men perform masculinities. There was rarely a notion in such work of people *not performing gender*. If the data did not 'look like' recognizable femininity or masculinity, the 'finding' was that gender identity is not what we thought it was, or that it is variable, inconsistent, multiple, or fragmentary (Edwards & Stokoe, 2004). Thus, the *performance* of gender was explained or accounted for in a somewhat circular fashion, leaving what Velody and Williams (1998) call a 'realist residue'. This type of 'constructionist' research, therefore, buys back into the sex difference framework that it was originally designed to replace and inadvertently reintroduces essentialism and determinist understandings of gender identity construction 'by the back door' (Stokoe, 2008).

The foundations of the constructionist wave, and performative work in language and gender more generally, owes some debt – whether explicitly or implicitly – to ethnomethodology, via Garfinkel's (1967) work on 'passing' (see particularly Kessler & McKenna, 1978; West & Zimmerman, 1987). But it was Sacks's work on membership categorization that, we argue, had a much more radical impact on understanding gender. This is because it implied a method, a set of criteria for a robust empirical approach. With regard to identity categories – gender or anything else – conversation analysts led by Sacks *invert* what previous language and gender researchers have done when they either rush to explain differences in language use or examine, in a circular way, the construction of gender identities, in some stretch of data. LeBaron (1998, quoted in Tracy, 1998: 15) summarizes the conversation analytic position:

> [W]e should not … say 'oh, look, here's a man and a woman talking; … oh, we can make these conclusions about gendered communication'. But rather we should say, 'gender only becomes an issue when the participants themselves make it one and we can point to different things about that'.

For Sacks, and particularly for Schegloff, any analysis of categories should be based in what participants do and say, rather than in what analysts take to be relevant as a function of their hypotheses, research questions, politics, or theory. From this perspective, then, to warrant an analytic claim that a particular category is relevant to any stretch of interaction, the analyst must be able to demonstrate that such identities are linked to specific actions. There are two key issues here for conversation analysts. First, the *problem of relevance*: Given the indefinitely extendable number of ways any person may be categorized, how should we decide which from a range of potential identities is relevant? The answer is to go by what is demonstrably relevant to participants 'at the moment that whatever we are trying to produce an account for occurs' (Schegloff, 1991: 50). Second, the issue of *procedural consequentiality*: If we can establish that a particular identity category is relevant, can we see that it is consequential for participants, in terms of its trajectory, content, character, or organizational procedures?

Conversation analysts, then, must be able to show that, and how, 'participants' production of the world was itself informed by these particular categorization devices […] that the parties were oriented to that categorization device in producing and understanding – moment-by-moment – the conduct that composed its progressive realization' (Schegloff, 2007: 475). If the participants do orient to gender, then that gives us grounds, as analysts, for making the claim that gender is 'procedurally consequential' for (that is, has a direct influence on) what is going on in the interaction. Conversely, if they do not orient to gender, then we do not have grounds for claiming that gender is relevant or consequential for the participants in the interaction at that moment.

For Sacks (1992: 597), any study of categorial topics must consider how categories – in our case, gender – 'might be relevant for the doing of some activity'. Key empirical and theoretical studies demonstrating this approach were published in the late 1990s, including Hopper and Le Baron's (1998) demonstration of the stepwise process through which 'gender creeps into talk'; that is, how gender gets 'noticed' and becomes focal, rather than peripheral, in talk. In a related study, Stringer and Hopper (1998: 213) analysed 'repair sequences' initiated by speakers' use of the generic 'he' when referring to 'sex-unspecified incumbents of traditionally male social categories'. In Edwards's (1998: 15) study of 'identity categories in use', he showed how gender is picked out as 'the relevant thing' about participants in marriage guidance counselling interaction, again often within a repair operation. Finally, I published the analysis of Transcript 6.2, and other instances from my PhD materials, about how gender may be invoked as a category as part of an action that is then relevant to the subsequent trajectory of that encounter (Stokoe, 1998).

Sacks's lectures provided a crucial foundation for the systematic analysis of membership categories and related phenomena. Starting with his often-idiosyncratic observations about membership categories, I decided to tackle head-on how to track categorial concerns in the same way that conversation analysts pursue sequential practices. In so doing, I provided a 'how to' for the systematic analysis of membership categories and argued that a reinvigorated focus on membership categories was essential for protecting and maintaining some of the most exciting aspects of Sacks's legacy (Stokoe, 2012a). In the broader ethnomethodological field, which has been sadly rife with tensions, caricatures, and fractures over the years, I argued for work on categorization to survive and be respected. To do this, one must address Schegloff's (2007: 477) concerns about embracing 'the rest of the field of which it is presumptively a part and what has been learned in it'. In the final section, we move on to bring Bogdana into our story, whose research provides an example of how to fulfil the call to action described above.

Scaling up from 'the relevant thing about her'

So far in this chapter, we have charted our journey from a problem – 'finding' gender in materials that did not support the prevailing paradigm of 'difference' via Sacks's framework for studying categories. The extract from my PhD data provides a powerful example of how gender and language can come together, and how analysts may establish 'the mechanisms by which a specific identity is made relevant and consequential in any particular episode of interaction' (Raymond & Heritage, 2006: 677). However, how do we capture sufficient moments like 'well secretary and female' to say something about *practices*? This issue is articulated by language researchers of all traditions:

> We cannot 'simply go into the field and observe how, when, where, and with whom people talk with others about [identity] groups ... Finding data ... would amount to a search for the proverbial needle in the haystack.
>
> (Van Dijk, 1987: 18, 19)

> Because we cannot know in advance when a person will explicitly invoke a ... category, there is no way to plan data collection of them ... collections ... in all likelihood, would not be instances of the same interactional phenomenon.
>
> (Pomerantz & Mandelbaum, 2005: 154)

Across numerous studies, we have shown that the answer to the 'scalability' problem is to collect multiple large datasets. In this way, one can identify uses of the same categories, in the same sequential environments, in the same turn design, doing the same action – thereby satisfying both categorization and sequential analysts. Derek and I began this work with our project on the relevance of identity to neighbour disputes and began to show how, in institutional encounters, recurrent actions were often composed with recurrent categorial practices. For example, we showed that the action of denying (e.g., suspects' denials in police interviews; people's denials of bad neighbour behaviour) was routinely built with categorial turn components (e.g., 'I wouldn't hit a woman' – see Edwards, 2006; Stokoe, 2009, 2010).

In 2014, Bogdana Huma joined Loughborough University's Discourse and Rhetoric Group. She wanted to dig further into the relationship between conversation analysis and psychology and continue the respecification project initiated by Derek and colleagues. For her PhD (Huma, 2018), she analysed several commercial sales corpora, including outgoing business-to-business 'cold' telephone calls in the technology industry and incoming calls from customers to buy new windows and doors. Her main focus was on the practices that comprised persuasive conduct, unpacking traditional social psychological notions of (and methods for studying) social influence.

However, we also began to notice, much like Derek and I had with our own institutional datasets, that the macro-organization of the calls provided a perspicuous setting for studying gender categories. For example, when analysing calls to a double-glazing sales company, we observed that, when callers take the first step towards becoming a customer (e.g., asking for a quote or making an appointment for window measurements to be taken), the seller must establish the name of their new customer (Stokoe et al., 2017). Transcript 6.6 is an example.

Transcript 6.6

WC-39
01 S: C'n I take your su:rname please.
02 (1.0)
03 C: I:t's Hanks.=Aitch ay en kay es.
04 (0.8)
05 S: °#Aitch ay en kay es.#

The customer supplies her surname in response to the salesperson's yes/no interrogative formatted request, thus responding to its function rather than its format. She also, immediately, spells out her surname, in an additional turn construction unit (line 03). Based on the perceptually available pitch of their voices, the customer is categorizable as a woman, although, of course, they might not be (Edwards, 1997; Jayyusi, 1984).

As our analysis unfolded, we came to focus on how category incumbencies were managed as salespeople elicited information about prospective customers. In particular, we examined the turn design of sellers' requests for names, and how men and women customers were asked for their titles (e.g., 'is it miss, missus or ms?'). We showed that these activities precipitated talk about the customers' domestic domain regarding who comprises 'the buyer' within the membership categorization device 'parties to a sale'. Although such requests were apparently mandated by the company, they often produced turbulence as salespeople implied, or attempted to avoid implying, the nature of customers' domestic relationships.

Our analysis also showed that, and how, such requests sustained the gendered nature of forms of address. For example, sellers sometimes initiated the first part of a collaboratively built *compound* turn construction unit (TCU; Lerner, 1991) to elicit names. That is, the seller constructs the first part of a TCU, and the customer supplies its second and completing part. Transcript 6.7 is an example.

Transcript 6.7

WC-45
01 S: #Let# me take some details,=You're mister,h
02 (0.2)
03 C: Mister Cai:n?

The caller completes the TCU, although he repeats 'mister' rather than just supplying 'Cain'. We found that compound TCUs requiring surname completion from customers occurred *only* with audibly male customers. That is, sellers did not routinely ask audibly female customers, 'You're missus ...?'.

Rather, they asked women customers to provide their titles. Transcript 6.8 is an example.

Transcript 6.8

WC-39
01 S: and ar- ↓sorry are you ↑miss missus or ↓mizz. Which do
02 you £prefer.£
03 (0.4)
04 C: Missus,
05 (0.3)
06 S: #Lovely.#

Thus, we found evidence of what feminist linguists (and cultural observers more generally) have objected to for many years: that 'mister', used across the dataset as a generic title for men, supplied no information about sexual orientation or marital status: it was used without risk of 'error' (see Weatherall, 2015). However, for women, 'missus' and 'miss' (and 'ms') were in regular use across the dataset, each containing a presumption about the woman's relationship status. We also found that women's titles became accountable in ways that men's did not.

Transcript 6.9

WC-140
01 S: Lovely,=Are you m- a(m-) is it ↑missus miss or
02 ↓mizz.=Which [do you prefer.
03 C: [Mizz ( )
04 (0.4)
05 S: Mizz:::. [A(h)ll ri(h)ght.=nh nh nh?=
06 C: [Yeah: mizz.
07 C: =heh heh
08 (.)
09 S: Right. No problem.

In contrast to the straightforward supply of 'missus' in Transcript 6.8, in Transcript 6.9, the customer selects 'mizz' (line 03), and some disaffiliation follows. The salesperson confirms the caller's selection at line 05, with emphatic and extended pronunciation followed by a laughed-through acceptance ('A(h)ll ri(h)ght. =nh nh nh?') and continued laughter particles (line 05). C confirms 'mizz' with somewhat delayed reciprocal laughter (lines 06, 07), thereby not being in strong affiliation with the caller. The salesperson closes the sequence with 'Right. No problem.' (line 09), displaying readiness to move on, but also – notice there is no laughter this time – the 'No problem' can be hearable as minimizing any perceived deviance in C's response, thereby highlighting marital status, and belonging to the 'ms' category, as an issue. 'No problem' also presupposes that there *might be* a problem, such that it is relevant to deny that there is one.

In our final case, the caller makes relevant the categorial inferences associated with the way the salesperson elicits her name.

Transcript 6.10

WC-91
01 S: >C'n I'ave your na:me< madam.
02 (1.3)
03 C: You ca:n.
04 (0.4)
05 C: Just don't call me madam.=I hate that,
06 (.)
07 C: Sorry.↑ [↑Heh he hh]
08 S: [( )- hh]
09 (0.2)
10 S: Heh heh
11 (0.2)
12 S: .hhh I'm [tryin't'sound clear and professional.
13 C: [Right I know you-
14 (0.6)
15 C: Sorry?
16 (0.2)
17 S: I'm tryin't'sound <clear> and profe:ssional. Heh
18 C: Oh right.[=w'll madam sounds like um .h
19 S: [Heh heh heh
20 (0.3)
21 S: .h[heh
22 C: [I dunno.
23 (0.5)
24 S: [Yeah.]
25 C: [I won't] go there but- [no..uheh]
26 S: [>No no< is i-] hhhh
27 (0.5)
28 S: ↑Ha ↑ha ↑ha heh. .hhh=
29 C: =.↑hhehhh
30 S: And' an' what's your address, please.
31 C: <Sorry my name is <Jane Dempsy>

Note what happens at line 18, as the caller accounts for her objection to the salesperson's use of 'madam': 'madam sounds like um .h'. She does not complete the turn; she does not explicitly unpack the category-bound features of 'madam', though both participants appear to share the same stance towards the unnamed inferences. At line 25, the caller further states 'I won't go there', orienting to the fact that there are meanings of 'madam' that they perhaps both share that are 'unsayable'. One possibility, of course, is that 'madam' connotes 'brothel-owner' and/or 'prostitution'. Later, however, the caller states that 'it's an expression of somebody called a right madam aren't they?'. Here, a 'right madam' carries a different set of inferences. Our job as analysts is not to pin down what members mean more precisely than members themselves do; language is a resource for doing inferential work, and this is clear from Transcript 6.10.

Overall, our research provides an empirical example of 'categorial systematics' (Stokoe, 2012b) – that is, how membership categorization analysis can be used to identify systematic gendered categorial practices that are embedded in sequences of action.

Concluding remarks

Our aim in this chapter has been to tell a story, across three generations of researchers, about how Sacks's work on membership categorization and conversation analysis inspired us to think differently about the relationship between language and gender. We argue that Sacks's work provides a framework for making powerful insights into the workings of gender, made all the more powerful because they are rooted in members', not analysts', ongoing production of social life. Analyses of gender grounded in participants' orientations resist challenges in ways that those in which gender relevance is asserted because the analyst 'knows' it do not. We are not arguing – perhaps especially as feminists in our personal lives – that we might 'feel' or 'see' gender relevance but are unable to pin it down. Rather, in a world where public discourse is saturated with plausible deniability, we argue that it is crucial to ensure that potentially politically charged research has as little misinterpretation wiggle room as possible.

Sacks's often idiosyncratic observations about the machinery of membership categorization have been exploited in systematic conversation analytic studies, including our own research. In contrast to the commonly held view that matters of identity are not 'capturable' as robust and recurrent practices outside experimental or otherwise researcher-elicited contexts, these studies show that, in fact, the opposite is true. We argue that not only is it *possible* to identify that, and how, people invoke gender categories in the design of turns that build courses of action, it is *vital* to do so for research integrity and the feminist endeavour. By adopting a theoretical and methodological commitment to avoid the a priori assumption of category relevance, conversation analytic research challenges the reproduction of gender stereotypes in scholarship. Instead, the relevance, logic, meaning, reification, and transformation of 'gender' and any categories are grounded in the empirical analysis of audio- and video-recorded talk 'in the wild'. Yet, despite these arguments being relatively commonplace in ethnomethodologically informed fields, gender difference remains a taken-for-granted starting point for much of science and social science. Further, in the internet age, in which Sacks did not work, with its overwhelming power to construct and maintain category-based stereotypes, it is crucial to restate his foundational insights. What we think we know about women and men, or any other category, is not a permanent state of affairs; categorization work is central to social change.

References

Beattie, G. (1983). *Talk: An analysis of speech and non-verbal behaviour in conversation*. Milton Keynes: Open University Press.

Cameron, D. (1997). Demythologizing sociolinguistics. In N. Coupland & A. Jaworski (Eds.), *Sociolinguistics: A coursebook and reader*. Basingstoke: Macmillan (pp. 55–67).

Curl, T.S., & Drew, P. (2008). Contingency and action: A comparison of two forms of requesting. *Research on Language and Social Interaction*, 41, 129–153.

Edwards, D. (1994). Script formulations: A study of event descriptions in conversation. *Journal of Language and Social Psychology*, 13(3), 211–247.

Edwards, D. (1995a). Two to tango: Script formulations, dispositions, and rhetorical symmetry in relationship troubles talk. *Research on Language and Social Interaction*, 28(4), 319–350.

Edwards, D. (1995b). Sacks and psychology. *Theory & Psychology*, 5(4), 579–596.

Edwards, D. (1997). *Discourse and cognition*. London: Sage.

Edwards, D. (1998). The relevant thing about her: Social identity categories in use. In C. Antaki & S. Widdicombe (Eds.), *Identities in talk*. London: Sage (pp. 15–33).

Edwards, D. (2006). Discourse, cognition and social practices: The rich surface of language and social interaction. *Discourse Studies*, 8(1), 41–49.

Edwards, D., & Potter, J. (1992). *Discursive psychology*. London: Sage.

Edwards, D., & Stokoe, E.H. (2004). Discursive psychology, focus group interviews, and participants' categories. *British Journal of Developmental Psychology*, 22, 499–507.

Garfinkel, H. (1967). *Studies in ethnomethodology*. Englewood Cliffs: Prentice-Hall.

Holden, C. (1993). Giving girls a chance: Patterns of talk in cooperative groupwork. *Gender and Education*, 5(2), 179–189.

Holmes, J. (2007). Social constructionism, postmodernism and feminist sociolinguistics. *Gender and Language*, 1(1), 51–67.

Hopper, R., & LeBaron, C. (1998). How gender creeps into talk. *Research on Language and Social Interaction*, 31(3), 59–74.

Huma, B. (2018). *The interactional organization of initial business-to-business initial sales calls with prospective clients*. Unpublished PhD thesis, Loughborough University.

Järviluoma, H., Moisala, P., & Vilkko, A. (2003). *Gender and qualitative methods*. London: Sage.

Jayyusi, L. (1984). *Categorization and the moral order*. London: Routledge & Kegan Paul.

Kelly, J. (1991). A study of gender differential linguistic interaction in the adult classroom. *Gender and Education*, 3(2), 137–143.

Kessler, S.J., & McKenna, W. (1978). *Gender: An ethnomethodological approach*. New York: John Wiley.

Kitzinger, C. (2008). Conversation analysis: Technical matters for gender research. In K. Harrington, L. Litosseliti, H. Saunston, & J. Sunderland (Eds.), *Gender and language research methodologies*. Basingstoke: Palgrave (pp. 119–138).

Lakoff, R. (1973). Language and woman's place. *Language in Society*, 2, 45–79.

Lerner, G.H. (1991). On the syntax of sentences-in-progress. *Language in Society*, 20, 441–458.

Pomerantz, A., & Mandelbaum, J. (2005). A conversation analytic approach to relationships: Their relevance for interactional conduct. In K. Fitch & R.E. Sanders (Eds.), *Handbook of language and social interaction*. Mahwah: Lawrence Erlbaum (pp. 149–171).

Raymond, G., & Heritage, J. (2006). The epistemics of social relationships: Owning grandchildren. *Language in Society*, 35(5), 677–705.

Sacks, H. (1992). *Lectures on conversation* (Vols. I & II, edited by G. Jefferson). Oxford: Blackwell.

Sacks, H., Schegloff, E.A., & Jefferson, G. (1974). A simplest systematics for the organization of turn-taking for conversation. *Language*, 50(4), 696–735.

Schegloff, E.A. (1991). Reflections on talk and social structure. In D. Boden & D. Zimmerman (Eds.), *Talk and social structure*. Berkeley: University of California Press (pp. 44–70).

Schegloff, E.A. (2007). A tutorial on membership categorization. *Journal of Pragmatics*, 39, 462–482.

Speer, S.A., & Stokoe, E. (Eds.) (2011). *Conversation and gender*. Cambridge: Cambridge University Press.

Stokoe, E. (1995). Gender differences in undergraduates' talk: Contrasting analyses and what they offer. *Feminism and Psychology*, 5(1), 99–104.

Stokoe, E. (2008). Categories and sequences: Formulating gender in talk-in-interaction. In K. Harrington, L. Litosseliti, H. Saunston, & J. Sunderland (Eds.), *Gender and language research methodologies*. Basingstoke: Palgrave (pp. 139–160).

Stokoe, E. (2009). Doing actions with identity categories: Complaints and denials in neighbour disputes. *Text and Talk*, 29(1), 75–97.

Stokoe, E. (2010). 'I'm not gonna hit a lady': Conversation analysis, membership categorization and men's denials of violence towards women. *Discourse & Society*, 21(1), 1–24.

Stokoe, E. (2012a). Moving forward with membership categorization analysis: Methods for systematic analysis. *Discourse Studies*, 14(3), 277–303. DOI: 10.1177/1461445612441534 2012.

Stokoe, E. (2012b). Categorial systematics. *Discourse Studies*, 14(3), 345–354. DOI: 10.1177/1461445612441543.

Stokoe, E. (2018). *Talk: The science of conversation*. London: Little, Brown.

Stokoe, E., Sikveland, R.O., & Huma, B. (2017). Entering the customer's domestic domain: Categorial systematics and the identification of 'parties to a sale'. *Journal of Pragmatics*. DOI: 10.1016/j.pragma.2017.05.006.

Stokoe, E.H. (1997). An evaluation of two studies of gender and language in educational settings. *Gender and Education*, 9(2), 233–244.

Stokoe, E.H. (1998). Talking about gender: The conversational construction of gender categories in academic discourse. *Discourse and Society*, 9(2), 217–240.

Stringer, J.L., & Hopper, R. (1998). Generic *he* in conversation? *Quarterly Journal of Speech*, 84, 209–221.

Tracy, K. (1998). Analysing context: Framing the discussion. *Research in Language and Social Interaction*, 31(1), 1–28.

Van Dijk, T. (1987). *Communicating racism: Ethnic prejudice in thought and talk*. London: Sage.

Velody, I., & Williams, R. (1998). Introduction. In I. Velody & R. Williams (Eds.), *The politics of constructionism*. London: Sage (pp. 1–12).

Vygotsky, L.S. (1978). *Mind in society: The development of higher psychological processes*. London: Harvard University Press.

Weatherall, A. (2015). Language planning (gender and sexuality issues). *The International Encyclopedia of Human Sexuality*, 649–719. DOI: 10.1002/9781118896877.wbiehs261.

West, C., & Zimmerman, D.H. (1987). Doing gender. *Gender & Society*, 1, 125–151.

7 A most remarkable fact, for all intents and purposes

The practical matter of categorical truths

Jessica Robles

Ordinary interactions are full of little mysteries. How do we hear a story as a story? How do we know when to lie? These questions may seem trivial, but they are at the heart of understanding how social life works (and why, sometimes, it does not). Harvey Sacks asked such questions, and his approach to answering them has played a central role in my investigations of everyday communication. One of my earliest "data obsessions" was from an audio recording, donated to me by friends, in which one jokingly proposes they make papier-mâché masks and sell them:

Transcript 7.1

1 Christa: we could sell them at a yard sale (1.8)
2 at the flea market >you know Mexicans
3 love that ki-< oh-
4 (2.0)
5 Val: n(h)o comment (.) r[((h)acist)]=
6 Chris: [re wind]
7 Val: =ass.
8 (1.0)
9 Chris: du:de,
10 Val: my boyfriend doesn't own a globe shut up

How is it that we can project what Christa was saying in lines 1–3? What made Christa stop mid-production of her utterance? Why does Valerie identify Christa's talk as problematic, and what on earth do flea markets have to do with Mexicans, or Mexicans to do with Valerie's boyfriend?

In this chapter, I consider how Sacks's ideas – particularly on categories and normative expectations of what should and should not be said – have contributed to my work on how social differences are interactionally organized. What do these concepts have to offer research, teaching, and impact? Sacks's approaches provide uniquely generative heuristics for investigating that which is implicit and implicated in talk, while providing an empirical basis for surfacing arrays of unspoken social practice.

The ordinary morality of categorization

When Sacks (1984) described ordinariness as a sort of job, he described the work of doing that job as involving a number of components: common-sense cultural knowledge, an ability to do the job at all (e.g., not being in prison), and so forth. He also, over the course of the lecture, discussed how this work involves distinctions between what to say and what not to say: for example, describing someone as "just a real, real nice guy," rather than describing "the set of his eyebrows, or the timbre of his voice" (p. 416). The odd result of this compulsion is that, despite monitoring our lives for storyability, we conclude "nothing much" (p. 417), and, even when catastrophes occur, people go to great lengths to interpret scenes as though "nothing happened" (p. 419). This nothing-in-particular orientation toward normalness was famously triggered in Garfinkel's (1967) breaching experiments, in which confederates deliberately violated social rules such as providing or pursuing exhaustive descriptions of ordinary events as though their particulars should not be taken for granted in service of social action. In other words, one "leaves well enough alone" to allow for life to get done, ordinarily. And, as Garfinkel showed, far from being neutral, this orientation to ordinariness is highly normative: violations produce trouble and even hostility.

Thus, from both ends, the morality of ordinariness is empirically visible in participants' conduct: (1) violations themselves are sanctioned, if they occur; and (2) possible violations are accounted for ahead of time, in some effort to minimize them. In research I conducted with colleagues around how people talk about their own and others' technology and social media use (Robles, DiDomenico, & Raclaw, 2018), participants carefully produced descriptions that emphasized the ordinariness of their own comportment. Consider the following examples:

Transcript 7.2

Fragment 1 (from Excerpt 1, p. 154)

```
10  Lila:    I: just- I juggle my phone (.)
11           because this one (.) when we're
12           in the car: (.) n'I'm like chillin
13           takin a selfie (.) goes like this
14           A[agh::]
15  May:       [(you know what)]
16  Lila:    >and< you know what happens? .hh
17           this happens I end up <juggling>
18           it, (.) and it ends up under the
19           seat=
```

Transcript 7.3

Fragment 2 (from Excerpt 2, p. 155)

```
25  Blake:   Aw:h. (4.0) so: my roommate is
26           trying to get me to: set up an O-K
```

27 Cupid account.
28 Ari: weird.
((5 lines deleted))
29 Blake: =>yeah and he< comes home one
30 night he's like >whadda ya< think
31 about online da:ting, and I'm
32 like- (.) are you: a
33 fifty year old divorced woman?

In both cases, participants initiate a telling by first describing their own blameless ordinariness in relation to what follows: Lila was "chillin takin a selfie" (lines 12–13) when she is interrupted by May's hand-waving and vocalization (mimicked in lines 13–14); Blake's own activities don't appear to warrant narrating, but he sets the scene with his roommate unremarkably coming home one night (lines 25–26) before asking the unexpected question "whadda ya think about online dating" (line 30–31). In both cases, the participants are merely going about the business of being ordinary, and this serves to account for already-articulated, or potential, attributions of non-ordinariness – for example, Lila was earlier accused of taking too many selfies and posting them on social media, and Blake is seeking to avoid the label of "weird" (line 28) or being comparable to a "fifty year old divorced woman" (line 33) before seeking advice about whether to respond to a woman who approached him through the online dating account his roommate allegedly set up for him without his consent.

Although these examples are relatively trivial, we do examine cases in which non-present parties' non-ordinariness is used to police the boundaries of the "normal" person in potentially problematic ways; for example, in a later excerpt, we analyze participants' denigrating talk about a woman's online images, to which they attribute "gross" sexuality and label her a "slut" (Robles, DiDomenico, & Raclaw, 2018, p. 164). Elsewhere (Robles, 2017), I have considered similar instances of gossip and gossip-like moralizing about non-present parties, and how these mobilize common-sense knowledge about what is culturally and locally acceptable. The following example has similar features to the ones described above:

Transcript 7.4

Fragment 3 (from Excerpt 3, p. 13)
10 Halley: She was li~ke "oh my go:sh I'm so:: drunk ha ha
11 ha ha ha" and then (.) Aaron was just like u↑u::h
((10 seconds later))
12 Halley: all the sudden (0.5) she like tells me about her
13 night=
14 Liz: =°oh [go:d°
15 Halley: [>n it's like<] she's already
16 disgusting >I mean I don't wanna know about that
17 shit<

In this fragment, Halley similarly presents herself as an unwilling participant in someone else's sanctionable conduct – she appears to have been "minding her own business" when "all the sudden" this person tells Halley about her night (lines 12–13). In cases like this, the moral component is more obvious because the assessments are so much more extreme. But the machinery that produces these judgments works in the same way.

Though I have not centered it in every publication, the core of how I understand these sorts of interactions is through Sacks's approach to categories: the membership categorization device (MCD). I encountered this concept for the first time when starting my graduate degree at the University of Colorado at Boulder. I can't say where I saw it first – whether it was in a class I took with Karen Tracy on discourse analysis or in the book she'd written (which I revised with her for the second edition) on everyday talk. The first of Sacks's own writings on this concept that I read was from his chapter "The baby cried. The mommy picked it up," as reprinted in *The Discourse Reader* (in Jaworski & Coupland, 2006). I found the idea instantly comprehensible, fascinatingly technical, and extremely applicable. The MCD basically describes the process by which categories or types of people are associated with particular activities (or traits/behavior as visible in their activities) and is deployed to do some work in situated interactions. Sacks describes a caller to a suicide helpline who provides examples of activities (hair styling, fashion) and then attributes a category with which the caller presumes the call taker might associate those activities ("you probably suspect – as far as the hair stylist and – either go one way or the other. There is a straight or homosexual, something like that"; p. 245). The caller indexes a body of cultural knowledge about categories of people, including relationships between gender, sexuality, sexual problems, preferences/interests/occupations, maybe even vocal quality (if the caller never stated their gender in the call). The MCD helps us understand how this knowledge is intelligibly produced and interpreted on the basis of a number of rules and maxims Sacks sets out across various writings.

The MCD is not exactly a little-known concept in research. Indeed, it may be the most popular of Sacks's contributions to the study of conversation, even having spun out into its own method (membership categorization analysis; e.g., Hester & Eglin, 1997; Housley & Fitzgerald, 2002; Stokoe, 2012). Perhaps, in part, this widespread use of membership categorization exists because it easily links up with ideas across disciplines, from cognitive categories in psychology (see Edwards, 1991) to social roles and status in sociology (e.g., Parsons, 1940). Furthermore, the MCD has the benefit of combining a set of clear techniques with a general heuristic that is easy to grasp and easy to see in everyday life. However, the same properties that make the MCD so useful can also contribute to its being applied inconsistently, even badly. One challenge is that nowhere does Sacks lay out all his views on the MCD: it is left for subsequent scholars to pull the gems of his writings and lectures together. Because of this, MCDs and ways of applying them in analysis are taken up in various ways and described with varying levels of completeness, detail, and accuracy. Another consideration is that there is the ongoing issue of "original intent" versus "current practice," and this applies not just to Sacks's ideas, but to the field of study in general (for instance, the view that conversation analysis, as the state-of-the-art in interaction research, may owe a debt of gratitude to Sacks, but renders his analytic tools obsolete). Furthermore, because MCDs are taken up in different areas for different purposes, and sometimes in applications beyond what Sacks himself might have considered, debates have emerged regarding not just whether MCDs should feature in analysis, but how they do so (e.g., Schegloff, 2007).

I've been writing about and applying MCDs in my research for at least 7 years now. Although it's a brief span compared with other researchers, I can say that, across the last 7 years, my own understanding and use of MCDs have evolved. In fact, there's at least one summary of the concept that I wrote in 2012 with which I now disagree (although I was simplifying the idea for an introductory, student audience, I think I simplified too much). I have never thought of myself as a membership categorization analyst – and yet, in most of the papers I have written, even when I have on occasion actively tried *not* to see the data through this lens, I end up writing about categories again. It is simply too useful sometimes, particularly when respecifying unempirical lay opinions or concepts from other traditions. The main context in which this was apparent to me, and in which I initially started focusing on MCDs in analysis, was when writing on the topics of racism, sexism, and stereotypes.

In these projects (Kurylo & Robles, 2015; Robles, 2015a; Robles & Kurylo, 2017), MCDs were the focal heuristic through which I sought to understand, and ground empirically, how racist/sexist or stereotyping practices are recognizable as such (as in research such as Rapley, 1998; Stokoe & Edwards, 2007; Whitehead & Lerner, 2009). The following example, mentioned at the beginning of the chapter (from Robles, 2015a), shows how recognizably racist content is oriented to in unfolding talk:

Transcript 7.5

Fragment 4 (from Excerpt 2, p. 7)

1	Christa:	we could sell them at a yard sale (1.8)
2		at the flea market >you know Mexicans
3		love that ki-< oh-
4 (2.0)		
5	Val:	n(h)o comment (.) r[((h)acist)]=
6	Christa:	[re wind]
7	Val:	=ass.
8 (1.0)		
9	Christa:	du:de,
10	Val:	my boyfriend doesn't own a globe shut up

The self-initiated self-repair in line 3 displays some problem with speaking, orienting to something underway that is potentially problematic. The specific placement of the self-repair – between the category "Mexicans" and the projectable activity comprising something they "love" (ostensibly, flea market wares) – displays an attentiveness precisely to the association that Christa is in the process of articulating. The silence (line 4) indicates some form of trouble, and the evidence of trouble is further displayed in Val's "no comment" in line 5 (which does a form of stance display by espousing no stance!) and is followed by a sanction of Christa. Though the sanction/insult is not entirely hearable, the attribution of "racist" is not necessary to see that the subsequent "ass" (line 7) is meant to label Christa negatively and, therefore, assess her previous turn as a problem. Christa's "rewind" (line 6), a sort of meta-repair, displays an orientation to having said something problematic and espouses a wish to "take it back" or undo it (possibly literally, as they are recording the conversation). After the silence and Christa's "dude" (lines 8–9), Val does another reproach of Christa, this time embedded in a refutation. Because the flea market-type wares Christa was describing just before this excerpt (indexed by "them" in line 1) were papier-mâché globes; because such globes were projected as the kinds of things "Mexicans" might "love" (lines 2–3); and because Val purports that the non-present party "boyfriend" does not own a globe (let alone love one; line 10), we can surmise that Val's boyfriend is a member of the category "Mexicans." Reaching this point, then, we can retrospectively uncover the unspoken shared knowledge that made Christa stop what she was saying in the middle of her utterance in line 3.

Thus, Sacks's MCD gives us a way of tracking the unsaid and, sometimes, the unsayable. This has always been a fascination of mine: how it is that so much gets done not just in spite of, but often because of, how interaction unfolds so implicitly and indirectly (see Drew, 2018). Often, as members, we have the experience of inferring certain things about situations and people and label certain identities and activities in particular ways; the MCD provides some basis for interrogating and accessing an empirical basis for such interpretations through its technical application. One way in which the MCD could be more usefully applied is by a return to some of its technical components, especially those less attended to in the literature. For example, in a project with a colleague and a doctoral candidate on the basis of the latter's dissertation research (Joyce, Robles, & Butler, 2018), we examined the use of partitioning as a resource for doing challenges, resisting challenges, and remedying conflicted interactions. Partitioning refers to how categories can be recategorized in various ways depending on the local contexts – Butler (2008) gives the example of a classroom, in which categories could be divided by institutional role (teacher/student), age (adult/child), or gender, all with different implications for who is in what category, and what is being done by categorizing in that way. One practice our analysis shows is how participants are able to bring off otherwise-sanctionable actions by using partitioning to recategorize actors and "cover" the potentially problematic action with a seemingly innocent one.

Therefore, another power of the MCD is not just that it makes the hidden observable, but that it provides another point of access into the normative dimensions of talk. As my primary interest in interaction has always been how it involves morality (see Robles, 2015b), the MCD has been a useful way of seeing how participants do moralizing activities when they rarely do so on record. For instance, in another project with colleagues (Robles, Xiong, & Yuan, 2018), I returned to focusing on issues of more obvious conflict, argument, and politics, now in the context of online discourse. Here we examined the use of quotation marks in online YouTube comments and microblog posts, in the USA and in China, in response to social-political events. One of the ways participants seem to use quotation marks is to do what we call "categorical mockery." In this tactic, the quotation marks enclose not a literal quotation ever said by a particular person, but an attributed "kind of thing" that a certain "type of person" would say. For example, in the following set of comments and replies posted in response to an interview between an American entertainment newscaster and a conservative commentator, P2 has repeated an assessment by an earlier poster (P1):

Transcript 7.6

Fragment 5 (pp. 10–11)

P.2 4 months ago
P1 gracious ? Man go jump off a cliff
P.3 4 months ago
P2 You provide NOTHING to this discussion, except "duhh.... I got a smart thing to say.... go jump off a cliff."

P1 called the conduct of conservative guest Tomi Lahren "gracious"; here, P2 replies by repeating this term and giving a nonserious injunction that refutes the positive assessment. P3 then responds to P2's comment, opening with a reproach of P2 that denigrates their contribution to the thread ("you provide nothing to this discussion"), followed by a quotation mark-enclosed utterance: "duhh ... I got a smart thing to say ... go jump off a cliff." Though the quoted content contains a direct (and easily confirmable) quotation of what P2 actually wrote ("go jump off a cliff"), it is preceded by an attributed quotation of the person's stance or hypothetical thought process leading up to their typed utterance; this preceding formulation labels its own talk as "smart" but is constructed as sarcasm (in comparison with how it is introduced as "providing nothing" as well as the "duhh," which marks the content as "stupid"). This produces an indirect description of P2 as an unintelligent and unproductive participant in the online discourse, but, furthermore, it castigates a certain category of online commenters, particularly those with which the speaker might disagree. This is shown even more clearly with examples such as "'LOL THE AUDIENCE BOOED HER AND CHEERED FOR HIM! SHE GOT REKT!' Thanks, MSM. Good luck in the next election," in which various opinions are presented in an extreme, parodied, and quoted form attributed to "MSM" (mainstream media), which is positioned by the speaker as a voice of liberal bias; and in an example from Chinese microblog comments responding to a standoff between an ordinary woman and officials over a flower stand: "Who said 'Say less?'" serves to call out the officials for their approach to the woman, followed by sarcastically suggesting that the officials "all should go to conquer the Diaoyu Islands" as they are "the hero" of this saga. In these and many other examples, a category of people is denigrated as a contrast with another category – for instance, a political affiliation – or a type of brave or intelligent person associated with another character in the drama being referenced, or the speaker of the utterance themselves. In these examples, the world of the argument is divided into two sides, right and wrong, and the use of quotation to categorize people by their positions contributes to this binary differentiation and polarization.

I propose that, in addition to Sacks's technical insights, we might find some practical insights for use in both teaching, and potentially improving, communication practices. Though Sacks's work (consistent with Garfinkel's) is rigorously focused on analysis over intervention, and in this way is apparently inconsistent with normative applications (see Craig, 2003), in the concluding section I nonetheless consider the possibility and value of the attempt.

Categorization and practical insight

In every class I have ever taught, I have taught the MCD. Sometimes it appeared as a minor point; other times it was a primary bit of instruction in a day, especially when using the book I co-authored, in which it features fairly prominently in one of the chapters (Tracy & Robles, 2013). I also covered it when teaching topics to which it seemed especially relevant (identity and culture, for example). One day in the autumn of 2015, in a largish class of about 90 students, after I'd come to the end of the lesson and solicited questions, a student at the front put his hand up. "What is the point of learning this?" he asked. "Why is this useful to know?"

What I said to him was that all of us will regularly encounter situations in which we have some interpretation of an event, but aren't sure how we got to that interpretation; and that, in various kinds of such situations (for example, during arguments), we might want to reconstruct, and have evidence for, a particular interpretation. There are a number of social problems that face, in one way or another, difficult empirical demands: subtle forms of racism/sexism and so on, and microaggressions, issues of sexual consent, disagreements over tone, and other phenomena that can be difficult to "prove" where the context (or a fussy interlocutor) might demand proof. In these situations, some assumption of ordinariness has been breached – and ordinariness itself then becomes a weapon to dismiss allegations.

We live in an interesting historical moment, grappling with the failure of assumptions of sharedness on which so much of practical everyday life depends. Although the central concerns about truth, interpretation, and value are not new, the exposure to their divergences – and the effects of their polarizations – are increasingly salient to everyone, members and analysts. "Truth" is explicitly interrogated in the public sphere and has become what Boromisza-Habashi (2010) might call an "essentially contested" term. For example, in response to a post on Twitter quoting Oprah Winfrey's comment "speaking your truth is the most powerful tool we all have" during the Golden Globe awards, American conservative commentator Ben Shapiro responded, "there is no such thing as 'your truth.' There is the truth and your opinion." In an age where we have more access to facts than ever before, the idea of truth remains elusive, and the means by which we can draw empirical support in its absence (while understood for decades in academia) has largely failed to assist the general public.

There is much in critical theory that claims to want to serve justice, but doesn't, as well as empirical sciences such as conversation analysis that disclaim the goal, for sound reasons. I have no wish to rehash that argument. But empirical studies of interaction and some of their concepts can indeed be "useful," not just to organizations and institutions (where applied work of this sort already exists; e.g. Craig & Tracy, 2014; Stokoe, 2014), but also to social problems at different scales and in less amenable places. Social problems are, after all, members' matters, and, if all social problems can be systematically analyzed in discourse, then there should be no topics declared a priori off limits or beyond scope.

The "radical project" of ethnomethodology within which Sacks's ideas were developed and to which they continue to contribute – a project largely forgotten in contemporary research in this vein, particularly in conversation analysis – rejected formal analysis in favor of concerning itself primarily with *lived phenomena* (rather than technical "constructive" analysis); it also rejected combinations with other methods, and reforming or correcting common sense (Lynch, 2016). Setting aside that I might adore and find Sacks's contributions remarkably technical, personally struggling with analyzing my own lived experience, and being a shameless borrower of whatever ideas broadly definable as discourse analysis serve my analytic purposes: I propose that the MCD (1) can address the gap between the intuitive accountability of conversation and the analytic characterizations of empirical analysis; and (2) that this is precisely what makes it useful for surfacing and allowing for correcting, if not actually reforming, common sense. I have no sophisticated theoretical or methodological basis for this proposal – only my own radical pragmatism that demands that, if a thing can be useful, then by all means use it.

At one point in his lectures, Sacks (1992) relates the "most remarkable fact" that we don't have to know how someone measures their day to understand what they mean when they respond to "how are you?" with "okay" or "fine" (p. 555). The "we" here refers to members, of course, but, on the surface, it refers to analysts too. After all, as Sacks noted in response to a student question during his lecture, what participants "'really mean' is what they say, for all intents and purposes" (p. 558), and empirical research on conversation has largely kept to this guiding principle. But the absence of obvious *saying* does not always rule out provable *meaning*, and it is in this space that MCDs can indeed be useful, on par (and perhaps ideally paired) with conversation analysis's next turn proof procedure. This space is the point at which *the generation of possible meanings* meets *the demonstrably possible meanings ratified by recipients*. This space is a members' and analysts' problem, and it is precisely where contestations get stuck. I don't suggest that an MCD can resolve the stuckness, only that it can make its properties visible for further scrutiny.

In his reading of ethnomethodology, Craig (2003) suggests that, contrary to Garfinkel's assumptions, social scientists can and almost certainly do have some impact upon ordinary actors' lives. What I argue is that members will use whatever resources to hand that will get something done for them. If this wasn't the case, to take a very small example, language would never evolve to accommodate new words and new meanings of words, and the entire area of pragmatics would not exist. As Craig points out, ethnomethodology is concerned with the recognition of social facts, but, if ethnomethodologists are members who can recognize things, then, I hope, so too can any member. And recognition in itself can be incredibly radical. I would suggest most interventions into practice never proceed without it.

Sacks (1992) describes something he calls the "reverse procedure": "in deciding among possible competing facts, one may decide that that fact occurred which has an explanation, and that fact that hasn't an explanation did not occur" (p. 121). Having the means to articulate reconstructions of possible facts should not solely be the domain of professionals and degree-carrying academics. And, unlike the (often, sometimes deliberately, misunderstood) normalization of social construction and relativism, MCDs have some protection against ideologization because ideology requires that the implicit remain hidden, and, contrary to theory and metatheory, MCDs demand explication.

Not all that relies on the work of ordinariness needs breaching. The world would be a difficult place if it were so. But sometimes, when things aren't working, a breach is precisely what is needed, and a conversation can (and probably should) involve a level of explicit metadiscourse about how possible meanings are taken up as categorical truths in conversation. As interaction is so normative anyway, we owe it to interaction – if not ourselves – to at least attempt to have a say in what that normativity should be.

References

Boromisza-Habashi, D. (2010). How are political concepts "essentially" contested? *Language & Communication*, *30*(4), 276–284.

Butler, C. W. (2008). *Talk and social interaction in the playground.* Aldershot: Ashgate.

Craig, R. T. (2003). Ethnomethodology's program and practical inquiry. *Research on Language and Social Interaction*, *36*(4), 471–479.

Craig, R. T., & Tracy, K. (2014). Building grounded practical theory in applied communication research: Introduction to the special issue. *Journal of Applied Communication Research*, *42*(3), 229–243.

Drew, P. (2018). Inferences and indirectness in interaction. *Open Linguistics*, *4*(1), 241–259.

Edwards, D. (1991). Categories are for talking: On the cognitive and discursive bases of categorization. *Theory & Psychology*, *1*(4), 515–542.

Garfinkel, H. (1967). *Studies in ethnomethodology.* Englewood Cliffs, NJ: Prentice-Hall.

Hester, S., & Eglin, P. (1997). *Culture in action: Studies in membership categorization analysis (No. 4).* Washington, DC: University Press of America.

Housley, W., & Fitzgerald, R. (2002). The reconsidered model of membership categorization analysis. *Qualitative Research*, *2*(1), 59–83.

Jaworski, A., & Coupland, N. (2006). *The discourse reader*. London: Routledge.

Joyce, J., Robles, J. S., & Butler, C. (2018). Exploiting the partition (submitted to the International Communication Association, for the convention in Washington DC, 2019).

Kurylo, A., & Robles, J. S. (2015). How should I respond to *them*? An emergent categorization of responses to interpersonally communicated stereotypes. *Journal of Intercultural Communication Research*, *44*, 64–91.

Lynch, M. (2016, June). Radical ethnomethodology. *Position Paper for Workshop on Radical Ethnomethodology, Manchester Metropolitan University, UK*, *22*(23), 6.

Parsons, T. (1940). An analytical approach to the theory of social stratification. *American Journal of Sociology*, *45*(6), 841–862.

Rapley, M. (1998). "Just an ordinary Australian": Self-categorization and the discursive construction of facticity in "new racist" political rhetoric. *British Journal of Social Psychology*, *37*(3), 325–344.

Robles, J. S. (2015a). Extreme case (re)formulation as a practice for making hearably-racist talk repairable [special issue on –isms in interaction]. *Journal of Language and Social Psychology*, *34*, 390–409.

Robles, J. S. (2015b). Morality in discourse. In K. Tracy (Ed.), *International encyclopedia of language and social interaction* (pp. 1032–1036). Wiley-Blackwell.

Robles, J. S. (2017). Exclusion in gossipy talk: Hijacking the preference structure for ingroup belonging. *Critical Approaches to Discourse Analysis across Disciplines*, *9*, 5–22.

Robles, J. S., DiDomenico, S., & Raclaw, J. (2018). Doing being an ordinary technology and social media user. *Language & Communication*, *60*, 150–167.

Robles, J. S., & Kurylo, A. K. (2017). "Let's have the men clean up": Interpersonally-communicated stereotypes as a resource for resisting gender-role prescribed activities. *Discourse Studies*, *19*, 1–21.

Robles, J. S., Xiong, B., & Yuan, Z. (2018). Quotation marking as a way to polarize political positions in online commentary (submitted to the International Communication Association, for the convention in Washington DC, 2019).

Sacks, H. (1984). On doing "being ordinary". In J. M. Atkinson & J. Heritage (Eds.) *Structures of social action: Studies in conversation analysis* (pp. 413–429). Cambridge, MA: Cambridge University Press.

Sacks, H. (1992). *Lectures on Conversation: Volumes 1 & 2*, edited by G. Jefferson. Oxford: Blackwell.

Schegloff, E. A. (2007). A tutorial on membership categorization. *Journal of Pragmatics*, *39*(3), 462–482.

Stokoe, E. (2012). Moving forward with membership categorization analysis: Methods for systematic analysis. *Discourse Studies*, *14*(3), 277–303.

Stokoe, E. (2014). The Conversation Analytic Role-play Method (CARM): A method for training communication skills as an alternative to simulated role-play. *Research on Language and Social Interaction*, *47*(3), 255–265.

Stokoe, E., & Edwards, D. (2007). "Black this, black that": Racial insults and reported speech in neighbour complaints and police interrogations. *Discourse & Society*, *18*(3), 337–372.

Tracy, K., & Robles, J. S. (2013). *Everyday talk: Building and reflecting identities*. New York, NY: Guilford Press.

Whitehead, K. A., & Lerner, G. H. (2009). When are persons "white"?: On some practical asymmetries of racial reference in talk-in-interaction. *Discourse & Society*, *20*(5), 613–641.

8 Sacks

Omni-relevance and the layered texture of interaction

Richard Fitzgerald

In a series of lectures during spring 1966, Sacks examines an introduction sequence from a group therapy session where a new member is introduced (Sacks 1995, pp. 268–312). The lectures follow on from Sacks's analysis of the beginning of a child's story, 'The baby cried. The mommy picked it up.' (Sacks 1995, pp. 236–259), where he first introduces the main elements of his membership categorisation apparatus (see Housley, this volume), before then introducing a section of transcript from a group therapy session and switching to examine how category and sequential work are mutually entwined. Over the course of these lectures, Sacks builds up a multilayered analysis starting from examining the introduction sequence as a sequential action before combining this with membership category work in order to demonstrate how the sequential action and category work are mutually entwined and made relevant to the overall context of the therapy session. In this chapter, I trace Sacks's analysis over the course of the lectures to highlight the way that Sacks artfully demonstrates the analysis of sequence and category work as mutually entwined. Moreover, the discussion also emphasises the importance of examining the way Sacks develops his analysis over the course of the lectures, highlighting an approach to reading the lectures as a series of interrelated analyses that build on each other.

Categorisation and the layered texture of interaction

In Sacks's analysis of the beginning of the child's story, taken from the book by Pitcher and Prelinger (1963), *Children Tell Stories* (Sacks 1974, 1995, see particularly 'Spring 1966', pp. 236–259), he introduces a number of terms and concepts including 'membership categories', 'membership category devices', 'category predicates' together with some rules of application and some maxims for observing members' category work. Through the analysis of these two short sentences,[1] Sacks identified and mapped many of the insights and principles that underpin the routine work of members' categorisation practices, and that would come to underpin the development of membership categorisation analysis (MCA; Hester & Eglin 1997; Fitzgerald & Housley 2015). Although the emphasis within MCA was on naturally occurring data and uncovering members' own category analysis in situ, this particular analysis is autoethnographic, relying on Sacks's own understanding of the story, and the data taken from a story published in a book of stories, rather than deriving from a piece of naturally occurring conversation.

However, in the series of lectures that follow *The Baby Cried* analysis, Sacks (1995, pp. 268–312) introduces volumes of transcribed recording of a group therapy session for teenagers in Los Angeles. This new form of data heralded both a shift in some of the analytic principles Sacks brought to the study of categorisation and an explicit reorientation to analysis grounded in the participants' actions and their orientation to the events (Lynch 2000). As Schegloff (1995) observes,

> There is a shift here in analytic stance and procedure, from the analyst's understanding as initial point of departure on the one hand to the coparticipant's understanding as initial point of departure on the other. In the former mode, the analysis begins with an asserted convergence of interpretations and recognitions by the analyst and the analyst's audience (for example, that something is a story, that 'the mommy' is 'the mommy of the baby,' that an utterance is doing an invitation, and so on). It proceeds by the provision of a methodical basis for both that convergence of understandings and the convergence between the 'understanders' and the producers of the to-be-understood 'in the data.' In the latter mode, analysis begins with an asserted observation (that not-overtly-engaged participants are attending, and, indeed, are obligated to attend to the talk), and then immediately grounds that observation in subsequent conduct by the co-participants in the episode being examined. That conduct is taken as displaying their orientation to, and understanding of, the setting and what has been transpiring in it. The site of analysis is located in the setting of the data at the outset. And further: the analysts' so treating the conduct of the participants is itself grounded in the claim that the co-participants so treat it.
>
> (Schegloff 1995, Vol 1, Introduction, pp. xliii–xliv)

The data that became known as the group therapy sessions comprised transcribed recordings of therapy sessions and became a regular source of data for Sacks's lectures (Sacks 1995; Harvey Sacks Papers 2017, Box 20, 46). Although there are a number of volumes of recordings, Sacks mainly focuses on an 11-minute segment of the transcript that he first gave as a handout during the spring 1966 lectures (Sacks 1995, pp. 136–143, pp. 270–280). In the series of lectures that follow, Sacks concentrates on one short section of the transcript where the therapist introduces a new patient, Jim, to the group.

Transcript 8.1

Roger :	On Hollywood Boulevard the other night they were giving tickets for dirty windshields. ((door opens))
Jim :	hh
Ther :	Jim, this is uh Al,
Jim :	Hi

Ther :	Ken,
Jim :	Hi
Ken :	Hi
Ther :	Roger.
Roger :	Hi
Jim :	Hi
Ther :	Jim Reed.
( ):	((cough))
Ken:	We were in an automobile discussion
Roger:	discussing the psychological motives for
( ):	hhhhhhh
Al:	drag racing on the street.

(Sacks 1995, Vol 1, p. 271)

As the analysis of this introduction sequence unfolds over the next three lectures (Sacks 1995, Vol 1, pp. 270–319),[2] Sacks focuses on both sequential turn actions and membership category work as layered within the sequence. Within this sequence, Sacks first establishes what the action is (an introduction sequence) and then examines what form the introduction takes, how it is organised, and how the participants orient to relevant identities, categories, and actions during the course of the introduction. By tracing through Sacks's analysis, it is possible to see how he develops the analytic principles introduced in the *Baby Cried* analysis when applied to naturally occurring interaction. In so doing, Sacks demonstrates the central principle and analytic potential of treating category work and sequential actions as mutually entwined with multiple categorial and sequential relevancies as the interaction unfolds.

Lecture 04.a: an introduction sequence

In Lecture 04.a (pp. 281–291), Sacks introduces the new data and focuses on the introduction *sequence* with an interest in examining how the sequence is organised and how it is possible to recognise when it has been completed and that it has been completed properly. Here, Sacks pays particular attention to the possible order of those being introduced as a sequence of introductions. He notes that, by looking at who is introduced first, the participants are then able to figure out the order of the introduction sequence and so to anticipate when it will be their turn and when the introduction sequence would be completed, and that after first establishing that it is an introduction organised around a particular sequence of formatted introductions, Sacks then begins to build up the analytic layers of the analysis. He first suggests that the series of introductions points to a *collection of people* being introduced.

Sacks first notes how the introduction sequence is managed by one person who is treated by everyone as the appropriate person to do this action. This then points to differential roles for and during the introduction sequence as one person initiates and manages the introduction while the others are the ones introduced. Sacks suggests that the actions of introducer and introduced point to a contextually relevant collection of categories, 'therapist–patient', and that these categories are part of an 'omni-relevant' membership device, 'therapy session' (see also Keel, this volume). For Sacks, 'omni-relevance' refers to categorial devices that are composed of collections of categories that are always *potentially* applicable and that, when invoked, have priority in terms of organising action within – and only in – situated interaction. Sacks was clear that one omni-relevant device does not preclude the relevance of other devices in the production of an interaction, and does not assume that an omni-relevant device is always in operation for the duration of an encounter, but that:

> Things may be going along, the device isn't being used; at some point something happens which makes it appropriate, and it's used. And when it is used, it's the controlling device, i.e., there is no way of excluding its operation when relevant.
>
> (Sacks 1995, Vol 1, p. 314)

Sacks's observation points to both the categorial and sequential relevance of the device in that, at any point in an interaction, someone can expectedly and relevantly invoke an omni-relevant device to accomplish an activity, or, in doing some activity, invoke an omni-relevant membership device. For the introduction, the device operates reflexively at an immediate sequential level when initiating the introduction and at the organisational level where the therapist is the relevant category to do this within the device 'therapy session'. Sacks goes on to flesh out the layered texture of the action in the next lecture where he examines how it is that the therapist is able to, seemingly without trouble, interrupt or suspend the course of the interaction at this point. For this, Sacks brings in the idea of there being some actions that can take *priority* over other ongoing actions.

Lecture 04.b: an introduction sequence (continued)

In Lecture 04.b (pp. 292–299), Sacks introduces the idea of '*priority items*', sequences or actions that can take priority in the ongoing interaction, without regard to what has been occurring prior to them being used. Here, the introduction sequence is seen as a 'priority item' as it is seemingly out of sequential place, occurring sometime after the session has begun.

> Can we say something like: Under some conditions there are conversational possibilities which can be called *priority items*, or priority sequences, and that they have *superseding relevance* over whatever it is that may be being done, or over somethings that may be being done? It does appear that there are some 'priority items', and they're priority items whose character is not given by the last thing that occurred, in the sense that given a question an

> answer may be a priority item, given a first greeting the second may be. But these seem to have rights and obligations to be done, perhaps without regard to what it is that has been taking place, under some proper conditions occurring. They don't have, in that sense, a 'place' in the conversation.
>
> (Sacks 1995, Vol 1, p. 296; original emphasis)

Here, Sacks observes how these actions do not have a 'place' in the conversational sequence, in that they are not part of the topical and sequential flow of interaction, yet they are not treated as interruptions when invoked, but as both a relevant action and something to be attended to by everyone in the setting. Although the lecture contains much more analysis and discussion, for the purpose here I highlight this point as part of Sacks's interconnected layering of strands of analysis. From noting that some actions may be priority items, he goes on to note that someone whose business it is to do the action may be seen as *relevantly* doing these actions by the participants; that such an action may be *tied* to particular identities, such as a 'host' at a party whose job it is to introduce the guests to each other.

Lecture 6, omni-relevant devices; cover identifications

In Lecture 6 (pp. 312–319), Sacks pulls the elements of the previous analyses together to focus on how the introduction is a *categorially relevant* sequence. That it was the *therapist* who initiated and conducted the introduction when he did. Here, Sacks fleshes out the idea of *omni-relevance* as *omni-relevant category devices*, devices which contain membership categories some of whom may have rights to introduce *contextually* relevant actions that may not be sequentially matched to the ongoing interaction. Sacks is then able to tie omni-relevant categories and devices to sequential actions such that sequentially relevant 'priority items' may be categorially ordered. Sacks describes the process of his own discovery:

> I had a sense a year ago that 'therapist/patient' is an omni-relevant device here. I didn't know how to show that this was so, or even how to find that this was so. There were bits of data that looked like it, but until, as it happened, I was working on these things without any intention of dealing with the issue of omni-relevance, not much was happening. It was when I was working on the priority character of those insertable sequences [Lecture 04. b], and asked, 'how is that priority invoked, and what allows this one or that one to do it?' that it became apparent that it was very much related to the phenomena of omni-relevance.
>
> (Sacks 1995, Vol 1, p. 316)

In this fascinating reflection, Sacks describes how omni-relevance was something that he had not been able to pin down until he examined this sequence more closely. That is, it was through his analysis of these new data as both transcribed interaction and a focus on the participants' actions that he was able to connect up previous observations on categorisation and omni-relevant devices. Thus, moving from the autoethnographic analysis of the *Baby Cried* to transcribed data and participant-focused analysis reveals a fundamental shift in Sacks's approach, which he also addresses at times in the course of these lectures (Sacks 1995, pp. 290–291, 292, 295, 300–301, 306). For me, this series of lectures provided the key to treating members' category work as entwined and layered within the sequential flow of interaction, where sequential and categorial relevancies are oriented to, invoked and made operative over the course of interaction.

Omni-relevance and membership categorisation analysis

Sacks's analysis of the therapist's actions as organised through an omni-relevant device has been picked up in further studies of other institutional contexts (Fitzgerald & Housley 2002; Schegloff 2007; Butler 2008) as part of the 'reflexive co-determination' of sequence and identity (Schegloff 2007). While this research tended to focus on omni-relevant devices invoked as appropriate to the sequential actions research has also examined instances where the lack of an action by an omni-relevant category is treated as a breach. For example, in McHoul and Rapley's (2002) study of a 'quality of life' assessment, they examine how a 'breach' occurs when a non-relevant category invokes a priority action. Taken from the beginning of the session, the person who is the subject of the assessment makes the request, 'shall we make a start then?'. McHoul and Rapley argue that this utterance invokes the situated relevance of their interaction and makes relevant that it is the professional who should initiate the beginning of the session. Similarly, Butler (2008) shows how the omni-relevance of a device used to organise a children's game based on 'playing schools' is invoked when a 'student' says, 'aren't I supposed to do my work now', when the 'teacher' has failed to allocate a next activity for the students. In this way, the 'student' displays her attention to the categories and actions that are relevant and consequential for the ongoing interaction, thus invoking a device that has omni-relevance for the episode but was not being done properly.

Instances where there was a hitch in the interactional work or the progressivity of the action offers the possibility of extending the study of omni-relevance and multilayering to non-institutional settings. Extending the analysis to non-institutional settings, however, brings with it particular challenges in terms of demonstrating participant relevancies. As Raymond and Heritage (2006) succinctly point out, although the focus on institutionally relevant identities highlights how institutions are talked into being 'much more severe analytical problems emerge once we are in the open sea of ordinary conversation' (p. 680). The challenge for studies of omni-relevance and non-institutional interaction is whether, where no explicit category or identity is mentioned, it is possible to make sound analytic claims concerning the relevance and consequentiality of the phenomena to the participants. As Hester and Hester (2012) argue, for such analysis, there need to be two forms of analytic sensitivity for it to be demonstrably relevant for the participants:

> The first concerns how the parties to some scene or setting demonstrate for one another that a particular sense of social context is relevant for them, while the second refers to the methodological problem for the analyst of how to demonstrate that a particular sense of context is relevant for those participants.
>
> (Hester & Hester 2012, p. 13)

In Raymond and Heritage's (2006) study, they focused on a telephone call between two people and how the identity of one of the speakers as a 'grandparent' is made demonstrably relevant and consequential in the production of assessments about her grandchildren. Focusing particularly on the primary epistemic rights of the category 'grandparent', the analysis examines the way such rights are demonstrably consequential for the participants through turn design, turn content, and the trajectory of the sequence. Whereas Raymond and Heritage's (2006) focus was on sequential actions, a more categorisation-focused body of work has been developed through studies including friends talking, family mealtimes and couples using video chat (Fitzgerald, Housley & Butler 2009; Butler & Fitzgerald 2010; Hester & Hester 2012; Fitzgerald & Rintel 2013; Rintel 2015).

These studies examined the possibility of analytically demonstrating an orientation to omni-relevant devices in non-institutional settings. In doing this, they also sought to demonstrate how categories and membership are not fixed, but rather once invoked and open to negotiation over the course of interaction; that categories and membership can change over the course of conversation; and that category membership can be reconfigured at any point. Returning to Sacks and his discussion of a herring attempting to be served to a recalcitrant relative (Sacks 1995), he highlighted how category membership, devices and category predicates are not fixed even within the interaction, in that relevant categories and categorial relevancies may emerge, or become 'operative', at some point as the event unfolds and may evolve over the course of the interaction (Sacks 1995; Butler & Fitzgerald 2010).

In Sacks's lecture titled 'The "old man" as an evolved natural object' (Sacks 1995, Vol 2, pp. 318–331), he examines an extended sequence of mealtime talk between a middle-aged couple, Ethel and Ben, their son, Bill, and Ethel's recently widowed stepfather-in-law, Max. In his analysis, Sacks notes how the operative identity of the 'old man' as an 'old man' and as a 'burden' was accomplished through the repeated attempts of the man's son and daughter-in-law to get him to eat some herring. What is interesting in this analysis – and related to the analysis of the introduction sequence discussed above – is how Sacks combines both the sequential organisation of talk (how an offer is followed by a request and then a threat, and so on) and the categorial organisation in the sense of the unstated categorial relevancies being made operative and oriented to by the participants. Here, Sacks demonstrates how unstated, tacit or implicit relationships between the parties can emerge into relevance over the course of the sequence and come eventually to drive it (Schegloff 1995, p. xxvii). Although this particular analysis is not couched in categorial terms, it further contributes to understanding how sequential and inferential orders of interaction can be examined together by treating category incumbency not as fixed, but in terms of how it can evolve and shift between interactional layers of relevance. Moreover, participants can shift membership in relation to different orientations within the interaction, and categories can become 'promiscuous' within interaction.

Promiscuous categories[3]

As the analytic understanding of the multilayered texture of interaction was explored further, it also became possible to examine the way a *single* category can have different meanings for different participants within interaction – for example, a category introduced or treated as a member of one device can be shifted to other devices within the interaction, and, in the process, collect different predicates and have different import for the interaction (Fitzgerald and Rintel 2013). To illustrate this categorial phenomenon, the brief analysis below examines how a story recipient gradually treated a character in a story differently as the story unfolded and eventually recategorised the 'lifeguard' as a 'bitch' at the end of the story.

The data come from a recording of a couple, Des and Kay, in a long-distance relationship; they would use video relay chat technology to talk to each other at the end of the day. During the routine work of catching up on the day's events, Des tells a story about what he did that day: he and his friend Lizzie sneaked into a residential complex in order to use the pool. As the story unfolds, Des introduces various characters, including a female character who is central to the story – the 'lifeguard'. The lifeguard is seen as a gatekeeper to the pool, and so Des describes his actions as having to 'play it- (0.3) do:wn low or whatever' in order to avoid being found out.

As the story continues, Des returns to the character of the lifeguard and adds more to his description, that the lifeguard is a 'girl' and she is 'super nice':

Transcript 8.2

51 Des: - =so we- we go in, (.) a:nd (.) >the lifeguard's this girl,
52 - and she's li:ke super nice,
53 so I started li:ke ta(h)lki(h)ng to h(h)e(h)r he .hh

In fleshing out the character of the lifeguard, Des builds on the professional category membership of lifeguard with personal attributes such that the lifeguard becomes a 'girl' who is 'super nice'. In the next line, Des mentions that he started to talk to her. Previously, at the beginning of the story, Des described how he and Lizzie had to be on the 'down low' to avoid being noticed by the lifeguard. Since then, the lifeguard has now become a super nice girl who he starts talking to.

Des continues with his story and how he continued his subterfuge when talking to the lifeguard by giving the lifeguard an apartment number and pretending it was his friend Lizzie's apartment, so that he was able to legitimately use the pool.

Transcript 8.3

54 Des: $an [I made up this whole sto:ry about like,$]
55 Kay: [@Smiles a little ((‘tightly’))@]
56 Des: how Lizzie lived in the building
57 and I was just mooching off her
58 to get the free poo::l a(h)n(h)d
59 (0.4)
60 Des: .hh
61 Kay: mh °hmhmh.°
62 Des: [$like all this] stu:ff,$
63 =like I gave a phony nu:mber and everyth(h)i(h)ng?
64 (0.4)
65 [an she like-]
66 Kay: [Wai:t, you gave] her a number to ca:ll you?
67 Des: No no a hou- uh >an apartment number,<
68 (0.4)
69 Kay: **L**°Oh.°
70 Des: >I j'st like, looked at some of them
71 when we were walking up the:re,<
72 (0.5)
73 Des: and I was like yeah I live in: thirty one
74 eig(h)h**t**(hi)ty hu.
75 Kay: Yo[u mean Lizzie lives there?]
76 Des: [and um er] >Lizzie lives
77 in °thirty one eighty.=yeah.° u:m (1.0) so:

After initially glossing his subterfuge (‘made up this whole story’; ‘and all this stuff’), Des produces a specific example of giving the lifeguard false information – he gave the lifeguard a ‘phony number’. At this point (line 66), Kay halts the story ‘wait, you gave her a number to call you?’. Kay's action halts the flow of the story and operates as a ‘priority item’, and that she is able to legitimately do this, and provides a subtle first glimpse of her treating the lifeguard as possibly more than only a character in a story. Suspending the story to clarify if he gave the lifeguard a *phone* number provides an analytic glimpse of a possible omni-relevant device being oriented to by Kay, that of *our relationship.* Within the omni-relevant device ‘our relationship’, the category of super nice female lifeguard who you gave a phone number to has potentially different meanings, different predicates, than the original category 'lifeguard' first introduced by Des. This mishearing points to a possible shift of the character 'lifeguard' from a character *within* the story to now *outside* the story, as a category relevant to Des and Kay's relationship.

While Des continues with the story, Kay begins to circle back within the story and to point out various discrepancies in Des's story about the lifeguard, such as wanting to be on the 'down lo' but then talking to her. Again, these actions point to the evolving recategorisation of the lifeguard from within the story to a category relevant to their relationship. While the story continues to the end, and it turns out the point of the story was that Des finds out they have mutual friends with the lifeguard, Kay provides a more explicit recategorisation for the lifeguard.

Transcript 8.4

Extract 3

142 Kay: Okay well now that you've
143 - flirted with the bitch a who:le day. hehehe.
144 Des: Yep yep yep

Kay's summary, then, recategorises the lifeguard explicitly in relation to the omni-relevant device 'our relationship' – the lifeguard is not welcome in the device 'our relationship'. Moreover, the device 'our relationship' takes priority over other actions, possibly because this is what is being oriented to through the call, of catching up with each other at the end of the day. That is, relating stories about their day are routine actions as part of relationship maintenance, but are subordinate to this omni-relevant device.

The analysis shows not only how categories can evolve within the interaction, but also how they can be treated as a member of two devices simultaneously. For Des, the category of the lifeguard was relevant to the story characters, to be revealed later as having mutual friends, whereas, for Kay, the lifeguard became relevant to their relationship as someone Des had 'flirted' with. That is, categories can be 'promiscuous' (Schegloff 2007) as they can be removed and repurposed within the interaction, irrespective of how they were originally introduced.

Summary

My aim in the chapter has been to highlight the continuing relevance and payoff of going back to Sacks's lectures, and, as I have pursued a particular methodological problem, Sacks so often provides the insight needed to push the analysis further. For me, the problem was how to analytically explore interaction as three-dimensional. I took this to be at the heart of Sacks's approach when he moved from the *Baby Cried* data to the therapy session data and where this new data produced a profound shift in both data and his approach to analysis. It might be argued that the shift to transcribed data provided Sacks with the solution to his data 'problem'. As he discussed in a seminar with Garfinkel in 1962, his interest was not so much in the study of the discipline of sociology, but the study of people doing sociology in their everyday actions (Harvey Sacks Papers 2017; Fitzgerald forthcoming), the problem was getting the data. Older technology had provided newspapers and published books, but the tape recorder provided the means by which to capture the actual lived problem solving of people doing sociology in action (Fitzgerald 2019).

Sacks then orients to data in two different, but interrelated, ways – as something that is interesting in itself as a phenomenon, but also as a way to solve analytic problems and develop his principles of analysis. This, for me, is the abiding relevance of Sacks: his constant demonstrations of creative ways to solve analytic problems, together with an invitation to develop upon his initial analysis. This invitation is made explicit by Sacks in a description of how he approaches his form of sociological inquiry. In a folder entitled 'Notes on Method' (Box 32), a draft document in the archive written for a volume of studies that was never published, Sacks introduces the studies that will follow as 'exercises' before describing how he goes about doing them and how the reader should understand them:

> The studies, let me call them more appropriately, the exercises that compose this volume … Let me note that the exercises tend to have a recurrent form. A presentation of some small fragment of transcribed conversation is followed by a quite bland, uncontroversial and unilluminating observation about a fragment, followed by an attempt to determine how the observed features might possibly be achieved or some such explanatory effort devoted to the observations, followed by some further observations which the attempted analysis generates, which further observations may well be news, may well be illuminating and interesting, and then further analysis devoted to explaining the presence or the operation of the newsy facts. The procedure of analysis generating new observations which provide for a further analysis can be carried on again and again, but I have happened to stop after one or two or three applications and to start over again on new materials, for fear that a sort of abstractness would be reached which would not permit the actual materials to control how I think about them.
>
> (Harvey Sacks Papers 2017, Box 32, File Notes on Method, pp. 2–3)

In this introductory passage Sacks makes clear that his analysis is only the start, it is to kick things off, as he then invites the reader, the analyst, to build on his work and take his analysis further. The lesson taken from this is that his analysis is to be treated as practical exercises that show the potential analytic power of this form of analysis and an invitation to continue developing upon and extending the analysis of social action wherever it occurs.

Notes

1 Sacks collected data from a range of different contexts including newsprint, overheard conversations, stories, children's street games, children's drawings, his own recollections, comic books, classic and contemporary research reports and, of course, transcripts of various forms of interaction (Fitzgerald 2019). The recorded interactions and transcripts include conversations between colleagues and between family members, shopping for a used car (where Sacks made 23, presumably secret, recordings of him visiting different used-car lots (Harvey Sacks Papers 2017, Box 20, File, Auto Shopping), transcripts from TV and radio phone-in programmes (Harvey Sacks Papers 2017, Box 121, File, Crandall), as well as the group therapy session (GTS) data (Harvey Sacks Papers 2017, Box 46, File, GTS 5. H.S. Copy).

2 It should be noted that Lectures 4a and 4b were not delivered in spring 1966 but in autumn 1966. However, as Jefferson points out, these two lectures are part of the sequence of analysis (Jefferson in Sacks 1995, Vol 1 p. 281 fn).

3 The term 'analytic promiscuous' is used by Schegloff (1995, 2007) in his critique of MCA where he cautions against analysts imposing their own understandings of the meaning of categories and predicates over those of the participants (see also Fitzgerald 2012; Stokoe 2012; Hester 2016). Indeed, Sacks's own work on categorisation had encountered this problem where he notes that he had dropped the term 'category bound activities' because his students would just invoke 'zillions' of predicates rather than those from the data (Harvey Sacks Papers 2017 Box 15, File Worktapes S72). Although 'analytic promiscuity' can, of course, be an issue for any form of analysis, including CA, our interest is in 'categorial promiscuity' as a members' phenomenon.

References

Butler, C.W. (2008). *Talk and social interaction in the playground.* Aldershot, UK: Ashgate.

Butler, C.W., & Fitzgerald, R. (2010) Operative identities in a family meal. *Pragmatics*, *42* (9), 2462–2474.

Fitzgerald, R. (2012). Membership categorisation analysis. Wild and promiscuous or simply the joy of Sacks. *Discourse Studies*, *14*(3), 305–311.

Fitzgerald, R. (2019). The data and methodology of Harvey Sacks: Lessons from the archive. *Journal of Pragmatics*, *143*, 205–214.

Fitzgerald, R. (Forthcoming) Sacks and Garfinkel: On ethnomethodology and sociological inquiry. In Carlin, A.P., Dennis, A., Jenkings, K.N., Lindwall, O., & Mair, M. (Eds.), *Routledge international handbook of ethnomethodology and conversation analysis.* Abingdon, UK: Routledge.

Fitzgerald, R., & Housley, W. (Eds.). (2015). *Advances in membership categorisation analysis*. London: Sage.

Fitzgerald, R., Housley, W., & Butler, C. (2009). Omni relevance in interactional context. Special Issue of *Australian Journal of Communication*, *36*(3).

Fitzgerald, R., & Rintel, S. (2013). From lifeguard to bitch: The problem of promiscuous categories in story telling in a long-distance relationship. Special Issue of the *Australian Journal of Communication*, *4*(2) (40.3).

Fitzgerald, R.H.W. (2002). Identity, categorisation and sequential organisation: The sequential and categorial flow of identity in a radio phone-in. *Discourse and Society*, *13*(5), 579–602.

Harvey Sacks Papers. (Accessed 2017). *Collection 1678*. UCLA Library Special Collections, Charles E. Young Research Library, University of California, Los Angeles, CA.

Hester, S. (2016). *Descriptions of deviance. A study in membership categorisation analysis*. Edited by P. Eglin & D. Francis. http://emca-legacy.info

Hester, S., & Eglin, P. (Eds.). (1997). *Culture in action: Studies in membership categorization analysis. studies in ethnomethodology and conversation analysis*. Washington, DC: University Press of America.

Hester, S., & Hester, S. (2012). Categorial occasionality and transformation: Analyzing culture in action. *Human Studies*, *35*(4), 563–581

Lynch, M. (2000). The ethnomethodological foundations of conversation analysis. *Text & Talk*, *20*(4), 517–532.

McHoul, A., & Rapley, M. (2002). 'Should we make a start then?': A strange case of (delayed) client-initiated psychological assessment. *Research on Language and Social Interaction*, *35*(1), 73–91.

Pitcher, E.G., & Prelinger, E. (1963) *Children tell stories. An analysis of fantasy.* New York: International Universities Press.

Raymond, G., & Heritage, J. (2006). The epistemics of social relations: Owning grandchildren. *Language in Society*, *35*(5), 677–705.

Rintel, S. (2015). Omnirelevance in technologised interaction: Couples coping with video calling distortions. In Fitzgerald, R. & Housley, W. (Eds.), *Advances in membership categorisation analysis*. London: Sage, pp. 123–150.

Sacks, H. (1974). On the analyzability of stories by children. In Turner, R. (Ed.), *Ethnomethodology*. Harmondsworth: Penguin, pp. 216–232.

Sacks, H. (1995). *Lectures on conversation, volumes I and II*. Edited by G. Jefferson with Introduction by E.A. Schegloff. Oxford: Blackwell.

Schegloff, E. (1995). Introduction Vols 1 and 2. In Sacks, H. (Ed.), *Lectures on conversation, volumes I and II*. Edited by G. Jefferson. Oxford: Blackwell, Vol. 1, pp. ix–lxii; Vol. 2, pp. ix–lii.

Schegloff, E.A. (2007). A tutorial on membership categorization. *Journal of Pragmatics*, *39*(3), 462–482.

Stokoe, E. (2012). Moving forward with membership categorization analysis: Methods for systematic analysis. *Discourse Studies*, *14*(3), 277–303.

9 Membership categorization and the sequential multimodal organization of action

Walking, perceiving, and talking in material-spatial ecologies

Lorenza Mondada

The work of Harvey Sacks has always fascinated me for its two indissociable facets, categorization analysis and sequential analysis. Early on – influenced by the work of J. Widmer (1986, 2010), who was the first person I ever talked with about ethnomethodology, when he came back from UCLA in the early 1980s – I began to explore multiple phenomena for which categorization analysis was particularly insightful – such as, in linguistics, the categorization of speakers, the linguistic resources they were using, and the language(s) they were speaking (Mondada, 1999, 2002a, 2002b). Later on, when I engaged in video studies within an EMCA perspective, the obvious challenge for me became how to integrate visual and embodied details within membership categorization analysis (MCA). This interest was developed from a constant challenge for categorization analysis: that is, how to demonstrate the relevance of participants' categories as a phenomenon locally observable in, and consequential for, the organization of their conduct. Following Harvey Sacks's invitation to consider categories as a constant accomplishment by the participants, my work has attempted to contribute to this issue by showing the relevance of visual and embodied resources in the situated establishment, maintenance, and challenge of relevant categories.

In this paper, I elaborate on how multimodal resources are exploited by participants to make sense of their categories, moment by moment, and on how this contributes to Sacks's MCA. On the basis of video-recorded guided visits, I reflect on how the detailed organization of embodied practices, such as walking, both exhibits and achieves the categories of the walkers. In this activity, the way in which the "guide" versus "guided" organize their walking, looking around and talking, accountably manifests their categories and, at the same time, reflexively, contributes to establishing them. Here, I focus on *embodied category-bound practices of walking* as a perspicuous phenomenon (Garfinkel, 2002). Participants are spatially positioned in ways that achieve and exhibit their categories of "guide" versus "guided"; some walk, and others follow; some initiate the walking, and some are responsive to it, and so on. This makes categories visible, but also possibly challenges them. Two episodes are analyzed, one in which the category of "guide" is confirmed and reproduced by the organization of the collective walk, and another in which a participant initiates an action that departs from the expected and established categories. These cases raise more general questions about the sequential and interactional organization of multimodally formatted actions, the relation between sequential organization and categorical organization, and the achievement and the negotiation of membership categories as they are implemented in accountable embodied micro-practices. In this sense, this chapter reflects on the consequences for MCA of the "embodied" or "video" turn in EMCA.

Categories in action

Membership categorization is achieved through lively situated practices that are indissociable from the sequential organization of talk and embodied action. In this chapter, I show the relevance of a multimodal analysis of embodied actions for the understanding of how participants establish and recognize themselves as belonging to a category and acting as such. The crucial issue is how embodied practices are formatted and interpreted as categorically accountable.

Following Harvey Sacks's seminal writings (1972a, 1972b, 1992), I focus on membership categories-in-action – that is, categories as they are observable for the analyst and for members alike, in actual courses of action and – consequently – in audio-video-recorded naturally occurring social interactions. Sacks himself used a variety of ethnographic, textual, and interactional materials to study membership categorizations; I focus here on the last type. Within this focus, categories are treated as members' phenomena – adopting the members' perspective, rather than an external, exogenous, etic perspective imposed by the analyst (Sacks, 1963). Two options have been broadly developed in the literature (see Hester & Eglin, 1997; Fitzgerald & Housley, 2015). A first approach focuses on categories that are explicitly *named* as such in the course of social interaction, mentioned in order to refer to absent third parties (as a "recognizable description"; Sacks, 1972a, 1992, I: 245) or, less frequently, from the perspective of the co-present first or second persons (such as when they refer to "we"; Sacks, 1992, I: 568). A second approach focuses on categories that are *enacted* through talk, within actions that make their doer recognizable as belonging to a specific category, with consequential rights and obligations characterizing that category. Enacted categories are implemented in situated actions and accountable as such thanks to the format, sequential environment, and actual context of that action. The relations between organization of action and relevance of membership categories have been investigated in various ways, following Sacks's insights:

(a) Categories are made relevant in talk and oriented to by the co-participants without having to be named, and this is accountable in how they shape subsequent actions, which reveal participants' understandings and normative expectations (Schegloff, 2007).

(b) Categories might be invoked but also accepted, amended, resisted, or rejected in interaction (Sacks, 1992, I: 114–8). For example, a participant may be *claiming* membership (e.g. to be a "hotrodder" by referring to cars in a specific way and telling specific stories about them) and *be challenged* by another (e.g. by being corrected about their way of talking about cars; 1992, I: 119).

(c) Participants may be recognized as engaging in "*category-bound activities*" (Sacks, 1972a, 1992, I: 241; emphasis added) – as shown by the example of "crying" as an activity "bound" to the category "baby", demonstrated by the fact that this category-bound character is exploited within procedures for praising and degrading members (1992, I: 249), or of "automobile discussion" as bound to "teenage boys" (1992, I: 301).

(d) Another way of incarnating categories is, for example, "*doing 'being ordinary'*", an expression used by Sacks to reflect how members "may be coordinatively engaged in assuring that each of them are ordinary persons, and that can then be a job that they undertake together, to achieve that each of them, together, are ordinary persons" (1992, I: 216; emphasis added). This reminds us that a category can only be constantly sustained and maintained in and through action.

(e) Beside *social categories* such as "mother", "Jewish", "activist", or "lesbian", categories can be directly generated by the organization of interaction – as demonstrated by Watson (1997a, 2015) with the notion of "*turn-produced category*", referring to categories such as "caller"/"called", or "performer"/"audience", which are generated by the turn-by-turn unfolding of talk and have a reflexive effect on the organization and the accountability of talk.

However, categories are not only achieved and made accountable through talk, but also through embodied action. Although this aspect remains largely under-investigated, a multimodal approach of categories in action, such as the one proposed here, reveals how, more generally, the embodied, and not only linguistic, shaping of actions reflexively elaborates categories' recognizability and intelligibility.

In this chapter, I point at the fact that an embodied practice such as walking is not only sequentially organized (Mondada, 2014a) but also categorically accountable. As such, walking contributes to the accountability of a range of social activities, such as the guided visit. The fact that categories are "visually available" was pointed out early on by Jayyusi on the basis of "the intelligibility of the categories of action and person visible in the photographed scene" (1992: 11). A series of studies by Lee and Watson (see Watson, 2005, 2015: 34) further show that "visibility arrangements" of bodies in public spaces provide for the accountability of their trajectories for other members. These practices are also crucial for the categorical visibility of "blind" people on the road (Relieu, 1994). Likewise, the visible disposition of queuing in space provides for the visible accountability of categories such as "first in line", "next", "last", and so on (Watson, 2015: 34). These observations show the fruitfulness of a *multimodal membership categorization analysis*: in this chapter, I elaborate on the embodied formatting of actions such as walking, stopping, leading, following, showing, and seeing as having a categorical accountability, incorporating rights and obligations, and being recognized (or challenged) as such by the co-participants.

To do so, I focus on an institutional setting – guided visits – characterized by talk, embodiment, specific interactional spaces and bodily arrangements, and mobility. The guided visit is an institutional event that is categorially organized, featuring participants recognizable as belonging to one of two parties, the "guide" and the "guided", forming a standardized pair. Despite these two categories often being recognizable and oriented to, they may also be challenged (Mondada, 2013; De Stefani & Mondada, 2014, 2017).

The embodied production and reproduction of categories

In guided visits, the categorical accountability of the participants' actions is not only verbally but also bodily produced and made recognizable. The guided visit examined here features a gardener (Luc) and three visitors (Yan, Elise, and Jean). We join the group as they walk through the garden. Although they all look around, admiring the surrounding landscape, Luc, walking ahead, is the participant who stops the walk to point at and show relevant details he spots in the trees. His gaze on nature not only refers to a "professional vision" (Goodwin, 1994), but is embodied in specific ways of positioning his body and of initiating new sequences of talk, recognizable as doing the "guide".

The extract begins as Luc notices a detail in a tree and shows it to the co-participants, modifying the "mobile formation" (McIlvenny, Broth, Haddington, 2014) they constitute in order to introduce a referent that will be identified, described, and explained:

Transcript 9.1

(3/13.34_graines_meta3,12.14_A_eli_51.35, A_jea_1.04.18)

```
1          #(0.4) ζ #(0.7)
    luc    >>walks ahead--->
    yan    >>follows->
    eli    >>follows->
    jea    >>follows->
    luc    ζlooks at tree->
    fig    #fig 9.1   #fig 9.2
```

2 LUC **>v'voξ⊥yez?<# !**
>y'see?<
luc ξpoints->
yan ⊥looks at tree->
eli !looks at tree->
fig #fig 9.3
3 **(0.2) * (0.6) # * (0.2)**
luc ->*turns twd tree and approaches*stops--->
fig #fig 9.4

9.4

9.5

4 LUC **voyez lesβ: #on pr- on parlait des% des deλs^abris%λ**
see the: we t- we talked about about about shelters
jea βlooks at tree->
eli ->%comes closer---%stops->
jea ->λstops----λ
fig #fig 9.5
5 **p+our% les inse!ctes. alors,**
for the insects. so,
yan ->+comes closer--->
eli ->%
eli ->!looks at tree--->
6 **(0.2)**
7 LUC **vous +avez+ # des:ξ ζ(0.3) cesξ ces graines⊥! #là,**
you have some these these seeds there,
luc -->ξtakes seed/fruitξshows seed in his hand->
luc ->ζlooks at seed/fruit->
yan ->+stops+
yan ->⊥gz at seed/fruit->
eli !gz at seed/fruit->
fig #fig 9.6 #fig 9.7

9.6

9.7

9.8

8 **(0.3) <.hhh .h (0.2) λ**
jea λcomes closer->

```
9   LUC     qui sontξ:# (0.6) λ
            which are:
    luc          -->ξhands over the fruit-->
    jea                        -->λ
    fig                   #fig 9.8
10  JEA     °ahξ φc'est quφoi° [°°ça°°?
            oh that's what       [°°this°°?
11  LUC                           [.hh
    luc     ->ξ
    jea          φ.......φtakes the fruit->
12          (0.2)
13  LUC     qui sont,ξ perforées par les oiseaux, φ (.) pour manger
            that are    perforated by the birds, (.) in order to eat
    luc              ξgest perforating-->
    jea                                          ->φempties shell on R hand->
14          les insectes (.) qui sontφ dedans. >ils mangent pas les<
            the insects (.) that are inside. >they don't eat the<
    jea                           ->φ
15          graiξnes, [(.) elles sont pas ξbonnes.ξ]
            seeds,     [(.) they are not good.]
    luc       ->ξ                         ξpointsξ
16  JEA                [et ça c'est quoi? c]          'est des grai[nes là?
                       [and that it's what? it]       's se[eds there?
17  LUC                                                            [ça c'est
                                                                   [that it's
18          les graines, oui. ζ [.hhh
            seeds,         yes.  [.hhh
    luc                    ->ζturns twd tree->>
19  ELI                          [i man!gent les inse[ctes: qui sont à l'intérieur
                                 [they eat the insecξts       that are inside
20  LUC                                              [i- les inseξct!es┴
                                                     [th- the insects
    eli                            ->!looks at Luc----------------!tree-->>
    yan                                                          ┴lk tree->>
    luc                                                       ξpoints tree->
21          qui qui ont passé l'hiver là-dedans,=
            that that have spent the winter inside there=
22  ELI     =j'ignorais qu'y avait autant
            =I ignored that there were so many
23          de:[: graines àξ insectes ou d'insectes [euh
            seeds with/for insects or insects [ehm
24  LUC        [.hh                                  [c'est fou hein? ξ
               [.hh                                  [it's crazy uh?
    luc                 ->ξpicks a new seed/fruit------------------ξ
```

At the beginning of the excerpt, the group is progressing in a specific "mobile formation", in which Luc walks ahead, Jean walks beside him at a little distance, and Yan and Elise walk behind (Figure 9.1). This mobile formation is adapted to the local ecology – a narrow footpath – but is also characterized by Luc not just "walking ahead" but also "leading" the group, whose members are "following" him. These constitute *category-bound ways of walking*.

The way of walking is also adjusted to the way of looking: whereas the other participants look around while progressing in their walk, with a panning gaze on the environment, Luc stares at a detail, beginning to reorient his body towards it (Figure 9.2). When he utters the verb "v'voyez?"/"you see?" (2), he also points at the tree (2, Figure 9.3), then pivots (3, Figure 9.4) and definitely stops (Figure 9.5). His entire body works as a pointer to what he is about to show.

His body, as well as his turn, reorganizes the walk and gaze of the co-participants: they slow their pace and turn towards the pointed-at tree. All align with his action. As Luc repeats the verb "voyez" (4), they look in the direction he indicates (Figure 9.5). At this point, although their attention is responding to his pointing, they have not yet stopped, and their bodies are still in motion. This might be the reason why Luc delays what is projected by the article introducing the object to see ("les:"/ "the:" 4) and, instead of a noun, inserts a reference to a topic they already talked about (4–5). As a matter of fact, during this insertion, the visitors slow down and modify their trajectories, ending up stopping (4–5). Their aligned responses are recognizable as category-bound, further confirming them as an "audience" of "guided" persons. Thus, while the "guide" sees, notices, spots details in the environment with his professional vision, and shows them, the "guided" respond to him and look at what he points at, in a form of instructed gaze.

The explanation of the detail pointed at progresses when the participants have stopped and are turned towards Luc (Figure 9.6). Despite his reference to previous talk (4–5), he introduces the object as a new topic with the verbal construction "vous avez"/"you have" (7) followed by the (previously projected but suspended) descriptor of the pointed-at referent: "des: (0.3) ces ces graines là"/"some (0.3) these these seeds there" (7), while he picks a fruit-like seed from the tree. This description is further expanded by a relative clause (9) while he shows the seed in the palm of his hand. This produces a more restricted focus of shared attention, with the participants coming closer and leaning over his hand (Figure 9.8).

In this way, Luc not only shows the spectacle of nature, but he also extracts relevant particulars from the exuberance of the garden and guides the vision of the visitors to details that cannot be otherwise observed – such as the seeds constituting a shelter for insects. In this way, he shows not only his knowledge, but also his way of bodily relating to the environment, including the collection of samples to be detached from it, to be inspected by the participants. The "guided visit" becomes a "lesson" in natural sciences.

The expertise of the guide contrasts with the displays of the other participants: Jean utters a question (10), which is introduced by a change-of-state token, and displays in its format ("c'est quoi ça?"/"it's what, that?", 10) a total ignorance of its object (Heritage, 2012). Luc does not answer the question, but continues his relative clause (13), explaining the nexus between the fruit-like seed, the insects, and the birds, describing in a few words a tangled system of botanical and animal life (13–15). Its completion is overlapped by a new, similar question from Jean (16), now expanded in a yes/no question offering a candidate answer (Pomerantz, 1988), confirmed by Luc (18). Another visitor, Elise, also offers a candidate answer (19), confirmed again by Luc (20). The contributions from the visitors display their epistemic positioning relative to Luc; they also manifest their progressive assimilation of the knowledge Luc is providing. Elise concludes the episode with a claim of (past) ignorance (22), summarizing Luc's lesson in a synthetic construction ("graines à insectes"/"seeds with/for insects", 23), aligned with by Luc's final assessment (24) seeking further consent.

In this extract, the participants produce embodied category-bound activities that accomplish the accountability of what they are engaged in as a guided visit, as well as the mutual recognition of them as belonging to the standardized relational pair "guide"/"guided". Luc is doing being the guide by implementing a variety of actions in a way that is categorically recognizable by the other participants. The latter align with them, doing being the "guided" – for instance, by following him, following his instructions, looking at what he shows, asking questions, and displaying lack of knowledge about what he is showing.

Challenging conduct: the subversion and re-establishment of categories

The relevance of the paired categories "guide"/"guided" is a constant accomplishment that is actively sustained by both parties in their actions (such as explaining vs listening, showing vs looking, etc.). This work through which categorical accountability, as well as the rights and obligations of the incumbents of the various categories, is maintained, and sometimes defended, becomes particularly noticeable when a member of a category engages in a conduct that might acquire an accountability other than expected from that category. The "subversive" character of that conduct is reflexively established and observable in the responses of other participants, aligning or misaligning, adjusting or re-establishing the previous categorical relevance – as visible in their embodied conducts.

In guided visits, this is the case with actions done by visitors who, instead of displaying lack of knowledge in asking questions – as the "guided" – initiate alternative courses of actions, such as describing, explaining, and so on, which display epistemic authority. These are category-bound activities that compete with activities typically initiated by the "guide" (De Stefani & Mondada, 2014, 2017; Mondada, 2013). In these cases, the co-participants respond to these actions by orienting to their categorical accountability – for example, when the guide reasserts his or her epistemic superiority or leadership.

Embodied actions can produce the same tension: for instance, when a member of the group other than the guide begins to walk in an alternative direction, followed by others, or when s/he begins to introduce and establish an alternative focus of attention, redirecting the visual and bodily orientation of the group. In this case, too, competing actions might be oriented as such by the guide, who might reaffirm authority and leadership. These moments make particularly observable the fact that categorical membership is neither a pre-existing feature nor a feature that is established once for all, but has to be constantly achieved, again and again, within the precise formatting of each action.

A case at hand is observable in the next fragment from the same corpus, in which a member of the group, Yan, notices something in the environment and reorients his walk, abandoning the initial trajectory that followed the guide. In this way, he initiates an alternative trajectory as well as an alternative set of actions, making relevant a different set of categories.

We join the action as Luc, the gardener, is leading the other co-participants across the park he is in charge of. The same group had already been in the same place several months before, during the winter, and Yan had particularly appreciated a specific area called the "research garden". As they are now walking along a footpath, Yan looks to his right, where this area is located, and produces a noticing:

Transcript 9.2a

(Jardivis 055_12.12=meta5_10.27-)
((the group is walking along a foothpath))

```
1          # (1.0) ⊥ (0.5) #
     fig   #fig 9.9       #fig 9.10
     yan          ⊥turns to his right->
```

9.9

9.10

```
2    YAN   aßhξ +ben si:↑ ça aß poussé↑ un peu# quand même.ß
           oh well yes:   it grew up   a bit   nonetheless
     yan        +walks out of the path, on the right-->
     jea                   ßlooks at Y------------------ß
     luc     ξlooks at Y------------->
     eli   ßlooks at Y--------->
     fig                                 #fig 9.11
```

9.11

```
3          λ(0.7) # (1.0)
     jea   λwalks to the right->
     fig         #fig 9.12
4    LUC   ah% oui,ξ ah ben↑ *on va aller# voir% effectivement on va aller
           oh yes, oh well     we'll go   to see   actually       we'll go
     luc        ->ξ
     eli                                   -->%
     eli     %walks to the right->
     luc                *walks to the right-->
     fig                              #fig 9.13
```

9·12

9·13

5 **voir le: (0.9) les jardins d'la recherche.**
to see the: (0.9) the research gardens (= name of the garden)
6 **(1.1)**

The group walks in silence along a footpath (Figure 9.9): Luc is ahead, Jean and Elise walk side by side, and Yan is a bit further away on the right. As in the previous fragment, the very fact that Luc walks ahead is recognizable as a category-bound activity: walking is categorically organized, making visible who is the "guide", and who are "guided", following him.

Yan turns his head to his right (1, Figure 9.10) and produces a noticing, referring to some prior experience (the change-of-state token manifests surprise but also recognition, the particles "ben si:"/"well yes:" respond to some potential or past utterance that is negated, the connective "quand même"/"nonetheless" also refers to a contradictory observation). In producing this turn with a louder voice, Yan treats his co-participants as able to hear and understand it.

While talking, Yan begins to walk away from the path, towards the place he noticed. His turn produces the accountability of this deviation from the ongoing collective trajectory. The co-participants' response is embodied. Their gaze shift constitutes a first response: they progressively look at Yan walking away (2, Figure 9.11). A further response is produced by Jean, Elise, and then Luc, all beginning to walk in the same direction (3, Figure 9.12). By so doing, they bodily align with Yan's noticing and treat it as an invitation to follow him.

Luc is the last participant who changes trajectory; he is also the only one producing a verbal response. By so doing, Luc does not merely "follow" Yan, as do the other members of the group. Rather, by producing a description of a future action ("on va aller voir […] les jardins de la recherche"/"we'll go to see […] the research gardens", 4–5), he explicitly formulates what was implicit in Yan's noticing; he orients towards the fact that proposing a walking trajectory is an activity bound to the category of "guide"; he transforms his initial move aligning with Yan into the action of "guiding" the group towards a *visitable* objective. Whereas Yan was uttering a noticing about a vague referent, Luc produces an invitation to go to a precisely named place. Luc's walk is adjusted to these actions: when he changes his trajectory (Figure 9.13), he accelerates the pace of his walk, orienting again towards the fact that he is late relative to the action of "guiding" (vs "following").

The fragment shows how walking is an interactionally, categorically, and sequentially organized practice, which raises issues concerning who initiates/responds, leads/follows, aligns/misaligns, and so on, in relation to the ongoing action (noticing, proposing, inviting to see something) and the categories it makes relevant (such as "guide", "guided"). In guided visits, it is generally the guide who achieves the actions of leading the group from one place to another, identifying relevant spots, objects, and details to be seen in the environment, stopping, and elaborating on them. Moving the group along a certain trajectory, as well as stopping it and rearranging it around an object are typical prerogatives of the guide. Here, we observe how other participants might initiate similar activities, but also how the guide revises their accountability, as well as engaging in actions that re-establish him as being the guide.

Besides the responsive and mutually adjusting actions of the participants and their reflexive categorical relevancing effects, camera work makes visible a first proto-analytic interpretation of what is happening (Mondada, 2014b). In this case, the camerawoman is confronted with a dilemma related to the sequential, categorical, and normative organization of the course of action. A change of trajectory raises a selection problem: who will be photographed by the camera? Does the camera stay focused on the guide or on the "deviating" participant? This has strong implications for how the scene is shot. The beginning of the fragment is shot by the camerawoman *anticipating* the walk led by the guide; after the change of trajectory, the camerawoman *follows* the participants. The camera is not only interpreting in real time what is happening, but also reflexively producing the record that will enable the researcher to understand and to analyze what happened.

Next, Luc engages in further actions that reorganize the walk, the attention, and the talk of the group around category-bound actions pertaining to the "visit" and led by him as the guide – further confirming himself as the leading category:

Transcript 9.2b

((continuation))
7 LUC **#voyezξ là,+ en-ξ quand┴ on met un peu d'eau↑ on arrive à: (0.4) voyez?**
see over there, in- when we give a bit of whater↑ we're able to: (0.4) see?
luc ξ.........ξpoints fwd, palm open, to the shrub->
yan -->┴looks at shrub-->
fig #fig 9.14

9.14

8 **on-% onλ crée des petites +*oasis↑ φcomme ça [mais: .h] #**
we- we create small oases↑ like that [but: .h]
luc -->*stops on the left of shrub->
eli ->%changes trajectory and walks to the right of the plant->
jea ->λchanges trajectory and walks to the right of the plant->

yan ->+stops/pivots back twd shrub->
jea φtouches plant->
fig fig 9.15#

9.15

9 JEA **[c'est] des lys?**
[are these] lily?

10 **(0.4) ξ**
luc ->ξ
11 JEA **c'est [quoi.]**
what is [this.]
12 LUC **[c'est d]es héφméro[*cal%les.**
[these are] hemerocallis.
13 JEA **[des %héξméro↑calles.**
[hemerocallis
eli -->%stops--->
jea -->φ
luc -->*approches the shrub->
luc ξgrasps and puts his glasses->
14 LUC **des *hémérocalles. τregardezξ # l'insecξte là↑⊥**
hemerocallis. look at the insect over there↑
luc ->*
luc τleans forward on the plant->
luc -->ξ ξpoints at and touches plant->
yan --->⊥...looks and leans over->
fig #fig 9.16

9.16

As Yan continues to walk ahead (Figure 9.14), Luc initiates a new sequence, even if he is still behind the other members of the group. With his turn, he introduces a shrub as a new referent to the co-participants, although the shrub is still far away from most of them (Yan is passing by it in Figure 9.6). In this way, Luc uses *verbal* resources for an early achievement of an action typical of the guide – that is, showing and constituting a new focus of attention – while *bodily* and *visually* he is not yet able to come closer to the object and to point at it. His turn accomplishes this by announcing that something will be seeable, without yet describing what it is (7): in this sense, the deictic expression works as an attention-getting device. What is projected by this emergent turn is suspended by another bipartite sentence (7), also suspended, before the perception verb is recycled (end of 7), and the second part of the sentence is realized (8). Towards the end of the turn, the object to be seen is named ("des petites oasis"/"small oases" 9), although the shrub is pointed at well before (7). This turn format shows how the introduction of the new referent is sensitive to the ongoing mobile formation: the participants are still walking, Yan has already passed the shrub, and Jean and Elise are coming closer. Thus, Luc is directing and guiding the gaze and the body of the participants, who were initially scattered around in a dispersed way, but who now respond by moving and rearranging their bodies, targeting the object pointed at.

The response of the participants emerges in real time: Yan, ahead, pivots back towards the shrub. Jean stops in front of it. Both Jean and Elise modify their trajectories, which were following Yan: they bifurcate towards the right of the shrub and stop (Figure 9.15). The participants slow down and position themselves around the shrub (Figure 9.16). They do so, even if Luc's walk is delayed and he cannot bodily guide and dispose them around the referred-to object. His invitation to look at something, uttered from a distance, achieves the guiding of the group.

Luc's action reorganizes the embodied and spatial arrangement of the participants. He re-establishes a series of relative positionings, constituting an interactional space (Mondada, 2009) recognizable as typical of the visit, in which the participants reorganize as a group and share a common visual focus around an object. The response of the participants is categorically organized: they align not only with the action he initiates – showing them something – but also with the global activity of the "guided visit". Their stopping constitutes the object as a target of the visit and not just a noticing *en passant*.

Once the group has stopped, a new interactional space is constituted around the common focus of attention, and a new sequence begins. It is initiated by Jean asking a question (11) about the name of the shrub. In this way, a participant further contributes to the recognition of the "guide", through an action typical of the "guided" – asking a question – occasioning a display of epistemic authority by the guide. Jean is actually the first to arrive at the plant and he touches it; Yan walked by and now turns back; Luc just arrived, and Elise is positioning herself to the right. They all look at the plant – gradually repositioning in space as a group.

Jean's question proposes a candidate answer ("c'est des lys?", 11); in the absence of a response (12), it is asked again, in an open way ("c'est quoi." 13), which now does not display any knowledge about it and rather treats it as unknown. Various epistemic stances are manifested here, as well as in Luc's answer, which offers, in overlap and without any hesitation, a technical name ("c'est des hémérocalles." 14), exhibiting the epistemic authority of the gardener.

Luc utilizes elements of the ecology of the garden to instigate control over the movement of the group by halting it around the "shrub", allowing him to catch up with the others, and by further focusing their joint attention on the "hémérocalles". By so doing, he guides the participants' embodied movements, visual perception, and discursive knowledge through the local territory.

This fragment shows how a competitive alternative to the organization of the action by the "guide" is initiated by a member of the group, Yan (Transcript 9.2a), and how Luc reorganizes his course of action in such a way to re-establish the relevance of the category of "guide" and its category-bound activities (Transcript 9.2b). This re-establishment is a joint achievement: for instance, by asking a question, another participant, Jean, displays a lack of knowledge and occasions an expert answer by the "guide"; by aligning with the instructions and the guidance of Luc, all the participants recognize him as a "guide" and respond as "guided".

Discussion and conclusion

This chapter aims to provide some hints to answer the question of how to demonstrate the relevance of categories on the basis of embodied evidences – contributing to a multimodal MCA based on video data.

The fragments analyzed show how the organization of *walking* as a sequential interactional phenomenon is categorically accountable – recognizable as constituted by ongoing trajectories of actions through which participants "align" with, "lead", or "follow" others. The interactional space that results is a spatial configuration designed by a visible arrangement of the bodies that aligns with the distribution of these categories. Likewise, the organization of *showing/looking* is categorically recognizable as initiated by a participant with the right to organize, establish, and maintain a common focus of attention, and co-participants aligning with it, within embodied actions such as "leaning over", "gaze following", "staring", and so on. The focus of attention might be an object that constitutes the center of the visible arrangement of the bodies, but also an object that one participant has the right to identify, point at, manipulate, give to inspect, name, and describe. Finally, the turns-at-talk produced by the participants also exhibit differential rights and obligations: the guide introduces new referents and elaborates on them, and answers the questions asked by the guided, within a distribution of knowledge that displays and reproduces their categorical asymmetry. These actions can also be challenged by the initiation of alternative courses of action and the adoption of embodied postures and gestures that are recognizable under different categorical aspects. This may be aligned with or resisted and rejected by the co-participants, re-establishing more normative orders.

Multimodal MCA is still underdeveloped within the current EMCA literature. Returning to Sacks, references to details of bodies and embodied actions are scarce (one beautiful exception is the description of the consequentiality of lighting someone's cigarette; 1992, I: 50 ff.). Nonetheless, the *visible* dimension of social life is treated through Sacks's notion of *viewer maxim* – which allows the making sense of ongoing actions as they are *seen* by the participants. The *viewer's maxim* tells that,

> if a Member sees a category-bound activity being done, then, if one can see it being done by a member of a category to which the activity is bound, see it that way. The viewer's maxim is another "relevance rule" in that it proposes that for an observer of a category-bound activity, the

> category to which the activity is bound has a special relevance for formulating an identification of its doer.
>
> (Sacks, 1992, I: 259)

The viewer maxim is further developed in Sacks's reflections about people exchanging glances about other people (1992, I: 81–94), orienting to their membership: "what persons see is a class member, for whole collections of classes. You see 'a girl', 'a Negro', 'a such-and-such'. That is, the class permits you to see what it is that's there. It permits you to see" (1992, I: 86). Elsewhere, Sacks speaks of categories that are *glance-determinable* (1992, II: 539) – such as being the older by far. Through these notes about the availability of some relevant categories *at a glance*, Sacks indirectly points at the fact that this relevance is crucially connected to the observable and, therefore, describable character of social life thanks to its visible embodiment in gesture, postures, movements, trajectories, and body arrangements – which are scrutinized, monitored, and witnessed by participants as well as bystanders (see also Goffman, 1963, 1971; Sudnow, 1972).

Detailed video studies enable us to further sharpen the responses to the double question of the demonstrable and publicly observable relevance of categorization practices within social interaction – for people and analysts alike. Considering how people bodily produce a recognizable categorizable action, and how people see a category at a glance, respond, align with, and adjust to it contributes to the understanding of action formation, of the rights and obligations associated with it, and of its visible accountability for the participants. Thus, video studies contribute to understanding not only of how the arrangement, posture, and movements of bodies are accountably produced, but also of how they are interpreted and oriented to by the co-participants.

The exemplary case of the guided visit, the reproduction and the subversion of its organizational and categorical order as practical, situated, moment-by-moment accomplishments show that – and how – categories are a constant achievement of the participants, not only in and through talk, but also in and through their visible and embodied arrangements. This casts a multimodal light on the intertwining of sequential and categorical orders, and on phenomena as diverse and fundamental as talking, perceiving, and moving.

Transcription conventions

Talk has been transcribed according to Jefferson's conventions used in CA.

An indicative translation is given in italics, line by line, which aims at helping the original to be understood.

Gestures and embodied actions are transcribed according to Mondada's conventions (see 2018 for a conceptual discussion, and www.lorenzamondada.net/multimodal-transcription for a tutorial):

* *	movement descriptions are delimited between
+ +	two identical symbols (generally one symbol per participant/type of movement)

% %	are synchronized with corresponding stretches of talk
>>	movement described begins before the excerpt's beginning
—>>	movement described continues after excerpt's end
*—>	movement described continues across subsequent lines
——>*	until the same symbol is reached
....	movement's preparation and emergence
——	movement's apex is reached and maintained
,,,,,,	movement's retraction
luc	identification of the participant doing the movement
fig	the exact point where a screen shot has been taken is indicated
#	with a specific sign showing its position within turn at talk

More particularly, the following symbols have been used for embodied features of each participant:

	LUC	**YAN**	**ELISE**	**JEAN**
Gaze	ζ	⊥	!	β
Walk	*	+	%	λ
Gesture	ξ			φ
Body posture	τ			

References

De Stefani, E. & Mondada, L. (2014). Reorganizing mobile formations: When "guided" participants initiate reorientations in guided tours. *Space and Culture*, 17(2), 157–175.

De Stefani, E. & Mondada, L. (2017). Who's the expert? Negotiating competence and authority in guided tours. In Van De Mieroop, D. & Schnurr, S. (Eds.), *Identity Struggles. Evidence from Workplaces around the World*. Amsterdam: Benjamins, 95–124.

Fitzgerald, R. & Housley, W. (Eds.). (2015). *Advances in Membership Categorisation Analysis*. London: Sage.

Garfinkel, H. (2002). *Ethnomethodology's Program: Working Out Durkheim's Aphorism*. Lanham, MD: Rowman & Littlefield.

Goffman, E. (1963). *Behavior in Public Places: Notes on the Social Organization of Gatherings*. New York: Free Press.

Goffman, E. (1971). *Relations in Public: Microstudies of the Public Order*. New York: Basic Books.

Goodwin, C. (1994). Professional vision. *American Anthropologist*, 96(3), 606–633.

Heritage, J. (2012). The epistemic engine: Sequence organization and territories of knowledge. *ROLSI*, 45(1), 30–52.

Hester, S. & Eglin, P. (Eds.). (1997). *Culture in Action: Studies in Membership Categorization Analysis. Studies in Ethnomethodology and Conversation Analysis*. Washington, DC: University Press of America.

Jayyusi, L. (1992). The reflexive nexus: Photo-practice and natural history. *Continuum*, 6 (2), 25–52.

McIlvenny, P., Broth, M., & Haddington, P. (2014). Moving together: Mobile formations in interaction. *S.I. of Space and Culture*, 17, 2.

Mondada, L. (1999). L'accomplissement de l'étrangéité dans et par l'interaction: procédures de catégorisation des locuteurs. *Langages*, 134, 20–34.

Mondada, L. (2002a). Pratiques de transcription et effets de catégorisation. *Cahiers de Praxématique*, 39, 45–75.

Mondada, L. (2002b). Pour une approche interactionnelle de la catégorisation des ressources linguistiques par les locuteurs. *Cahiers de l'Institut de Linguistique de Louvain*, 28(3–4), 23–35.

Mondada, L. (2009). Emergent focused interactions in public places: A systematic analysis of the multimodal achievement of a common interactional space. *Journal of Pragmatics*, 41, 1977–1997.

Mondada, L. (2013). Displaying, contesting, and negotiating epistemic authorities in social interaction. *Discourse Studies*, 15, 597–626.

Mondada, L. (2014a). Bodies in action: Multimodal analysis of walking and talking. *Language and Dialogue*, 4(3), 357–403.

Mondada, L. (2014b). Shooting as a research activity: The embodied production of video data. In Broth, M., Laurier, E., & Mondada, L. (Eds.), *Video at Work*. London: Routledge, 33–62.

Mondada, L. (2018). Multiple temporalities of language and body in interaction: Challenges for transcribing multimodality. *Research on Language and Social Interaction*, 51(1), 85–106.

Pomerantz, A. (1988). Offering a candidate answer: An information seeking strategy. *Communication Monographs*, 55, 360–373.

Relieu, M. (1994). Les catégories dans l'action. L'apprentissage des traversées par des élèves non-voyants. *Raisons pratiques*, 5, 185–218.

Sacks, H. (1963). Sociological description. *Berkeley Journal of Sociology*, 8, 1–16.

Sacks, H. (1972a). On the analyzability of stories by children. In Gumperz, J. J. & Hymes, D. (Eds.), *Directions in Sociolinguistics: The Ethnography of Communication*. New York: Holt, Rinehart & Winston, 325–345.

Sacks, H. (1972b). An initial investigation of the usability of conversational data for doing sociology. In Sudnow, D. N. (Ed.), *Studies in Social Interaction*. New York: Free Press, 31–74.

Sacks, H. (1992). *Lectures on Conversation*. Oxford: Blackwell, 2 vol.

Schegloff, E. A. (2007). A tutorial on membership categorization. *Journal of Pragmatics*, 39, 462–482.

Sudnow, D. (1972). Temporal parameters of interpersonal observation. In Sudnow, D. (Ed.), *Studies in Social Interaction*. New York: Free Press, 259–279.

Watson, R. (1997a). Some general reflections on "category" and "sequence" in the analysis of conversation. In Hester, S. & Eglin, P. (Eds.), *Culture in Action*. Washington, DC: University Press of America, 49–76.

Watson, R. (2005). The visibility arrangements of public space: Conceptual resources and methodological issues in analysing pedestrian movements. *Communication and Cognition*, 38(3–4), 201–229.

Watson, R. (2015). De-reifying categories. In Fitzgerald, R. & Housley, W. (Eds.), *Advances in Membership Categorisation Analysis*. London: Sage, 23–49.

Widmer, J. (1986). *Langage et action sociale. Aspects philosophiques et sémiotiques du langage dans la perspective de l'ethnométhodologie*. Fribourg: Editions universitaires de Fribourg.

Widmer, J. (2010). *Discours et cognition sociale. Une approche sociologique*. Paris: Editions des Archives Contemporaines.

10 Revisiting Sacks's work on greetings

The 'first position' for greetings

Christian Licoppe

In this chapter, I will try to reconsider Sacks's discussion of greetings in his lectures. Greetings occupy an interesting position in Sacks's work. They straddle his earlier, more ethnomethodological focus on the intelligibility of actions in social encounters and his later emphasis on sequentiality which proved crucial to the emergence of conversational analysis as a field of its own. Regarding the first aspect of Sacks's work on greetings (for example, in Lecture 12, 1964–1965, 1992) and his recurrent interest in the management of entry into interaction, several points stand out. There is a place for greetings. Greetings have an 'ahistorical' character. There is no exclusion rule for greetings. The exchange of greetings might constitute an instance of a minimal conversation or encounter. However, in the later, more conversation-analytic part of his work (for instance in Lecture 4, Winter 1970), there is a shift of emphasis in the points Sacks now makes with respect to greetings. They are recognizably adequate complete answers. They come in pairs and they may be considered as adjacent pairs, although of a particular sort (they display a lower susceptibility to 'separability'). Finally, they occur at the 'beginning of beginnings', so that they are also constitutively tied to the overall structure of the conversation in ways that 'ordinary' adjacent pairs are not. One salient feature of this evolution in Sacks's thinking is that he becomes progressively less interested in the place for a (first) greeting and more interested in the way greetings are produced as adjacent pairs embedded in systematically organized opening sequences.

In the second part of this chapter, I will show the fruitfulness of revisiting Sacks's early work, and particularly his initial concern with the 'place for greetings'. I will describe how video-mediated call openings commonly display multiple greeting sequences, a phenomenon which makes particularly salient and relevant Sacks's interest in understanding what may make a greeting a relevant next action in the first place. I will define 'appearance events' as 'multimodal contextures' providing such a 'place for greetings' – that is, as occasions which are oriented-to as making conditionally relevant the production of a first greeting. Finally, I will argue that this whole approach, inspired by Sacks's work, may be particularly important today to understand the emergence of social interaction in digital ecologies, where other participants may and do appear often, and in many different technology-mediated ways.

A shift in Sacks's analytic stance regarding the production of greetings

Early lectures: the 'greeting place'

Sacks's first extensive treatment of greetings came in his series of lectures given in 1964–1965, and particularly in Lecture 12. Sacks's initial interest was in what makes a conversation recognizable as a conversation. He first explored the possibility of identifying minimal sequence units, made of recognizable, self-contained, 'adequate complete utterances', which we could describe today as 'sequentially implicative'. Such units prefigure the notion of 'adjacency pairs' he was to develop later, the idea being that, should one be able to identify such minimal sequence units, then any assemblage of such units would constitute 'something that will be, recognizably, "a conversation"' (Lectures, p. 96).

Another approach would be to look for invariant parts, with the occurrence of such invariants meaning that a conversation has occurred. Unfortunately, as he remarks, there is no such thing, with perhaps the exception of greetings, which might approximate such a concept. Indeed, greetings are standardized (or formulaic), such that their design makes them recognizable as greetings; they constitute 'adequate complete utterances' which project responsive talk for the addressee at their recognizable completion; and, finally, 'greetings are paired', so that the proper response to a first greeting is a return greeting. 'It might therefore be the case that such a minimal exchange of greetings provides us with an instance of a "minimal conversation"' (ibid.). We might then be tempted to say that any stretch of talk containing a greeting exchange is a conversation. This may often be so. However, not all conversations contain greetings, and, as Sacks remarks, 'it's not invariably the case that "greeting items" such as "hello" occur as "greetings"' (Lectures, p. 97).

So, as we see, Sacks's early interest in greetings stems from his early reliance on the 'intuitive recognizability of the conversational objects being analyzed' (Lynch, 1993, p. 216), in this case, the recognizability of conversation itself. As is often the case in Sacks's lectures, these observations provide him with an opportunity to go off on a tangent to another topic and to discuss greetings in more detail. For instance, now that he has established that greetings do not always occur at the beginning of conversations, he may wonder what makes a greeting sequence relevant and intuitively recognizable as such.

Sacks starts by making a very important observation, namely that we must distinguish between a 'greeting item' and a 'greeting place' (Lecture I, p. 97). A greeting item is something which is morpho-syntactically designed as a greeting and can be categorized as such. However, understanding greetings as greeting items only in this sense would be akin to attempting to label and categorize speech acts in the spirit of analytic philosophy (such as Searle, 1975, 2010). By making sequential positioning a crucial resource in the everyday recognizability of greetings, Sacks made a daring move away from earlier approaches such as speech act theory, which goes beyond greetings per se (for a recent treatment of action recognition, see Enfield & Sidnell, 2017). It also makes unavoidable the requirement of looking at actual data.

Coming back to the question of greetings, the concept of a 'greeting place' points to a recognizable configuration in the flow of embodied conduct which is crucial to their intelligibility as such:

> Then, something is a 'greeting' only if it's a 'greeting item' occurring in a 'greeting place'. If a greeting item occurs elsewhere it's not a greeting, and if some other item occurs in a greeting place, it's a greeting, though some items which are closed to greetings might take on the character of a greeting by occurring in a greeting place.
>
> (Ibid.)

As he notes, when 'hello' occurs far down after the beginning of a conversation, and therefore not in a greeting place, it is not a greeting, but may be an attention-getter.

At that time, Sacks's interest seemed, therefore, to lean more towards the place of greetings, and in particular the kind of place that makes a greeting relevant. Several of his observations in these early lectures clearly point towards such an interest. First, one finds his claim that there is no 'exclusion rule for greetings', which makes them relevant for any conversation. Their occurrence is subject to relevance rules, so that their absence is potentially noticeable. Second, in the 'everyone has to lie' lecture, he observes that greetings are 'ahistorically relevant' compared with, say, introductions, which are no longer appropriate between any two people after they have been gone through once (or perhaps more times by mistake). Where greetings are concerned, however, there is no rule that says 'on the n + conversation, no longer begin the conversation with a greeting. Instead, any conversation they ever have – they can have been married for 40 years – can begin with a greeting' (Lectures, pp. 551–552). This is another facet of the absence of an exclusion rule for greetings:

> 'To say that "greetings" are ahistorically relevant is not to say that every conversation must begin with greetings, but that there's no exclusion rule for greetings'. And, 'if they (greetings) do occur, they properly occur at the beginning of a conversation'.
>
> (Ibid.)

One could, therefore, say that, at the time, Sacks was more interested in the initiation of a greeting exchange, a question which necessarily involved the way in which a first greeting may be made relevant. According to his reformulation of this point in the 1966 lectures, there is a 'greeting place', a 'first position', which makes greetings relevant:

> They are only greetings if they occur in the greeting place. And that's a pretty good way to see that we have a greeting place. And the greeting

> place is what we could call 'first position'. If the item occurs there, then it's a 'greeting'.
>
> (Lectures, p. 308)

But, as we will see, his interest will move elsewhere, and Sacks, therefore, leaves us with several open questions regarding such a 'first position' for greetings. How is a 'position for greetings' recognizable as such? As the occurrence of such a position may not involve any talk, but just embodied motions or material events, what kind of relationship may exist between such a 'greeting configuration' and a potential first greeting? How are particular configurations recognized as 'first positions', and how do they make a (first) greeting relevant?

The later lectures: a growing concern with sequential organization and adjacency

As the years go by, Sacks's interest seems to shift. When he mentions the greeting place, it is now in regard to an increased reliance on phone conversation data and a concern with the overall structure of conversation. For instance, he notes in the 1968 lectures that there is a place for greetings (which makes notable their absence), just to add that,

> Greetings occur at the beginning of conversation. It's not just a part anywhere in a conversation, look for it maybe you'll find it, but you can say where to look for it. It has in that sense, a structural place in conversation.
>
> (Vol. 2, Part II, p. 36)

In the winter of 1970, he stresses the formulaic and predetermined character of the first greeting, an 'utterly normative first move' which he compares to the first move in a chess opening and which he deems to be almost universal for phone conversations (Vol. 2, Part III, p. 159). He starts to think of the implications of the greeting sequence for the unfolding conversation: 'one can think of the tactics of the greeting sequence as possible ways to, e.g. control who gets a first chance to raise a "first topic"' (Ibid.).

The discussion of the 'first position' for greetings disappears completely, for the placement of greetings is now envisioned as the place of a greeting sequence within the overall structure of the conversation:

> A first thing about greetings is their placing. They go right at the beginning of beginnings. Putting that into productional terms we could say that, for greetings, their placing is of highest priority. And greetings have highest priority for initial placement in a conversation.
>
> (Vol. II, Part III, p. 188)

Because he has now elaborated the concept of adjacent pairs, the pairing of greetings becomes a more salient issue. Paired greetings are discussed as a special case of adjacent pairs, less separable and vulnerable to the development of side sequences than other adjacent pairs further down the conversation (Ibid., p. 189). Eventually, he stresses the difference between first greeting and second greeting in terms of adjacent pair organization:

> Greetings come in pairs … 'first greetings' and 'return greetings' are different objects … A simple way to see this is, whereas a first greeting gets a second greeting, a second greeting does not work in the same way a first greeting does, to get another greeting in return.
>
> (Ibid., p. 189)

Sacks now thinks of greetings almost only with respect to their relevance to adjacent pairs and overall conversational structure organization, two tenets of conversation analysis (CA), as this analytic perspective is later developed by his collaborator Emmanuel Schegloff (see, for instance, Schegloff (2007) as an attempt to delineate CA as a field for professional analysis). This brief discussion of the evolution of Sacks's reflections on the production and organization of greeting sequences vindicates Michael Lynch's (1993) argument about a shift in Sacks's approach from a focus on the naïve intelligibility of interactional moves (a perspective from which may stem an interest in the position for a first greeting) to the establishment of CA as a discipline (actualized in the case of greetings as a preoccupation with the way they constitute an adjacent pair and the place of greeting sequences within the organization of openings). This move left unanswered some questions initially opened by Sacks regarding the 'first position' for greetings and its recognizability. In the remainder of this chapter, we will pick up on this early preoccupation of Sacks's regarding the way a first greeting may be made relevant. I will explore some of the configurations which make a greeting relevant and the conditions under which they are treated as 'first positions' (for greetings) and try to identify some research questions this line of questioning may lead us to today.

Schegloff's analysis of conversational openings

In his discussion of the few first seconds of phone conversations (Schegloff, 1972, 1986), Schegloff provides a kind of paradigmatic account for how a separate and retrospectively identifiable 'first position' for greetings can be made sequentially relevant in phone conversations, such as in Transcript 10.1.

Transcript 10.1 (from Schegloff, 1986)

1 Phone ring
2 Ava : H'llo
3 Bee : hHi:
4 Ava : Hi:?

Schegloff discusses the first four lines of this phone opening as a succession of adjacent pairs, a summons–answer sequence, followed by an exchange of greetings. The second turn provides not only an answer to the summons, but also an identification sample. Summons–answer adjacent pairs are non-terminal (Schegloff, 1972), and so some further action is projected, and in phone openings that action is precisely a greeting. Schegloff is interested here in the overall organization of greetings. He discusses the greetings as a pair, a ritual exchange (Schegloff, 1986), in which the first greeting claims recognition (Schegloff, 1979). Globally his interests are aligned with the sequential interests of the later Sacks. A question which might, however, have interested the earlier Sacks would have been, for instance, to understand what makes relevant a greeting in Line 3. Or, in what sense does the summons–answer sequence in ordinary phone conversations provide a 'place for a greeting', so that an action accomplished in such a position would be oriented to as a potential greeting? Saying that the summons–answer sequence is not terminal (Schegloff, 1972) does not say which kind of action might constitute a relevant next. The caller actually treats its achievement as an opportunity to greet the call recipient in Line 3. In other words, it provides a 'first position' for greetings in a phone conversation. From the caller's perspective, Lines 1 and 2 have established a configuration in which the communication channels have been opened and in which a recognizable recipient has displayed her availability and orientation towards further interaction. This provides for what we could call here, as well an appearance, a phone opening configuration which makes conditionally relevant a greeting as a next action.

It may be the case that, though a valid point, this was not worth pursuing further in the case of phone conversations. However, while working on video-call conversation openings, I found it remarkably fruitful to get back to Sacks's earlier work, as I will try to show now.

Revisiting Sacks's 'place for greetings': 'multiple greeting sequences' in interpersonal Skype calls

Whenever looking to a particular phenomenon involving talk-in-interaction, I always find it useful to go back to Sacks's Lectures on Conversation and look up what he might have said about it (and he looked at so many things). This was particularly the case when I started to study the openings of ordinary video calls. The reason for that is that, in video calls, it was relatively common to find multiple greeting sequences, much more common than in phone conversations where it is rare, and co-present interactions where it may be occasionally observed (see Pillet-Shore, 2012, for an example). And, of course, if one gets video-call data with multiple greeting sequences, one has to wonder what made those successive greetings relevant, what they each might do in such a video setting, This makes salient again Sacks's initial interest in the place for greetings as, wherever multiple greetings are observable, there are multiple 'places for greetings' as a phenomenon. Transcript 10.2 provides one instance of this phenomenon.

Transcript 10.2

01 ((rings))
02 Art Art's control image appears on screen
03 Art moves Skype window to center of screen#
04 Fig # Figure 10.1

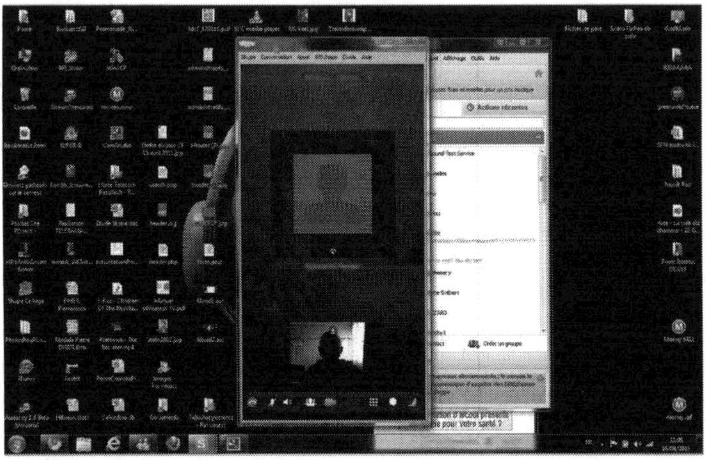

05 (7.0)
06 Audio noise starts
07 (3.0)
08 Art Bib/
09 Bud quoi?
what?
10 Art bonjour
hello
11 Bud's image becomes visible to Art#
12 Fig # Figure 10.2

13 Art bonjour Bibi
hello Bibi
14 ((waves hands emphatically for 2.5 seconds#))
15 *Fig* # Figure 10.3a, b and c

Figure 10.3a

Figure 10.3b

Figure 10.3c

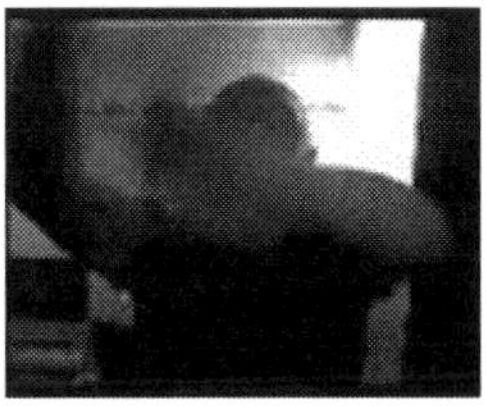

16 Bud bonjour (said as art gestures with his hands)
hello
17 Art ça va ?
how are you?

Art treats the advent of background noise as a cue that they might hear one another and as a slot to speak, though Bud's image is not yet visible on his screen. He provides an address term with an upward prosody, trying for a response ('Bib/', Line 8). Being responsive to an event which can be understood as possibly establishing a perceptual field of mutual audibility, Art's address term works and can be recognized as a greeting, though its form is slightly unconventional. Bud's response ('what?', Line 9) demonstrates the establishment of the mutual perceptual field (he has heard something), but could be understood in this context either as a repair initiation (indicating, for instance, that he might not have heard properly) or as a treatment of the previous address term as a summons ('what' then being taken as a kind of shorthand for 'what do you want with me?'). Art responds to this with a conventionally designed greeting term (Line 10), which confirms retrospectively that his opening turn was to be heard as a greeting, a greeting that was oriented to the establishment of a mutual auditory field.

At that moment, Bud's image appears on Art's screen. Art orients to this by uttering a new greeting followed by the same greeting term, claiming some sort of recognition. Because identification has already been made, such recognition has to be oriented to a change in the way Art appears in the situation. It is also interesting that he does so 'immediately' (in the sense of not waiting for Art's expected completion of the previous greeting exchange), thus displaying his being geared to pay particular attention to that kind of visual appearance and its timeliness, From Bud's perspective, this new greeting turn is shaped as being occasioned by some appearance allowing some additional form of recognition. It is, thus, not just prolonging the previous sequence, but constitutes a new greeting, responsive to a different event than in the previous greeting sequence. Art will, moreover, make it even clearer that this is a visually oriented greeting by gesturing widely with his hands (Line 14 and Figure 10.3), turning the greeting into an embodied visual performance. When Art smiles and provides a greeting of his own, the participants move on with the sequence, displaying their understanding that a proper beginning has been achieved.

So what makes successive greetings relevant here? In his discussion of early encounters between acquaintances, Goffman relates the normative relevance of a first greeting to the mutual visual appearance of the participants through the following rule: 'upon newly *coming into sight* of someone with whom one is acquainted, there is an obligation to make one's presence felt by exchanging a greeting' (Goffman, 1971, p. 84; my emphasis). While attributing some other functions to greetings,[1] Goffman relates the initiation of a greeting sequence to the establishment of a state of heightened mutual access, a 'communion of a face engagement' (Goffman, 1964, p. 100) or an 'ecological huddle' (Goffman, 1964, p. 135), based on visual appearances. Similarly, Danielle Pillet-Shore remarks that, 'participants to incipient encounters visibly hold off doing the action of greeting until they see "who's there", displaying their orientation to identification/recognition via visual inspection as prerequisite to producing a co-present greeting' (Pillet-Shore, 2012, p. 377). How can we get a more precise account of how such a 'coming into sight' makes a first greeting relevant? And which of the two participants thus coming into sight should initiate the first greeting?

Within the field of linguistic anthropology, Alessando Duranti has built on both Sacks and Goffman to identify some universal properties of greetings (Duranti, 1997). He streamlines these into six points, which I have slightly reordered below:

(a) Neat boundary occurrence
(b) Establishment of a shared perceptual field
(c) Implicit establishment of a spatio-temporal unit of interaction
(d) Adjacency pair format
(e) Relative predictability of form and content
(f) Identification of the interlocutor as a distinct being worth recognizing.

Points (d) and (e) are aligned with Sacks's later interest in sequential analysis, and (f) highlights issues of identification and recognition, as well as acknowledgement and welcoming. However, the first three features provide an outline for understanding the 'first position' for a greeting: events leading to an interactional configuration recognizable as instantiating a discrete and marked shift in mutual perceptual access, the establishment of an interaction-relevant 'ecological huddle', which I will call here 'appearance events'. The coming into sight of someone in a social situation provides a paradigmatic instantiation of such 'appearance events', involving (a) a neat boundary occurrence, (b) the establishment of a shared perceptual field, (c) the implicit establishment of a spatio-temporal unit of interaction and (d) the identification of the interlocutor as a distinct being worth recognizing. This provides for a potential place for a greeting. Such an irruption makes conditionally relevant a first greeting which, when produced, appears responsive to such an 'appearance' event. When we greet a surly and silent teenager coming to the family breakfast with a 'good morning to you too', we retrospectively index his/her appearance as providing a place for a first greeting, which here is treated as missing.

The case of multiple greetings in video communication shows how discrete shifts in mutual accessibility and the establishment of a mutual perceptual field in the opening of the call may each be treated as 'appearances' that make a greeting conditionally relevant. This fits with Goffman's idea that, 'greetings are rituals that mark a change in degree of access' (Goffman, 1971, p. 79). An orientation towards treating those shifts as sequentially implicative constitutes a powerful resource in the establishment of a joint interaction frame in video calls. In such complex openings, which are common in video calls, seizing the sequential opportunity that such an event enacts is also a simple way to signal to the co-participant that some progress has been made in the establishment of a joint interactional frame and to test whether it is mutual (Licoppe, 2017). There are, therefore, local and situated reasons to treat such stepwise video 'appearances' as Sacks's 'places for greetings' and to achieve multiple greeting sequences in the openings of video calls.

Conclusion

Sacks's work on greetings in his early lectures displays a concern for the recognizability of 'first positions' for greetings. In the later lectures, this interest recedes, and he focuses more on some key notions of nascent CA as a discipline, such as adjacent pairs and the overall structure of conversations. Greetings then become a special case for adjacent pair sequences, and the production of greetings as sequence is now investigated with respect to its relevance with respect to the overall organization of conversation. Therefore, Sacks's seminal intuitions about the analytical relevance of a 'first position' for greetings somehow faded out from conversation-analytic concerns regarding the organization of openings in social encounters.

I took up a phenomenon commonly observed in the openings of video-mediated conversations – that is, 'multiple greeting sequences' – as an example of why it is almost always fruitful to return to the lectures and, in this case, Sacks's initial preoccupation with specifying the 'place for greetings'. It leads to the conceptualization of 'appearance events' – in which the sudden irruption on a social scene of another identifiable/recognizable actor makes potential interactants oriented to the initiation of an encounter and able to interact in some way – as making conditionally relevant the production of a greeting. 'Appearance events' defined as such are, therefore, potential 'places for greetings'. Such appearance events are best understood as complex 'gestalt contextures', involving embodied conduct, talk-in-interaction and the local organization of material/perceptual ecologies as constitutive elements.

Respecifying Sacks's notion of a 'place for greetings' in this way raises some important questions for CA: How may sequentially organized interaction emerge from continuous streams of embodied behavior? Or what kind of pragmatic relationship must we posit between the 'appearance event' and the potential greeting that is responsive to it? Conditional relevance might suggest an adjacency pair structure. However, an adjacent pair also projects a next speaker, whereas an entry onto the social scene may be simultaneously available to multiple participants without one of them necessarily being selected as a recipient. Another approach could be to highlight the immediate relationship between the perception of such an 'appearance event' and a relevant next action and, therefore, to treat the former as an 'affordance' (Gibson, 1986), but this latter notion does not necessarily involve semiotics. It is perhaps the sign-response 'enchronic' relationship (Enfield, 2011) which might capture in a better way the kind of conditional relevance through which an 'appearance event' may be oriented to as a 'place for greetings'.

More work is clearly needed to analyze the ways in which different types of 'appearance events' might make greetings relevant. Should we, for instance, make a difference in terms of sequential implicativeness between the continuous approach of co-present parties in an open space (Kendon, 1990) and the quasi-instantaneous materialization of a potential co-participant on screen (a 'pop-up' appearance) at the beginning of a video call? 'Pop-up appearance events' minimize the resources for prior mutual, moment-by-moment co-orientation and open up an agency gap separating the 'appearer' and his 'apparition' from the recipient as an 'appeared-to'. Focusing on the particular forms of sequential implicativeness of 'pop-up' contextures may be important because digital technologies provide us with an increasing number of occasions on which remote others may meaningfully pop into in our screen-based ecologies. Digital ecologies make such quasi-instantaneous 'pop-up' appearances proliferate. Therefore, revisiting Sacks's notion of a 'place for greetings' becomes a crucial resource to deal with some current questions regarding social interaction and the initiation of encounters in our technology-saturated environments.

Note

1 For Goffman, two further important aspects of greetings are the way they display concerns for identification and their ritual character. Greetings express and display the delight and mutual pleasure participants feel in their coming together, the acknowledgement of relative statuses, and also trust and reassurance (particularly for unacquainted parties; Goffman, 1971, p. 75). In that perspective, greetings are more than just salutations. There is a sense that greetings also involve something which philosophers such as Heidegger have called 'welcoming' (Ronell, 2007).

References

Duranti, A. (1997). "Universal and Culture-Specific Properties of Greetings." *Journal of Linguistic Anthropology* 7(1): 63–97.

Enfield, N. J. (2011). Sources of Asymmetry in Human Interaction: Enchrony, Status, Knowledge and Agency. In T. Stivers, L. Mondada & J. Steensig (Eds.), *The Morality of Knowledge in Conversation* (pp. 285–312). Cambridge: Cambridge University Press.

Enfield, N. J., & Sidnell, J. (2017). *The Concept of Action*. Cambridge: Cambridge University Press.

Gibson, J. J. (1986). *The Ecological Approach to Visual Perception*. Boston: Houghton Mifflin.

Goffman, E. (1964). "The Neglected Situation." *American Anthropologist* 66: 133–136.

Goffman, E. (1971). *Relations in Public. Microstructure of the Public Order*. New York: Harper & Row.

Kendon, A. (1990). *Conducting Interaction. Patterns of Behavior in Focussed Encounters*. Cambridge: Cambridge University Press.

Licoppe, C. (2017). "Showing Objects in Skype Video-Mediated Conversations: From Showing Gestures to Showing Sequences." *Journal of Pragmatics* 110: 63–82.

Lynch, M. (1993). *Scientific Practice and Ordinary Action. Ethnomethodology and Social Studies of Science*. Cambridge: Cambridge University Press.

Pillet-Shore, D. (2012). "Greeting: Displaying Stance through Prosodic Recipient Design." *Research on Language and Social Interaction* 45(4): 375–398.

Ronell, A. (2007). The sacred alien: Heidegger's reading of Hölderlin's "Andenken". In D. Davis (Ed.), *The ÜberReader: Selected Work of Avital Ronell* (pp. 205–226). Chicago: University of Illinois Press.

Sacks, H. (1992). *Lectures on Conversation*. Cambridge: Cambridge University Press.

Schegloff, E. A. (1972). Sequencing in Conversational Openings. In D. Hymes & J. Gumperz (Eds.), *Directions in Sociolinguistics. The Ethnography of Communication* (pp. 346–380). New York: Holt, Rinehart & Winston.

Schegloff, E. A. (1979). Identification and Recognition in Telephone Conversation Openings. In G. Psathas (Ed.), *Everyday Language: Studies in Ethnomethodology* (pp. 23–78). New York: Irvington.

Schegloff, E. A. (1986). "The Routine as Achievement." *Human Studies* 9: 111–151.

Schegloff, E. A. (2007). *Sequence Organization in Interaction. A Primer in Conversation Analysis*. Cambridge: Cambridge University Press.

Searle, J. R. (1975). Indirect Speech Acts. In P. Cole & J. L. Morgan (Eds.), *Syntax and Semantics* (Vol. 3, pp. 59–82). New York: Academic Press.

Searle, J. R. (2010). *Making the Social World: The Structure of Human Civilization*. Oxford: Oxford University Press.

11 Sacks, silence, and self-(de)selection

Elliott M. Hoey

Among the paths leading people to conversation analysis (CA), one is populated by those interested in the mundane scenes and seemingly inconsequential facets of social life. For those of us with an attraction to sociality writ miniature, the distinct perspective developed by Harvey Sacks offers a license to indulge that impulse, as well as a method for doing so. For, if there is 'order at all points' (Sacks, 1984), then there is a way for the apparently trivial to be systematized and for the frivolous to be ennobled. Sacks's analyses of absences and silences stand as a paradigm case of this. In this chapter, I discuss how Sacks's investigations of silence produced some of CA's foundational discoveries and connect these observations to my own research on lapses in conversation. Through a close reading of Sacks's descriptions of the turn-taking organization, I identify a form of silence which had largely been overlooked and which served as inspiration for me as a graduate student casting about for a dissertation topic. I then offer an analysis of turn-taking and silence through a consideration of self-deselection, or those practices whereby participants recognizably pass up the chance to self-select.

Sacks and silence

Harvey Sacks's interest in silence emerged from a more general concern with absences. According to Schegloff (1992: lvii–lviii), this dated to discussions in 1962–63 about why Marxist revolutions were not occurring as predicted. For Sacks, the very observation of such an absence pointed to the existence of something that gave that absence shape and substance. How, he wondered, could some state of affairs be the outcome of something else not happening? This question was part of his broader critique of the social sciences, which he saw as relying on absences in an unexamined way:

> If you're going to make a statement which proposes that something is absent, then you can't in any serious way propose that X is absent unless you have some way of discriminating the absence of X from the assertable absence of millions of things.
>
> (1992b: 35)

We see Sacks developing his ideas on absences as early as his first lecture. He observed that callers to suicide hotlines could methodically avoid giving their names in the place provided for doing so (1992a: 7).[1] In Sacks's account, one could only see that callers' 'avoidance' was being done by reference to a 'slot' where name-giving could properly occur (after 'This is Mr Smith'). This kind of analysis of 'contingently relevant events' (Sacks, 1992a: 265) would form the basis for his investigations of absences. Across his lectures Sacks repeatedly returned to the idea of something being 'noticeably absent' (Sacks, 1992b: 35) to illuminate the social logic of various activities, such as not returning a greeting after receiving one (Sacks, 1992a: 97, 262) or skipping a person/party in a round-organized activity (p. 293). He identified meaningful absences operating in various corners of social life: the absence of ceremonials (e.g., 'Would you like to go to dinner with me?') can index intimacy in relationships (Sacks, 1992a: 18), radio silence between friends is routinely understood as 'no major news to report' (Sacks, 1992a: 777, 1992b: 164), and the inability to produce a second story can betoken the lack of particular life experiences (Sacks, 1992a: 782).

Sacks's interest in meaningful absences led to penetrating and influential investigations of silence in conversation. He understood that silence, by virtue of being found everywhere in conversation, would require some account. 'There's a lot of talk going on in conversation. There is also a lot of silence going on. How can we turn silence in to a thing that can show something?' (Sacks, 1992a: 672). He began these investigations by positioning silence in terms of several interrelated practical problems: how to notice silence as an event-in-the-conversation, how to render silence as occurring outside conversation, how to attribute silence to someone, how to convert 'my silence' into 'your silence', how to minimize inter-turn silence, and so on. Through these inquiries, Sacks, along with Gail Jefferson and Emanuel Schegloff, developed much of the technical apparatus that has come to define CA research. His investigation of, for example, 'how to render silence as occurring outside the conversation' (Schegloff & Sacks, 1973; Sacks, 1992b: 364) yielded the notions of adjacency pairs, noticeable absences, pre-closing sections, adequate utterance completion, and transition-relevance. Similarly, in taking up the matter of 'how to minimize inter-turn silence' (Sacks, Schegloff, & Jefferson, 1974; Sacks, 1987), Sacks and his colleagues developed the concepts of turn-constructional units, the turn-taking ruleset, speaker-selection devices, silence classification (pause, gap, and lapse), and the preference for agreement. These analyses of silences in conversation have been central to the development of CA as a discipline. The pause/gap distinction, for example, is marbled through many interactional domains. Pauses are key components in the organization of self-repair, turn-construction, and action formation, and gaps are crucial to nearly every analysis of preference, affiliation, and turn-timing.

For Sacks, *that* silence could be significant occasioned investigations of what structured that significance. The orderliness that he was able to unearth showed silences to be social objects in their own right, standing in systematic relationship to other forms of interactional conduct. By wresting from 'nothing' a rich assembly of social practices and common-sense understandings, Sacks demonstrated the possibility of studying silence in an empirically grounded way that could productively reveal its articulations with other domains of social life. I have tried in my work to extend this line of research on silence in social interaction. In what follows, I build on Sacks's pioneering observations by tracing the contours of an overlooked form of silence—lapses in conversation. I then consider how participants arrange participation during such silences, focusing in particular on practices for self-deselection.

An underspecification in the turn-taking organization

In Sacks's discussion of turn-taking, he makes the striking pronouncement that, 'under the more general rule of the turn-taking techniques we're dealing with, silence is a terrible thing. The turn-taking rules say that somebody should be talking all the time; not more than one person, but somebody' (Sacks, 1992a: 225). The nature of this problem became clearer in the turn-taking paper. For one, not all silences are 'terrible'. Silences that occur before a first transition-relevance place (TRP; within-turn 'pauses') are treated as belonging to the current speaker. So, despite the absence of speech, somebody is still 'talking', and there is no problem. Silences which *do* present a problem occur after possible turn completion and before the start of a next turn (between-turn 'gaps') and are typically taken to indicate 'someone not responding' (Schegloff & Sacks, 1973), which may be problematic for reasons related to preference and social solidarity (Pomerantz, 1984; Sacks, 1987; Clayman, 2002).

Although this distinction between intra-turn and inter-turn silences isolates problematic ones, it remains underspecified with reference to sequential implicature (Schegloff & Sacks, 1973) and speaker selection (Sacks et al., 1974). Interactants' understanding of a given inter-turn silence depends on whether the prior turn implicates a determinate range of next actions (sequential implicature) and, relatedly, whether a particular party has been designated to act next (speaker selection). Put simply, participants care about what should happen next and who should/could do it. We may thus distinguish three inter-turn silences: see Table 11.1.[2]

Most of the literature has focused on Type I silences, which occur between first and second pair-parts. Many practices are oriented to the infelicities associated with such silences, such as pursuits (Davidson, 1984), turn increments

Table 11.1 Types of inter-turn silences

	Type I	*Type II*	*Type III*
Prior action implicates determinate range of next actions	✓	✓	
Prior action restricts range of next speakers	✓		

(Schegloff, 2016), and various turn-initial hedges (Pomerantz, 1984). Type II silences have also been addressed—though to a lesser degree, perhaps because they require multiple potential respondents. For example, teachers may ask a question which any student may answer (McHoul, 1978), and any diner may respond when the server asks, 'Is everything all right?' (Lerner, 1993). By contrast, Type III silences remain virtually unexplored.

The turn-taking system provides for the occurrence of Type III silences, which I refer to as 'lapses'. Lapses occur when (a) no speaker-selection device was employed in the prior turn, followed by (b) all participants refrain from self-selection, which results in (c) a silence composed of 'rounds of possible self-selection' (Sacks et al., 1974: 715).[3] For Sacks, Schegloff, and Jefferson, lapses account for the fact that conversations can be discontinuous, with lapses serving as the intervening silence. However, beyond specifying the mechanism for the development of lapses, Sacks and colleagues left much unexplained—namely, what, if anything, are conversational participants to do without an apparent next speaker? This problem can be compared to its inverse condition: overlapping speech (Schegloff, 2000). The turn-taking system provides for overlap by allowing any party to self-select at a TRP before which no current selects-next technique was used. But, if multiple participants self-select, more than one speaker will occupy the place where just one should be. Similarly, the turn-taking system allows participants to refrain from speaking; rules 1b and 1c are optional. And, if all participants avail themselves of that option, a silence constituted by rounds of possible self-selection emerges. There is less-than-one speaker in the place where one should be. So both conditions violate the one-at-a-time feature of conversation, but do so in opposite directions.

The possibility that the turn-taking system yields a silence with no next speaker dovetails with a systematic possibility in the organization of sequences. Sequence organization concerns how a series of turns/actions cohere into intelligible courses of collaborative action (Schegloff, 2007). What propels the production of each action is the current utterance's sequential implicativeness, which projects the relevance of a determinate range of actions to occur next (Schegloff & Sacks, 1973: 296). Turns that lack sequential implicativeness tend to indicate the practical completion of a sequence (Schegloff, 2007). The potential ending of a sequence is a special environment because it affords participants the opportunity to go on to something else (a prior matter, a new topic, etc.). However, it is also a structurally provided possibility at possible sequence completion that there is nothing in particular to talk about—that the current turn bears little in the way of sequential implicativeness, and the interaction-so-far provides little direction in terms of what comes next.

The twin organizations of turn-taking and sequence may, therefore, conspire to produce a particular kind of silence where it is unclear who should speak next and what they should do. As a PhD student in search of a topic, what I took from this was the possibility of using silence as a way to investigate a structural position in talk. Inspired by how Sacks was able to 'make, of the phenomenon of silence, something' (Sacks, 1992a: 672), I have tried to describe the properties of lapses as a particular kind of social object. I've examined the recurrent ways in which participants arrive at such lapses (Hoey, 2015), verbal and bodily practices for dealing with them once they've emerged (2017, 2018a), and the methods they use to end the lapse and reinstate turn-by-turn talk (2018b).

As an extension of this research on lapses, the remainder of the chapter addresses some regular forms of conduct observed during such silences. Participants are recurrently seen shifting their gaze, producing weak acknowledgement tokens, and taking up minor side involvements. I argue that these behaviors are oriented to matters of turn-taking and constitute practices for *self-deselection*, or observably passing on the opportunity to speak. Self-deselection stands as an alternative to self-selection in moments where speaker selection is at issue. It is a method for avoiding the turn space, and, through that recognizable avoidance, other participants are given the opportunity to speak.

The data are video recordings of natural interactions in American and British English. These recordings feature mostly mundane interactions between friends, peers, and intimates. Inspection of these materials yielded a collection of more than 250 lapses, which were operationalized as intervals without talk, minimally 500-ms long, before which no speaker-selection device was used and during which all participants remained visibly committed to the interaction (see Hoey, 2017). Transcription conventions follow Jefferson (2004) for verbal/vocal conduct and Mondada (2016) for visible conduct.

Self-deselection

Three methods for self-deselection in a lapse are shown: displays of availability, sequence recompletion, and disengagement. Each of these orient to the relevance of turn-transfer in a lapse in conversation by recognizably passing up that option.

Display of availability

Absent verbal forms of speaker selection such as address terms, participants in a lapse are somewhat at a disadvantage when it comes to locating a next speaker. What is still available, however, is gaze and body orientation (see Lerner, 2003; Stivers & Rossano, 2010). During a lapse, participants can orient their bodies to another participant through a display of availability (Heath, 1984). Although this does not *select* them as next speaker, it does *nominate* them. It treats the gazed-at participant *as if* they might speak next and positions the gazer as someone who could listen. With such a display, participants show preparedness for talk from the nominated participant.

Transcript 11.1 shows a display of availability done after a lapse emerges. Lex, Marie, and Rachel are eating and chatting in an apartment. The transcript begins as Marie concludes a cute story about how her mother reunited with an old friend, after which the story-recipients provide their assessments (lines 1–3).

The story-telling then comes to possible completion once Marie ratifies those assessments (line 4). The participants have now reached a point where they could move on to something else—for instance, a second story (Sacks, 1992a, 1992b) or a new topic (Maynard, 1980). But, rather than continuing with talk, all of the participants refrain from self-selection, and so a lapse develops (line 5).

Transcript 11.1

(1) GB07-7_2600
01 MAR: And that's h*ow like they reunited.=
*gazes to food->
02 LEX: †=[°Aa:::[h.°
03 RAC: =[That's cut[e.
04 MAR: [Yeah(p).
†rests chin on hand->
05 (1.6)#*(0.7)#Δ(0.4)
mar *brings food to mouth->
ΔΔgazes to LEX->
fig #11.1a #11.1b

Figure 11.1a and 11.1b Marie gazes toward Lex

06 LEX: †.h* Oh my go:[:d,
07 MAR: [Mm hm,
†moves hand away from mouth->
mar ->*chewing->>
08 LEX: †ThaΔsso ni:ce,
†gazes at food->>
mar ->Δwithdraws gaze->>

During this lapse, Marie gazes at her food and Lex rests her chin on her hand, as if 'contemplating' the cute story that just concluded (Figure 11.1a). This lapse continues for 1.6 s before Marie brings her food to her mouth and gazes at Lex (Figure 11.1b). This display of availability reveals Marie's analysis of the present moment as one in which Lex might talk next. It serves as a form of self-deselection in that Marie shows herself as a ready recipient if Lex chooses to speak. It targets the less-than-one problem by nominating Lex as someone who could speak next. And, indeed, Lex observes that she is being gazed at and responds by producing a reappreciation of Marie's story (line 6). Displays of availability thus reveal a 'slot' for a next speaker in a lapse and propose participatory roles for that slot. This orients to silences without a next speaker by proposing who might speak next and who might not.

Sequence recompletion[4]

Another technique for self-deselection in a lapse is sequence recompletion. Just as participants can bring turns-at-talk to completion more than once—for instance, through increments (Schegloff, 2016)—so too may they bring a sequence to completion more than once (e.g., Schegloff, 2009; Mondada, 2015). A speaker recompletes a sequence by providing something which constitutes another possible sequence ending. By bringing a sequence to possible completion again, the social logic goes, the relevance of beginning another one is also renewed. In this way, sequence recompletion highlights the opportunity for another participant to self-select. This is commonly done with things such as acknowledgements, agreements, assessments, laughter, and affective vocalizations. Two of these are seen in Transcript 11.2, which begins as Kelly finishes up a funny story about how her grandmother forgot her husband's (Kelly's grandfather's) birthday (lines 1–4). As she delivers the final line of her story, the story-recipient, Heather, gasps and heartily laughs in response (line 5). Both participants then laugh together affiliatively (Holt, 2010) and break off mutual gaze (Rossano, 2013), which brings the sequence to possible completion. Neither elects to speak again right away, and so a lapse develops (line 6).

Transcript 11.2

```
(2) RCE28_0803
01  KEL:  and then like (.) she'd completely forgotten that it
02        was his birthda:y, and I was like >how long have you
03        (been) married- >she's like< .MTKh like fifty yea:::rs,
04  KEL:  [>%°I was like< [      OOO*H +gheheh
05  HEA:  [((gasp)) (.)    [HAHAHAHA*::+: .H
                                      +withdraws gaze->
    kel                              *withdraws gaze->
06         (1.1)
07  HEA:   N:i:ce.
08         (0.3)
09  KEL:   °mh mhh°
10         +(0.5)*(0.6)
    hea   ->+inspects fingernail->>
    kel         ->*gazes to HEA's hands->>
```

11 HEA: Yea:h_
12 (2.1)
13 HEA: +.mhhh (0.5) .mtk I'm picking it off slowly and surely.
14 KEL: Is that the sa:me from from like last wee:k,

The two participants sit in silence for more than a second, indicating that both understand the telling as complete and in need of no further expansion. They've arrived at an environment where moving on to something else would be possible and appropriate. However, what we observe instead is a prolongation of the period where nothing is sequentially implicated to come next. Heather is first to break the silence with an assessment *N:i:ce* (line 7), presumably voicing her own sarcastic reaction to her grandmother's forgetfulness. This assessment extends the storytelling activity by just a bit, providing another piece that could constitute its ending. Although this satisfies the need in conversation for there to be someone speaking, it is relatively anemic in its sequential implicativeness. In response to this small story extension, Kelly produces muted laughter (line 9). Neither Heather's assessment nor Kelly's laughter engenders more talk, and so the lapse continues (line 10).

During this silence, both participants gaze at Heather's hands as she inspects her fingernails, adumbrating the topic shift to come (lines 13–14; Maynard, 1980). Heather then produces a flatly intoned acknowledgment token *Yea:h* (line 11; see Jefferson, 1983). Like her previous turn, *N:i:ce*, this token is retrospectively oriented. Although it acknowledges Kelly's laughter, it does nothing to develop the sequence further. It recompletes the prior sequence and allows her to pass on the opportunity to initiate a next one. Finally, after two more seconds of silence, Heather ends the lapse by shifting their talk to the subject of her crumbling nail polish (lines 12–14).

With sequence recompletion, participants produce 'something' in the place where 'something' is due, but defer to someone else the task of starting up something new. This reveals an orientation to the continued relevance of talk in that space, while at the same time deflecting the obligation to do more than that. As a technique for self-deselection, it paradoxically offers a way for speakers to speak so as to show that they won't speak any more.

Disengagement

A third technique for self-deselection in a lapse is through disengagement from interaction. The mechanism for this is disattending the conversation in favor of some non-talk involvement, typically an auto-involvement, or a self-directed, self-absorbing act of withdrawal from interaction (Goffman, 1963; Goodwin, 1981). Disengaged participants display a decreased ability or preparedness to speak, and, by a process of elimination, the option to self-select is then passed on to the other participants. This is seen in Transcript 11.3. Maureen, Abby, and Terry have paused a board game so that another player, Pat, could take a phone call. They've been chatting about Pat's nephew, who had recently sent her and

Terry a card, thanking them for hosting him earlier that year. Just prior to transcript below, the participants joked about how his sending the card around Christmastime was a strategic reminder for them to send him Christmas gifts. The transcript starts as Abby and Maureen both produce upshots of that situation (lines 1–2). And then their talk comes to possible completion as both Terry and Maureen confirm those upshots (lines 3–4; Schegloff, 2007).

Transcript 11.3

(3) GameNight_0411
01 ABB: at le[ast he didn't send his list t#o San][ta.]
02 MAU: [no sense in sending it in Au:#gust.]
03 TER: [tha]t's right#=
fig #a #b
04 MAU: =°yeah.°
05 (1.1) # (1.6) # (0.2)
fig #c #d
06 ABB: .nhh (.) Hhhh ((a sniff followed by a sigh))
07 PAT: #I'll be# there ve:ry sho:rtly.
fig #e #f

Figure 11.2 Auto-involvements in a lapse (L–R: Maureen, Abby, Terry).

All participants are demonstrably oriented towards their interactional huddle as the sequence comes to a close (Figure 11.2a). In this environment, Terry withdraws her gaze (Rossano, 2013), and Maureen moves her hand to her eye (Figure 11.2b). These disengagements contribute to the conclusion of the sequence of talk and anticipate the relevance of turn-transfer. The participants display that they will neither continue with that topic nor advance a new one. All participants pass up the chance to speak, and so their conversation lapses (line 5).

During the lapse (lines 5–7), each participant engages in her own auto-involvement. Maureen rubs her eye; Abby drinks, returns the glass to the table with a sniff and a sigh (line 6), and then crosses her arms while gazing downward; and Terry stretches her shoulders, scratches her cheek, and wipes her nose (Figures 11.2c–11.2f). The occurrence of auto-involvements here, in the place where turn-transfer is relevant, shows them to be an alternative to self-selection (Goodwin, 1986). Momentary withdrawal from interaction renders the participants less available to speak. When this happens in a lapse, the auto-involved participant shows herself as non-next speaker. These kinds of self-directed acts allow the participants to remain visibly committed to the interaction and, at the same time, offer them a temporary departure from it. They amount to a display of disinterest in speaking next and render the moment as 'one where I do not speak'.

Participants may thus disengage from interaction as a way to deal with a silence where no next speaker is apparent, and yet one is called for. Disengagement operates on the participation framework through the formation of negative space. Participants remove themselves from the set of possible next speakers, leaving it to the remaining participants to speak next.

Discussion

Reviewing Sacks's work on silence and turn-taking, this paper identified an underspecification regarding one kind of silence: lapses in conversation where no next speaker is apparent. I described how such lapses emerge, the kinds of issues they present, and a set of practices (self-deselection) aimed at their resolution. I have argued that techniques for self-deselection operate on the participation framework by marking non-next speakers.

These findings contribute to Sacks's analyses of silence and turn-taking by specifying how 'turns are valued, sought, or *avoided*' (Sacks et al., 1974: 701; emphasis added). The three methods for self-deselection analyzed above each betray a particular stance towards the ongoing relevance of talk in a lapse. Through displays of availability, participants show initiative in scaffolding a potential participation framework by isolating a possible next speaker through gaze and bodily comportment. Through sequence recompletion and disengagement, participants display reluctance to assume speakership. With sequence recompletion, participants leverage the inherent pliability of sequence endings to renew the relevance of self-selection for other participants. And, with disengagement, participants use the permissibility of engaging in alternative involvements to momentarily depart from interaction, leaving others to deal with the obligation to self-select. So, just as there are methods for the resolution of overlap (Schegloff, 2000), so too are there methods aimed at locating a speaker where none is apparent.

The analyses above also build on Sacks's early recognition that conversationalists may falter in their recurrent obligation to coordinate turn-transfer, resulting in silence without an apparent next speaker. This was mentioned in 'Opening up closings', where he and Schegloff formulated their concern in that article as 'how to coordinate the suspension of the transition relevance of possible utterance completion, *not how to deal with its nonoperation while still relevant*' (1973: 295; emphasis added). In other words, they acknowledged, but deferred dealing with, the problem of silence where turn-transfer should have occurred—less-than-one speaker in the place provided for one. I have argued that lapses embody this problem, and that self-deselection furnishes a (partial) solution (see Hoey, 2018b).

One of the principal joys of doing conversation analytic research is discovering how 'detailed study of small phenomena may give an enormous understanding of the way humans do things and the kinds of objects they use to construct and order their affairs' (Sacks, 1984: 24). The profusion of orderliness that Sacks uncovered in his analyses of silence demonstrated this in abundance. The analyses presented above and much of my research program as a whole are rooted in the legacy of Sacks's singular genius as an observer and systemetizer of social life and testify to the continued liveliness of his ideas.

Notes

1 Schegloff identifies the start of conversation analysis in the ideas and analytic mentality found in this lecture (Sacks, 1992a: xvi–xvii).
2 Although a fourth type is conceptually available (prior action only does speaker selection), it is difficult to imagine what that would look like.
3 I acknowledge the terminological ambiguity here. Such silences are gap-like in that they occur between turns, but also lapse-like owing to the fact that they are composed of rounds of possible self-selection. I refer to them as lapses for this latter reason, and also because 'gap' has been conventionalized as referring to inter-turn silences of Types I and II.
4 This section partially reproduces the analysis in Hoey (2017).

References

Clayman, S. E. (2002). Sequence and solidarity. In S. R. Thye & E. J. Lawler (Eds.), *Advances in group processes* (pp. 229–253). Bingley: Emerald.

Davidson, J. (1984). Subsequent versions of invitations, offers, requests, and proposals dealing with potential or actual rejection. In J. M. Atkinson & J. Heritage (Eds.), *Structures of social action* (pp. 102–128). Cambridge: Cambridge University Press.

Goffman, E. (1963). *Behavior in public places*. New York: Free Press.

Goodwin, C. (1981). *Conversational organization*. New York: Academic Press.

Goodwin, C. (1986). Gestures as a resource for the organization of mutual orientation. *Semiotica*, *62*(1–2), 29–50.

Heath, C. (1984). Talk and recipiency: Sequential organization in speech and body movement. In J. M. Atkinson & J. Heritage (Eds.), *Structures of social action: Studies in conversation analysis* (pp. 247–265). Cambridge: Cambridge University Press.

Hoey, E. M. (2015). Lapses: How people arrive at, and deal with, discontinuities in talk. *Research on Language and Social Interaction*, *48*(4), 430–453.

Hoey, E. M. (2017). Sequence recompletion: A practice for managing lapses in conversation. *Journal of Pragmatics*, *109*, 47–63.

Hoey, E. M. (2018a). Drinking for speaking: The multimodal organization of drinking in conversation. *Social Interaction: Video-Based Studies of Human Sociality*, *1*(1). https://tidsskrift.dk/socialinteraction/article/view/105498

Hoey, E. M. (2018b). How speakers continue with talk after a lapse in conversation. *Research on Language and Social Interaction*, *51*(3), 329–346.

Holt, E. (2010). The last laugh: Shared laughter and topic termination. *Journal of Pragmatics*, *42*(6), 1513–1525.

Jefferson, G. (1983). Notes on a systematic deployment of the acknowledgement tokens 'yeah' and 'mm hm'. In G. Jefferson (Ed.), *Two papers on transitory recipientship* (pp. 1–18). Tilburg: Tilburg Papers in Language and Literature 30.

Jefferson, G. (2004). Glossary of transcripts symbols with an introduction. In G. H. Lerner (Ed.), *Conversation analysis: Studies from the first generation* (pp. 13–34). Amsterdam: John Benjamins.

Lerner, G. H. (1993). Collectivities in action: Establishing the relevance of conjoined participation in conversation. *Text*, *13*(2), 213–246.

Lerner, G. H. (2003). Selecting next speaker: The context-sensitive operation of a context-free organization. *Language in Society*, *32*(02), 177–201.

Maynard, D. W. (1980). Placement of topic changes in conversation. *Semiotica*, *30*(3/4), 263–290.

McHoul, A. (1978). The organization of turns at formal talk in the classroom. *Language in Society*, *7*, 183–213.

Mondada, L. (2015). Multimodal completions. In A. Deppermann & S. Günther (Eds.), *Temporality in interaction* (pp. 267–307). Amsterdam: John Benjamins.

Mondada, L. (2016). Conventions for multimodal transcription. Accessed March 14 2018. https://franzoesistik.philhist.unibas.ch/fileadmin/user_upload/franzoesistik/mondada_multimodal_conventions.pdf

Pomerantz, A. (1984). Agreeing and disagreeing with assessments: Some features of preferred/dispreferred turn shapes. In J. M. Atkinson & J. Heritage (Eds.), *Structures of social action* (pp. 57–101). Cambridge: Cambridge University Press.

Rossano, F. (2013). Gaze in conversation. In J. Sidnell & T. Stivers (Eds.), *The handbook of conversation analysis* (pp. 308–329). Malden: Wiley-Blackwell.

Sacks, H. (1984). Notes on methodology. In J. M. Atkinson & J. Heritage (Eds.), *Structures of social action* (pp. 21–27). Cambridge: Cambridge University Press.

Sacks, H. (1987). On the preferences for agreement and contiguity in sequences in conversation. In G. Button & J. R. E. Lee (Eds.), *Talk and social organisation* (pp. 54–69). Clevedon, UK: Multilingual Matters.

Sacks, H. (1992a). *Lectures on conversation, volume 1*. Oxford: Blackwell.

Sacks, H. (1992b). *Lectures on conversation, volume 2*. Oxford: Blackwell.

Sacks, H., Schegloff, E. A., & Jefferson, G. (1974). A simplest systematics for the organization of turn-taking for conversation. *Language*, *50*(4), 696–735.

Schegloff, E. A. (1992). Repair after next turn: The last structurally provided defense of intersubjectivity in conversation. *American Journal of Sociology*, *97*(5), 1295–1345.

Schegloff, E. A. (2000). Overlapping talk and the organization of turn-taking for conversation. *Language in Society*, *29*(1), 1–63.

Schegloff, E. A. (2007). *Sequence organization in interaction: A primer in conversation analysis*. Cambridge: Cambridge University Press.

Schegloff, E. A. (2009). A practice for (re-) exiting a sequence: And/but/so + uh(m) + silence. In B. Fraser & K. Turner (Eds.), *Language in life and a life in language* (pp. 365–374). Bingley: Emerald.

Schegloff, E. A. (2016). Increments. In J. D. Robinson (Ed.), *Accountability in social Interaction* (pp. 239–263). Oxford: Oxford University Press.

Schegloff, E. A., & Sacks, H. (1973). Opening up closings. *Semiotica*, *8*(4), 289–327.

Stivers, T., & Rossano, F. (2010). Mobilizing response. *Research on Language and Social Interaction*, *43*(1), 3–31.

12 “Using observation as a basis for theorizing”

Children’s interactions and social order

Susan Danby

Everyday social interactions occur so quickly, and so mundanely, that they are often taken for granted. All of what we do is inherently social. In most instances, we are talking with others, children, family, friends and colleagues; our mundane and everyday activities are accomplished in the flow of social interaction. And, perhaps because they happen so quickly, so fleetingly, and because they are so mundane, it is too easy to overlook them. Our social actions count in the context in which they are produced – is it a wink or a blink? When someone says hello and we don’t say hello back, are we rude for not answering, or perhaps we didn’t hear? It is only when there is some problem or issue that occurs doing the interaction (such as not being heard or mishearing) that we stop to examine and possibly repair what just happened. Harvey Sacks was interested in such social interactions, pioneering the study of how “humans do things” (Sacks, 1984a, p. 24).

Sacks’s method of close observation of human social interaction is the basis of understanding how people go about building and maintaining their social worlds. Sacks brought these methodological insights into understanding children’s everyday lives to observe, for example, how they participated within adult social orders. His lectures are punctuated with narratives of the *in situ* social competence of children as they participated in everyday life with adults, peers and family members.

At the time of the delivery of his lectures, children were viewed predominantly through a developmental lens that conceptualised children on a life trajectory being socialised into adult worlds. Sacks’s perspective took a different turn, as his work recognised the active and agentic work of children as they actively participated in the social orders of everyday life – his focus was on “kids’ culture and kids’ talk” (Garfinkel, Girton, Livingston, & Sacks, 1982). In recognising the child in the here-and-now, and not as one who is incomplete and developing into adulthood, his work inspired scholars who respecified “the child” from one who is developing to one who is being a competent member in their own kids’ culture (Mackay, 1974; Speier, 1971, 1973, 1974). His profound view was that children had the measure of adult culture, and that adults had to attempt to report back to the adults “seriously … on the kids’ behalf” (Garfinkel et al., 1982, p. 8). His theoretical position was that, "instead of the 'developmental' point of view being treated as an account of what ties are between kids and adults, one might better approach it as the competent adult's version of the encounters between kids and adults" (pp. 8–9).

The upshot of Sacks's theorisation was that children's own activities were to be taken seriously "as a sociological account of orderliness of children's enterprises" (Garfinkel et al., 1982, p. 9). Sacks's programme of investigations of kids' culture was based on a methodology of "using observation as a basis of theorising" (Sacks, 1984a, p. 25), and this work has informed and inspired a body of work in childhood studies (cf., Butler, 2008; Cromdal, 2004; Danby & Baker, 1998; Waksler, 1991). Sacks's theorisations of kids and their cultures were the basis of my doctoral studies and have informed my research; they have been hugely significant in producing a programme of research that recognises children as competent actors in their own social worlds, with implications for how others, including family members and educators, provide accounts of children's social enterprises.

This chapter takes up Sacks's methodology of "close observation" to investigate the social interactions of young children. This approach seeks to know more about the complexity and competence of children's interactions with each other and with adults through closely examining how children's social orders and identities were assembled, moment by moment, and built and realigned through social interaction. As Sacks opened up new understandings of the competent ways that children organise their everyday worlds, his insights became a springboard for investigating children's social interactions across a range of settings, including classroom talk (Bateman, 2011; Butler, 2008; Cekaite, Blum-Kulka, Grøver, & Teubal, 2014; Church, 2009; Danby & Baker, 2000; Gardner & Mushin, 2013; Theobald & Danby, 2012). Close observation makes visible the children's interactions and social orders underway.

Undertaking studies of children through Sacks's observational methodology

The problem with analysing interactions involving children is that what they do is often familiar to us as adults. After all, we were each a child once and we draw upon those experiences. Additionally, as parents, we draw on our social network of other parents to try and understand, or confirm, what our children are doing. We typically and in a common-sense way draw upon these strategies to describe the actions of a scene involving children. As a consequence, it is difficult to interpret the scene from the perspectives of the members, the children. Although Sacks's method of observation was not to try to understand or interpret some inner child, this approach makes possible observations of children to show how they put together their social orders, turn by turn, and to describe what some of the practices can be like.

How do we start to explicate children's social orders? Sacks (1992) started by looking at what he found interesting in the data: "I have to sell what I can do, and the interestingness of my findings. So, we've got this fragment of conversation … I want to start picking it apart" (Vol 2, p. 3). Picking the data apart was an approach also taken up in the work of early ethnomethodologists investigating children's social interactions (Mackay, 1974; Speier, 1971), and by conversation analysts in the 1990s to study children's talk as social action (Cromdal, 2001; Evaldsson & Corsaro, 1998; Goodwin, 1990; Hutchby & Moran-Ellis, 1998).

My early research focus was on the fabric of social order in the preschool. "Within educational sites, as elsewhere, social order is most insightfully viewed, not as a precondition of interaction, but as an accomplishment of interactive activity and, therefore, open to revision, settlement, disruption and resettlement" (Danby & Baker, 2000, p. 91). A study of social order became a study of interweaving courses of action among children and between them and the teachers. Social order from this perspective is not a structural precondition of interaction but a locally produced arrangement (and rearrangement) of identities and relationships organised around and through activities. Thus, any local here-and-now social order is reflexively tied to the work of members of a particular social space, particularly as identities and relationships are assembled and reassembled in the course of interaction. Carolyn Baker (2000), following Sacks's ideas, proposed a series of key questions that can help understanding of culture-in-action: What are we, as members of society, doing in social interaction? How do we make sense of conduct, everyday practices, and each other? How is interaction mutually achieved? How do we shape and construct our practices? How do participants orient to institutional practices?

An analytic interest in examining children's social practices and interactions that often go unnoticed and, therefore, unexamined is a focus on making visible what was previously invisible. As Sacks (1984a, p. 25) observed:

> We will be using observation as a basis for theorizing. Thus we can start with things that are not currently imaginable, by showing that they happened. We can then come to see that a base for using close looking at the world for theorizing about it is that from close looking at the world we can find things that we could not, by imagination, assert were there. We would not know that they were "typical" … Indeed, we might not have noticed that they happen.

Drawing on this understanding as a starting point, observations of classroom interaction can make visible the social order of the classroom – and the identities and relationships that are reflexively tied to it – as an always-underway project and, therefore, much more revealing of the intricacies and complexity of the children's work of constructing social order. Detailed analysis of what appears initially to be chaotic can produce understandings of children's orderly social action.

Close looking at preschool children's interactions

When I began studying preschool classroom interaction, the research problem was *not* that the preschool classroom looked chaotic, as other researchers such as Corsaro (1985) described it. Rather, the classroom had an order to it with which I was very familiar – I was an insider in that I had been an early childhood teacher. My goal, then, was to make the familiar strange – what I knew so well was to be made unfamiliar. I needed a new analytic lens to do this, and reading the work of Sacks and the early ethnomethodologists and the child studies researchers provided the tools for bringing a different kind of observational lens to my analysis.

My research was informed by Sacks's view that, "it is possible that detailed study of small phenomena may give an enormous understanding of the way that humans do things and the kinds of objects they use to construct and order their affairs" (Sacks, 1984a, p. 24). One strategy, then, is to examine a single episode of social interaction. The aim of analysing a single episode is not to generalize, but to show the complexity of the social interaction (Whalen, 1995) and to disrupt "our craving for generality" (Wittgenstein, 1958, p. 17). This perspective is known as a "situated perspective" (Heap, 1990), which directs the analyst to investigate the situated activity, focusing on specific events to show what counts as social order and how the children and teachers locally accomplish those social orders. Explicating the visible and audible moment-to-moment relational encounters, and not a child's inner mental representations, shows how children co-construct their social orders.

Sacks argued for two sorts of observational data for understanding kids' culture: "(1) Kids' enterprises of which Kids Talk was an essential part; and (2) Adults' access to Kids' Enterprises" (Garfinkel et al., 1982, p. 10). In this chapter, I provide an example of each: (1) boys using fast talking and action in the block area, and (2) children using imaginary mobile phones that show the differing social orders of the children and the teacher. Sacks argued that children had to be witnessed undertaking these enterprises, and that these "ethnographically accountable 'fragments'" (p. 10) had to be observable through repeated viewings. The use of video-recordings allows for multiple viewings and detailed transcription to make visible and public what is happening in the interaction (Heath, Hindmarsh, & Luff, 2010; Mehan, 1993).

Boys in the block area of the preschool

The block area in the preschool was a place where boys aged 3–5 years built with large wooden blocks, while also assembling their social order. This place was outside the teacher's gaze, and it became a strategic space of their own to engage without teacher intervention unless someone invited the teacher in (Danby & Baker, 1998, 2000). At first glance, the boys' interactions appeared chaotic, with seemingly little semblance of order among the players. Closer observation and analysis, though, revealed a finely organized social order taking place, organised through conflict and dispute talk.

Transcript 12.1 shows a group of boys in the block area arguing about another boy's entry into the area. David argues against this proposition, whereas Alan and Andrew argue for Matt to remain. Their talk becomes heated and loud. First impressions of the boys' video-recorded interactions suggested that they talked over each other with no gaps between turns, and that they did not wait until one had finished their turn before another started. The talk gave the appearance of speaker turns being unorganised and jumbled. Yet, close observation made visible that their interactions were not chaotic, but, rather, ordered and systematic, that there was an "orderliness of [the] children's enterprises" (Garfinkel et al., 1982, p. 9). To be able to participate in block area disputes, members needed smart talking that was ordered, sequential and purposeful.

A fundamental aspect of turn-taking is an examination of the talk of any one speaker at any one time, requiring fine coordination. A turn's projection involves some sense of a turn closure, making possible a next possible speaker (Schegloff, 1987). Elsewhere, I have discussed the boys' turn-taking and overlaps in the talk, and tactics for interjections in relation to the speaker's main message (Danby & Baker, 2000). The boys used a strategy identified as recycled turn beginnings (Schegloff, 1987) to gain the floor to be fully heard. When one boy ceased his turn of talk, another would recycle what they had just previously said in overlap with the previous speaker. In this way, their entire message could be heard by the other boys. Transcript 12.1 shows the recycled turn beginnings in action.

Transcript 12.1 (Danby & Baker, 2000, p. 109)

42	Alan	No you're [not* ((has walked behind David and is now on David's right ; he starts building with the blocks))
>43	David	[yep* he's going away [if he goes away* I won't smash it down
44	Andrew	[we're we're strong* ((walking over to Matt; pointing his finger at him))
45	David	If he doesn't go away [I won't smash it*
>46	Allen >	[( )* you are a ( ) bash you right down ((pointing at David))
47	Andrew	YEAH (0.5) ((points and leans towards Alan)) I'm going to get a monster shark's shark and it will ea:t him A:::::LL up! ((Andrew grins and begins a jig, turns towards the camera.)) [hee hee hee hee* ((laughing gleefully
>48	Matt	[And I'll get a get a ro(.)bot* I'll get a robot shark crocodile monster and eat you °up°

Shown in Danby and Baker (2000), David (line 43) overlaps Alan's turn (line 42), by first gaining the floor with "yep" and speaking over Alan. Andrew next overlaps David's turn (line 44). As David's turn was disrupted by Andrew talking over the top of him, David repeats the middle part of his utterance (turn 45) to ensure that his main message from his previous turn (43) was fully heard. Another recycled turn is heard when Matt, in turn 48, overlaps Andrew's turn (turn 47). Matt's repetition of his original message (I'll get a robot shark), as soon as Andrew finishes his utterance, is produced as the only speaker on the floor. His message is now available to be heard by all the boys.

Transcript 12.1 shows that slowing down analysis to examine turn-by-turn talk showed the children's use of the strategy of recycled turn beginnings to gain the speaking floor – the very same strategies that adults use in their everyday interactions. This close observation and analysis of the boys' talk made visible social order in a way that was not previously visible. The boys' talking over each other was not an action of *not* knowing how to produce turn-taking behaviour, but rather a strategic initiative to gain the floor and to have their main message heard by the others.

This finding was ground-breaking for me. We knew from Schegloff's (1987) work that adults routinely talk over each other to gain the floor for speaking, and this analysis had just identified that 3- and 4-year-old children also did this to gain the floor! The analytic resources of Sacks's approach of close observation and conversation analysis made visible the social structures in which the children operated, highlighting their *in situ* competency.

Child and teacher social orders

Pretend play is a well-known activity associated with young children. An investigation of children's games and activities shows how they prepare for, and practise, everyday social life – but from within their own culture (Butler, 2008; Danby, Davidson, Theobald, Houen, & Thorpe, 2017; Sacks, 1992). As Sacks (1992) points out, children's engagement with playing games is "an environment for learning and demonstrating criterial matters in real world action" (Sacks, 1992, Vol 1, p. 501). In other words, children's activities make visible their social and cultural life in action.

Sacks's interest was in showing how children's games were produced and framed by orienting to the children's local culture in action (Sacks, 1980, 1992). He wrote about how rules were produced that oriented to a "category set of game events", which allowed children to monitor the activities for observing the rules, as well as the infringements of the game underway (Sacks, 1992). Games are a series of actions, and "the simplest of children's games have two parts" (Sacks, 1992, Vol 1, p. 496). Using an example of children kicking a ball to each other, he observes that kicking and catching actions are expected to happen, and he identifies these games as relying upon the children's knowledge that there is an "expectable next event" (p. 497).

There are other games that children play that are less reliant on knowing to expect the next event. Known as imaginative or pretend play, these activities rely on peer interactions, but ones that rely on improvising actions in a pretend frame (Sawyer, 1997). Speier (1973) observed that children's interactions, such as pretending to play families, are an "interactional and cultural activity in their own right" (p. 156). Children, when engaging in pretence, are not simply imitating adult life; rather, they use cultural objects in ways perhaps not possibly anticipated by adults to actively build and construct their own "kids culture" (Garfinkel et al., 1982). Children constitute their social orders within and outside the social and physical spaces produced by adults (Gracey, 1972).

In the study of how children make sense of their everyday social worlds, play itself comes to be treated "as a topic for investigation" (Whalen, 1995, p. 317). The analyst decides categories that are assignable to the speakers and hearers by observing how participants assign the categories to each other (Speier, 1972). As Baker (1998) describes, "the relevant category-pair is often taken to be 'teacher'–'children', which assigns a generational relevance to what is said and done … this frame then informs the hearings that are made as well as the physical presentation of the transcript" (p. 113).

Pretend play is a normative activity that constitutes the here-and-now social worlds of young children. In considering pretend play activities, we could describe these practices as children working at "being ordinary" (Sacks, 1984b). Such work is accomplished by participants using their own membership resources. In order to understand participants' methods, Sacks (1985) suggests: "For members, activities are observables. They see activities … And that poses for us the task of … [f]inding how it is that people can produce sets of actions that provide that others can see such things" (p. 20). His central point here is that, "the inference-making machine" (Sacks, 1985) is not simply to make inferences, but rather for analysts take into account how members orient their talk and actions towards the event. Speier used Sacks's work on membership categorization to note that, "analysts use available identifiers … *as members of the culture they are observing*" (1972, p. 404). Analysts use the same resources as members themselves to make sense of the activity, and, more specifically, the analyst's role is to treat seriously, as a sociological account, "the orderliness of children's enterprises" (Garfinkel et al., 1982, p. 9)

Transcript 12.2 is drawn from a single episode of children's peer interactions in a preschool setting and what happens when the teacher arrives. Drawing on understandings of pretence and reality frames (Hester & Francis, 1997), this transcript shows the children's action through a pretence frame, whereas the teacher produced a reality frame. Each framing is made visible to the others. The episode starts with a group of children sitting on large rocks in the preschool playground. With small rocks in their hands, children are pressing their thumbs on their small rock as if writing a text message on a mobile (cell) phone. As the teacher arrives, one child calls out, "Please can you go out with me". The teacher hears this and asks how to send a message. From this point, the children and teacher orient to differing moral orders. The teacher does not participate in the pretend play as a member of the social order initiated by the children. Rather, she initiates a different adult-oriented order as she seek accounts of, and makes assessments about, the children's activity of texting.

Transcript 12.2a

```
001   Ch1   Please could you go out with me.
002   Tea   Please could you go ↑out↓ with m:ee.=
003         =o:hh.=
004   Ch1   =.he >>he he he ha::<<
005   Tea   ↑How do you do that¿
006                (0.9)
007   Tea   How do you text someone.(0.2) a message.
008                (0.9)
009   Ch?   [but miss Hannah     ]
010   Ch2   [.hh You do it on the] pu:tar.   ] ((computer))
011   Ch1   [((pretends to text using rock)) ]
012   Ch?   Miss Hanna[h,
013   Tea             [Do it on the computer?]
014   Ch3             [I do soccer           ]
015   Ch1             [Dot com dot a:] u:.   ]
016   Ch2   [((nods))                 ]
```

Lines 17-21 omitted

```
022   Tea             [Dot com] dot a u:? ]
023         [And where do you ]find dot-]
024   Ch4   [((lowers arm))     ]
025   Ch5   [Are we gonna                  ][go in:s       ]i:de?  ]
026   Ch4                                   [((C4 pushes C5 aside))]
027   Tea   Not yet. ((to C5 nearby))
028         (0.3)
029   Tea   [Where do] you find dot com [dot a u  ]
030   Ch4   [I do-    ]
031   Ch1                               [my mum] told me.
```

Transcript 12.2a begins with Child 1 texting on a small rock, where the rock is standing in as an object standing for another, the mobile phone. The teacher arrives and repeats the child's explanation of her activity (line 2), that she was texting someone to go out with her, and asks about how to text. At this point, several children respond (lines 10 and 15), at which the teacher further asks about dot.au (lines 22, 23 and 29); she receives a response from Child 1, who shifts from a pretence frame to a reality one in order to answer the teacher's question, that her mum told her (line 31).

Transcript 12.2b

039	Ch2	[Well- I can do- a thousand on my mobile]
040	Ch1	[I':M THE ONE WHO'S DRI:VING]
041		[((pretending to hold steering wheel))]
042	Tea	Alri::ght. ((singsong voice))(0.3)
043		What can't- [can you drive and text at the same ↓time,]
044		[((starts pointing to C1))]
045	Ch?	[Hey look what I can do]
046	Ch2	[I'M DRIVING] WHEEL WITH ONE HAND]
047	Ch2	[((LH: rock; RH: pretending to hold steering wheel))]
048	Ch?	[Look at me, Miss Hannah look at me]
049	Tea	[>°ha ha ha ha°<((looks at researcher))]
050	Ch?	Miss Hannah look at me:¿
051	Ch1	[(°beep beep°) [°shu shu] shu shu shu°]
052		[((continues pretending to steer and text))]
053	Ch7	[((steps forward to TA))]
054	Tea	[Ar:hh, lovely Jack_]
055	Ch7	look [me have pockets]
056	Ch?	[Can you-]
057	Ch1	[(All for-) ↑WE'RE HE:ERE↓.] ((continues pretending))

At the beginning of Transcript 12.2b, Child 1 shifts the topic of conversation back to pretend mode to call out loudly that she is driving (line 40) and pretends to hold an imaginary steering wheel. The teacher maintains her reality frame, raising the issue of texting and driving at the same time (line 43). Child 1 continues to maintain her pretend frame of driving through elaborating on her actions: driving with one hand (line 46), beeping the horn (lines 51–52) and arriving at the destination, the soccer field (line 57).

Transcripts 12.2a and 12.2b make visible the teacher's work as she oriented to the children's spontaneous pretend activities. Whereas the children's activities are embedded within a pretend frame, the teacher draws on an alternative frame to the children's one of pretence; rather, she draws on a reality frame, as shown through questions related to how to send a text message and why you can't drive and text at the same time. Her reality frame is a pedagogic order that displays culturally proper understandings of adult-formulated rules related to knowledge of how to use digital devices, and road safety and driving. At the same time, we see children's competence as they concurrently participate as members of kids' culture of pretence while also participating in the teacher's reality frame.

As Sacks (1992) noted, "children's games are describables, and in deeply interesting ways" (Vol 1, pp. 497–498). Here, the describables show the children pretending that a rock is a mobile phone, and that they are driving to soccer. Close observation showed the complexities of how this game was played. The children's competences were seamlessly displaying their continuing engagement with the game and how they shaped the social activity. They simultaneously participated as members in their social worlds of pretence while also participating in the teacher's reality-framed agenda.

Conclusion

A normative quality of childhood is engaging in pretence, where young children's activities are embedded within imaginary frames where they draw on the cultural and material objects around them, while also competently managing their social interactions. Competence here refers to the concept that children are competent observers of their own worlds, and that they understand the social structures in which they operate (Cicourel, 1970; Mackay, 1974). Children operate across multiple social orders; they simultaneously participate as members in their social worlds of pretence and participate within the adult reality-framed agendas. Further, not only are children competent to use adult rules, they use them to accomplish their own agendas and in ways not necessarily sanctioned by the teacher (Danby, 1998; Danby & Baker, 1998, 2000; Sacks, 1974)

My reading of Sacks's observations of kids' culture and kids' talk opened new ways for me to understand the interactional work and social worlds of children. "Picking apart" everyday social life made visible children's accomplishments in ways that were not visible before. Sacks's theorization of kids' culture opened a new research room, made possible through new concepts such as "competence" and "social order" and "kids' culture". I had a new analytic toolbox of language concepts accompanied by a new set of methodological and analytic tools to observe and describe children's everyday activities in order to understand how they accomplish social life. To recognise that 3- and 4-year-old children use recycled turn beginnings – just as adults do – to gain the speaking floor showed how even young children engage in the complexity of social interaction and understandings of adult social structures.

In our society, the developmental perspective is so persuasive that it is very easy to think that the practice of children talking over each other was because they had not learned to take turns at talk. Yet adults talk over each other all the time, and they aren't seen as being developmentally immature. It was exciting to empirically show the precision of the children's turns of talk in how they gained the floor and then retained the speaking floor with their full message being heard. It is this form of social competence that is often overlooked in a developmental view of children, where they are still viewed as somehow developing those skills.

Beginning with the notion that childhood is a social construct rather than beginning with childhood as a developmental phase, there flowed a very different research programme based on different categories of interpretation. Sacks's writings provided an alternative theoretical framework to draw upon, a shift from developmental theory to a field that allowed me to embrace a different theoretical perspective and a different understanding of childhood as kids' culture. Without this theoretical lens, I could not have imagined the complexity of young children's talk and action.

Sacks's view was that observation was a powerful tool: "I want to encourage the sense that interesting aspects of the world, that are as yet unknown, are accessible to observation" (Sacks, 1992, Vol 2, p. 420). Children's everyday encounters are "all so momentary and fleeting, so intricate and elaborate, so spontaneous and immediate, that we find it difficult to attend to them" (Shotter, 1996, p. 404). Sacks's own observations shone the spotlight on children as members of culture through recognising that observation of everyday practices can make possible understandings not otherwise available. In this way, drawing on his methodology, "we can start with things that are not currently imaginable, by showing that they happened" (Sacks, 1984a, p. 25). This approach makes possible insights into to how all members, including children, engage in their everyday activities through close looking and making visible what previously was invisible.

References

Baker, C. D. (1998). Transcription and representation in literacy research. In J. Flood, S. B. Heath, & D. Lapp (Eds.), *A handbook for literacy educators: Research on teaching the communicative and visual arts* (pp. 108–118). New York: Macmillan.

Baker, C. D. (2000). Locating culture in action: Membership categorisation in texts and talk. In A. Lee & C. Poynton (Eds.), *Culture & text: Discourse and methodology in social research and cultural studies* (pp. 99–113). St Leonards, NSW: Allen & Unwin.

Bateman, A. (2011). Huts and heartache: The affordance of playground huts for legal debate in early childhood social organisation. *Journal of Pragmatics*, *43*, 3111–3121.

Butler, C. W. (2008). *Talk and social interaction in the playground.* Aldershot: Ashgate.

Cekaite, A., Blum-Kulka, S., Grøver, V., & Teubal, E. (Eds.). (2014). *Children's peer talk: Learning from each other.* Cambridge: Cambridge University Press.

Church, A. (2009). *Preference organisation and peer disputes: How young children resolve conflict.* Farnham: Ashgate.

Cicourel, A. V. (1970). The acquisition of social structure: Toward a developmental sociology of language and meaning. In J. D. Douglas (Ed.), *Understanding everyday life: Toward the reconstruction of sociological knowledge* (pp. 136–168). London: Routledge & Kegan Paul.

Corsaro, W. A. (1985). *Friendship and peer culture in the early years.* Norwood, NJ: Ablex.

Cromdal, J. (2001). Can I be with? Negotiating play entry in a bilingual school. *Journal of Pragmatics*, *33*(4), 515–543.

Cromdal, J. (2004). Building bilingual oppositions: Code-switching in children's disputes. *Language in Society*, *33*, 33–58.

Danby, S. (1998). The serious and playful work of gender: Talk and social order in a preschool classroom. In N. Yelland (Ed.), *Gender in early childhood* (pp. 175–205). London: Routledge.

Danby, S., & Baker, C. (1998). How to be masculine in the block area. *Childhood*, *5*(2), 151–175.

Danby, S., & Baker, C. (2000). Unravelling the fabric of social order in block area. In S. Hester & D. Francis (Eds.), *Local educational order: Ethnomethodological studies of knowledge in action* (pp. 91–140). Amsterdam: John Benjamins.

Danby, S., Davidson, C., Theobald, M., Houen, S., & Thorpe, K. (2017). Pretend play and technology: Young children making sense of their everyday social worlds. In D. Pike, S. Lynch, & C. A'Beckett (Eds.), *Multidisciplinary perspectives on play: From birth to beyond* (pp. 231–245). Singapore: Springer.

Evaldsson, A.-C., & Corsaro, W. A. (1998). Play and games in the peer cultures of preschool and preadolescent children: An interpretative approach. *Childhood*, *5*(4), 377–402.

Gardner, R., & Mushin, I. (2013). Teachers telling: Informings in an early years classroom. *Australian Journal of Communication*, *40*(2), 63–81.

Garfinkel, H., Girton, G., Livingston, E., & Sacks, H. (1982). *Studies of kids' culture and kids' talk*. University of California, Los Angeles, CA. Unpublished paper.

Goodwin, M. H. (1990). *He-said-she-said: Talk as social organization among black children*. Bloomington, IN: Indiana University Press.

Gracey, H. L. (1972). Learning the student role: Kindergarten as academic boot camp. In D. H. Wrong & H. L. Gracey (Eds.), *Readings in introductory sociology* (pp. 243–254). New York: Macmillan.

Heap, J. L. (1990). Applied ethnomethodology: Looking for the local rationality of reading activities. *Human Studies*, *13*(1), 39–72.

Heath, C., Hindmarsh, J., & Luff, P. (Eds.). (2010). *Video in qualitative research: Analysing social interaction in everyday life*. Los Angeles, CA: Sage.

Hester, S., & Francis, D. (1997). Reality analysis in a classroom storytelling. *British Journal of Sociology*, *48*(1), 95–112.

Hutchby, I., & Moran-Ellis, J. (Eds.). (1998). *Children and social competence: Arenas of action*. London: Falmer Press.

Mackay, R. W. (1974). Conceptions of children and models of socialization. In R. Turner (Ed.), *Ethnomethodology: Selected readings* (pp. 180–193). Harmondsworth: Penguin Education.

Mehan, H. (1993). Why I like to look: On the use of videotape as an instrument in educational research. In M. Schratz (Ed.), *Qualitative voices in educational research* (pp. 93–105). London: Falmer Press.

Sacks, H. (1974). On the analysability of stories by children. In R. Turner (Ed.), *Ethnomethodology: Selected readings* (pp. 216–232). Harmondsworth: Penguin Education.

Sacks, H. (1980). Button button who's got the button. *Sociological Inquiry*, *50*(3–4), 318–327.

Sacks, H. (1984a). Notes on methodology. In J. M. Atkinson & J. Heritage (Eds.), *Structures of social action: Studies in conversation analysis* (pp. 21–27). Cambridge: Cambridge University Press.

Sacks, H. (1984b). On doing "being ordinary". In J. M. Atkinson & J. Heritage (Eds.), *Structures of social action: Studies in conversation analysis* (pp. 413–429). Cambridge: Cambridge University Press.

Sacks, H. (1985). The inference-making machine: Notes on observability. In T. A. van Dijk (Ed.), *Handbook of discourse analysis: Discourse and dialogue* (Vol. 3, pp. 13–23). London: Academic Press.

Sacks, H. (1992). *Lectures on conversation* (G. Jefferson, Trans. Vols. I and II). Oxford: Blackwell.

Sawyer, R. K. (1997). *Pretend play as improvisation: Conversation in the preschool classroom*. Mahwah, NJ: Lawrence Erlbaum.

Schegloff, E. (1987). Analyzing single episodes of interaction: An exercise in conversation analysis. *Social Psychology Quarterly*, *50*(2), 101–114.

Shotter, J. (1996). "Now I can go on": Wittgenstein and our embodied embeddedness in the "hurly-burly" of life. *Human Studies*, *19*, 385–407.

Speier, M. (1971). The everyday world of the child. In J. D. Douglas (Ed.), *Understanding everyday life* (pp. 188–217). London: Routledge.

Speier, M. (1972). Some conversational problems for interactional analysis. In D. Sudnow (Ed.), *Studies in social interaction* (pp. 397–427). New York: Free Press.

Speier, M. (1973). *How to observe face-to-face communication: A sociological introduction*. Pacific Palisades, CA: Goodyear.

Speier, M. (1974). The everyday world of the child. In B. Berger (Ed.), *Readings in sociology: A biographical approach* (pp. 55–60). New York: Basic Books.

Theobald, M., & Danby, S. (2012). "A problem of versions": Laying down the law in the school playground. In S. Danby & M. Theobald (Eds.), *Disputes in everyday life: Social and moral orders of children and young people* (Vol. 15, pp. 221–241). Bingley: American Sociological Association and Emerald.

Waksler, F. C. (Ed.). (1991). *Studying the social worlds of children: Sociological readings*. London: Falmer Press.

Whalen, M. R. (1995). Working toward play: Complexity in children's fantasy activities. *Language in Society*, *24*(3), 315–348.

Wittgenstein, L. (1958). *The blue and brown books*. Oxford: Basil Blackwell.

13 Membership categorisation and the notion of "omni-relevance" in everyday family interactions

Sara Keel

During my studies at the University of Geneva, I had the chance to spend a year as an exchange student in the Sociology Department of the University of Manchester. There, I took Rod Watson's course "Conversation Analysis". Discussing conversation analytic papers, key notions and analytic resources, joining in data sessions and making my first attempts to transcribe audio-recordings of naturally occurring interactions impacted my way of doing sociology in a profound and lasting way. When I began my doctoral research on pre-schoolers' socialisation a few years later, it was clear to me from the outset that conversation analysis would be my approach. For that project, I thus aimed to juxtapose Pomerantz's work on adults' assessment sequences (1975, 1984) with ones identified in everyday parent–child interactions. My goal was to determine whether adults' preference organisation, as revealed by Pomerantz (1975, 1984), also held for sequences initiated by young children in everyday parent–child interactions.

When I discussed the idea with my former professor, Rod Watson, he advised me to take into account an unfinished and unpublished research project by Garfinkel, Girton, Livingston and Sacks titled "Studies of Kids' Culture and Kids' Talk" (1982). Following his advice and participating in a reading group on Sacks's lectures (1992 I) with Esther Gonzalez-Martinez, Alain Bovet, Fabienne Malbois, David Rossi and Philipp Sormani (see Bovet, Gonzalez Martinez & Malbois 2014) allowed me to see how Sacks's lectures[1] laid the groundwork for Garfinkel, Girton, Livingston and Sacks's (1982) central argument for *respecifying* the study of socialisation.

In what follows, I will be outlining Sacks's reflections on children's unique position in society (Sacks 1992 I: 223–266, 1972) and Garfinkel et al.'s (1982) suggestion to "respecify" the study of socialisation by examining parents'/adults' and children's orientations to the "developmental scheme" (next section). Pursuing my account of how Sacks's work inspired my own research, I will then discuss the notion of "omni-relevance" as introduced by Sacks (1992 I) in his spring 1966 lectures (third section). Arguing that EMCA studies of parent/adult–child interactions have so far paid little attention to these two research endeavours initiated by Sacks, I will analyse two short transcripts of parent–child food-preparation activities in order to show what gets lost when the omni-relevance of participants' orientations to the developmental scheme is merely claimed instead of being tested and examined in its own right.

Criticising and "respecifying" conventional studies of socialisation

In their joint research project "Studies of Kids' Culture and Kids' Talk", Garfinkel et al. (1982)[2] focus on a classic topic of sociological investigation – socialisation – understood as the process "through which people become skilled in the ways of society" (Cromdal 2006: 462). To begin with, the authors remark that conventional social and human sciences investigate the processes of socialisation by adopting a sense-making device based on common sense, the developmental scheme. This scheme partitions the observed population (parent/adult–children) into two asymmetrically related categories: those who are "*not-yet-fully competent*" (children) versus those who are "*competent*" (parents/adults).

Although the authors consider ordinary members' frequent use of this sense-making device as understandable or even reasonable, they criticise its unexamined application in socialisation theory and studies (Garfinkel et al. 1982: 4). It results in observing, analysing, understanding and explicating children as "deficient" (Garfinkel et al. 1982: 2; Mackay 1975:181; Watson 1992: 264) and "naturally, normally, obviously, objectively, really and observably faulted" (Garfinkel et al. 1982: 4) when compared with adults. The unexamined use also engenders a view of the socialisation process as being "one-way" and precludes researchers from examining what children might competently contribute to the orderly organisation of intelligible interaction.

Moreover, as Mackay argued (1975: 182), instead of treating the ordinary use of the developmental scheme as a "topic" of investigation, conventional sociologists and psychologists use it as a "glossing resource" to make their own (scientific) description coherent and intelligible. This "has resulted in the unavailability for sociologists of interactions between adults and children as a phenomenon of study" (Mackay 1975: 182). Or, as Sacks puts it, when criticising conventional sociology more generally:

> All the sociology we read is unanalytic, in the sense that they simply put some category in. They may make sense to us in doing that, but they're doing it simply as another Member. They haven't described the phenomena they're seeking to describe – or that they ought to be seeking to describe.
>
> (Sacks 1992 I: 41–42)

In contrast, respecifying the study of socialisation, as proposed by Garfinkel et al. (1982: 2, 35–39), involves investigating parents' and children's observable orientation to and constitution of the developmental scheme, and its constitutive categories – the "not-yet-fully competent" child and the "competent" parent/adult – as a "topic" of investigation in its own right (Keel 2014, 2016: 26–53; see also Watson 1994). Sacks argued that as a *members' phenomenon*, the use of the developmental scheme and its interactive implications have to be taken as seriously as other "interpretative resources and methods of sense-making" that interactants deploy to organise their activities with those of others (from a speech by Sacks, cited in Garfinkel et al. 1982: 9).

In his lecture "The Baby Cried. The Mommy Picked it Up" (Sacks 1992 I: 236–266), Sacks observes that young children around the age of 3 begin their talk, when addressing adults, with an open question: "You know what, Daddy?" or "You know something?" (Sacks 1992 I: 256). He argues that this type of beginning does not reflect a lack of linguistic (or other) competences on children's part, and that it, in fact, indexes their understanding of their particular position with regard to parents/adults. As Sacks puts it (1992 I: 263): "Kids have restricted rights to talk", and they consist of a right to begin, to make an initial statement, and not much more. For this reason, he says, "starting to talk to adults is, for small children, a rather special matter". By beginning their talk with an open question, children show their ability to deal with their "restricted rights to talk" in a competent and effective manner: they make relevant another open question from the addressed parent/adult – "What?" – that is distinctive in that it gives them the full right to say whatever they wanted to say "in the first place" and to talk extendedly (Sacks 1992 I: 265). Sacks discusses another method of acquiring extended rights to talk that consists of announcing a trouble that is relevant to the addressed recipient: "The baby cried" (Sacks 1992 I: 265). Whereas the first method draws on sequential resources, the second one mobilises categorial resources ("baby") and a category-bound activity ("cried").

Inspired by Sacks's work, a few studies on parent–child interactions have revealed other interactive methods with which adults manifest their orientation towards children as inferior, deficient and "not yet fully competent". Speier's analysis, for example, argues that, whenever parents/adults answer or talk for a child rather than letting the child speak for himself or herself (Speier 1971: 195), and particularly when they enforce silence upon a child while talking to another adult (Speier 1976: 101), they are not taking the child's competences into consideration (Speier 1971: 209–216). Butler and Fitzgerald (2010) focus on a situation in which a family is invited to lunch at a friend's house. They discuss how the host's offer, "Do you want a s:eparate plate for him?", is accomplished in a way that attributes the right and responsibility of responding to the offer to the parents and not to the child (2010: 2466). As such, it makes the host's understanding of invitees' distinct membership categories, and the specific rights and responsibilities bound to them, locally relevant. Analysing in detail how the parents and the child treat the host's offer in turn allows the authors to show how membership categories and predicated rights and responsibilities "are not simply invoked and displayed [...] but are transformed, challenged and perhaps even undermined in the fine detail of talk-in-interaction" (2010: 2467).

To sum up: Garfinkel et al.'s (1982) respecification of the study of socialisation consists on the one hand of examining members' orientation to and constitution of the developmental scheme and its contrastive categories – "fully competent" versus "not-yet-fully competent" – as they become available in the sequential turn-by-turn organisation of their interactions. They thus treat socialisation as a members' phenomenon that needs to be studied in its own right. On the other hand, this respecification implies focusing on children's talk and other conduct in *terms of competences* that they mobilise to come to terms with their particular position in society (see also Sidnell 2010). Ultimately, the goal with respecifying the study of socialisation is to provide sociological explanations for children's other-than-adult conduct and to reveal how children participate in their own socialisation in a non-trivial way (Garfinkel et al. 1982: 19).

Asymmetry in parent–child interactions and the notion of "omni-relevance"

With the encouragement of my dissertation supervisor, Lorenza Mondada, I, therefore, paid as much attention to embodied conduct as to talk in my research on parent–child assessment sequences (see introduction). Her invaluable insight and support in this analytic endeavour (Mondada 2009, 2018) allowed me to revisit Pomerantz's work on assessment sequences as I identified young children's displays of embodied competences in addressing assessments to their parents and, more importantly, in obtaining responses to them (Keel 2015, 2016: 77–116). Moreover, juxtaposing a detailed examination of parents' embodied responses to young children's initial assessments (Keel 2011, 2016: 117–124) with Pomerantz's account of preference organisation of adults' assessment sequences (1975, 1984), I uncovered phenomena casting doubt upon the supposed omni-relevance of epistemic asymmetries in parent–child interactions.[3]

Since Garfinkel et al.'s proposal to respecify the study of socialisation, an impressive number of EMCA studies have examined children's competent participation in social interactions. These convincingly demonstrate that very young children already mobilise language, gesture (pointing), gaze and other embodied resources to produce intelligible actions and understand those of others (Corrin 2010; Filipi 2009; Forrester 2008, 2013; Forrester & Cherington 2009; Kidwell 2005, 2009, 2011; Kidwell & Zimmerman 2006; Laakso & Soininen 2010; Walker 2017; Wootton 1997, 2006, 2007, 2010). However, Garfinkel et al.'s proposal to investigate participants' orientation to and/or constitution of the developmental scheme as a "members' phenomenon" in its own right has still largely been neglected (but see Butler & Fitzgerald 2010; Butler & Wilkinson 2013; Speier 1971, 1976; Wootton 1981). Studies on parent/adult–child interactions do not reflect much upon, let alone focus on, members' observable orientation to it as a topic of investigation (see also Forrester 2017: 18). Instead, it has generally been taken for granted that the developmental scheme device is "omni-relevant" for the interactants themselves and, thus, consequential for the sequential organisation of parent/adult–child interactions.[4]

In three lectures Sacks gave between the spring of 1966 and the spring of 1967 (Sacks 1992 I: 312–319, 515–522, 590–596), he uses transcribed extracts taken from audio-recordings of a "group therapy session" to discuss the "generic relevance" of a particular setting for the orderliness of social interaction (Schegloff's introduction to Sacks 1992 I: xlvii), thus tackling another fundamental question for sociological investigation. Sacks criticises conventional sociologists for presuming that, for social interaction to be accomplished in an orderly and intelligible way, participants must "formulate their role relationships and systematically invoke their consequences" (Sacks 1992 I: 517) and for attributing to themselves "special rights to assign name-formulations to the actions, upon, say, occasions when they are not assigned by participants" (Sacks 1992 I: 517). He then raises the question of whether it is:

> possibly the case that, first, the phenomenon of a "setting" needs be recognized as also a Members' phenomenon, and not, for example, one of those things which, as social scientists, we construct and manage?
>
> (Sacks 1992 I: 516)

Using the group therapy transcriptions, Sacks begins his argument by observing that members recognise and make sense of each other's actions and also accomplish and prioritise actions effectively *without* necessarily formulating their role relationship, the activities they are engaged in and/or the setting in which they interact. He concludes that members might deploy methods to invoke "the pure fact of settinged activities, without having to formulate a setting" (Sacks 1992 I: 516) or, put differently, "without having to say who you are and who I am for now, or what we're really doing for now" (Sacks 1992 I: 517).

Following this observation, Sacks introduces the possibility of omni-relevance, meaning two things:

> On the one hand there are some actions which, for their effectiveness, involve categorial membership in that collection, and on the other hand, until the course of action is ended, one can't rule out the further use of that collection (i.e., even if it isn't being used right now it might well be needed or invoked at any point up until the end of that course of action; e.g., the "session").
>
> (Sacks 1992 I: 594)

Moreover, instead of merely presuming or claiming that a specific institutional setting such as group therapy or "a course" is omni-relevant for the sequential and categorial organisation of interactions, Sacks insists on the necessity of developing analytic methods that make it possible to determine whether a membership categorisation device, such as the developmental scheme, is treated as omni-relevant by participants themselves, and to evidence this if it is the case (Sacks 1992 I: 315, 462–463).

Sacks mentions that, as he began working on transcripts of group therapy sessions, he soon got the sense that the categories "therapist/patient", as constitutive parts of the group therapy collection, were omni-relevant for the organisation of the setting. However, it was only when he began to focus on the "priority character of insertable sequences" that he was in a position to show and account for the omni-relevance of the device (Sacks 1992 I: 316).

The interactive accomplishment of the priority character of insertable sequences

Using certain extracts, Sacks (1992 I: 313–315) explains what he means by "priority character of insertable sequences". In the group therapy session, adolescent patients might be in the middle of talking about cars when a new arrival, the therapist, "*qua therapist*", inserts a sequence to greet the patients and introduce himself or herself. Sacks also gives another example: a teacher and a group of students might be distributed loosely throughout a seminar room when, upon the teacher's announcement of a break, everybody leaves the room and goes to the cafeteria. In both cases, the omni-relevance of the category collection "therapist/patients" or "teacher/students" is made clear by the members' interactive organisation of the inserted sequence. "Patients" or "students" might be fully engaged in an activity for the orderly accomplishment of which the "therapist/patient" or "teacher/student" collection is not relevant. As soon as the therapist qua therapist or the teacher qua teacher launches a new activity – a greeting/introduction, a closing of a session or the taking of a break – "patients" or "students" ratify the new course of action by prioritising the newly proposed activity and dropping the activity they were engaged in before.

Sacks thus argues that, even if a category collection such as "patient–therapist" is not used throughout a longer stretch of talk, its omni-relevance implies that, when invoked, it constitutes the "controlling device", or, to put it differently, the priority characters of these insertable sequences "are controlled by reference to that device" – "group therapy" or "seminar" – and its constitutive categories – "therapist/patients" or "teacher/students" (Sacks 1992 I: 314–315):

> Things may be going along, the device isn't being used; at some point something happens which makes it appropriate, and it's used. And when it's used, it's the controlling device, i.e., there is no way of excluding its operation when it is relevant.
>
> (Sacks 1992 I: 314)

Moreover, the participants' *mutual* orientation to the group therapy or seminar device as constituting an omni-relevant device is key. The priorities that some participants, "located via the 'omni-relevant device'" – the "therapist" or the "teacher" – set need to be ratified by other participants, "located via" this same device – the "patients" or the "students" – at every other following occasion (Sacks 1992 I: 313–314). Sacks makes his point about the priority character of insertable sequences "even more exquisite" by showing that, in the transcribed extract, "'the therapist' [is] actually only hinting at the 'session's' closure, and one of the more experienced patients [is] interpreting that hint for a new patient." (see Schegloff's introduction in Sacks 1992 I: lvi).

Sacks concludes his discussions of "inserted sequences" by pointing out two additional things (Sacks 1992 I: 315). The first is that evidence of the omni-relevance of one membership categorisation device does not rule out the existence of other devices, such as "adult"/"teenager", that are omni-relevant for the same setting (Sacks 1992 I: 593). The impacts of alternative "omni-relevant devices" on the interactive organisation of some other activities occurring in the same setting thus need to be examined in their turn. The second is that other analytic methods can be used to evidence a collection's omni-relevance.

The stability of temporal or spatial indicator terms

In his lecture "Omni-relevant devices; Settinged activities; 'Indicator terms'" (1992 I: 515–522), Sacks suggests that showing members' "stable" uses of "temporal or spatial indicator" terms, such as "now", "later", "here", and so on, across a longer stretch of interaction, is another method with which the omni-relevance of a particular category collection can be evidenced (Sacks 1992 I: 520).

By "stable uses", Sacks means that an indicator term can be used on several occasions in a single course of interaction, thereby being treated as obviously referring to a single context and/or component of the context across all the uses:

> people can be producing strings of talking in which, say, "here" is occurring, and in which there seems to be no question about what it means, and it seems to be invoking something extremely similar across its uses, whatever that may be.
>
> (Sacks 1992 I: 519)

Sacks argues that the "abstractness" of indicator terms, such as "here" or "now", makes them available for referring at the same time to spatial and temporal components of a context (1992 I: 519), thus invoking "the sheer fact of the setting" – such as group therapy or a seminar or their constitutive categories, such as "therapist/patients" or "teacher/students" – without having to specify or formulate the context and/or its components on every following occasion.

In summary, in his lectures, Sacks provides researchers with three analytic methods for evidencing that participants themselves treat a collection, such as group therapy and its constitutive categories "therapist/patient", as omni-relevant and for accounting for the way members make a particular setting (context) recognisable to each other without formulating the setting "as a such-and-such" (Schegloff in Sacks 1992 I: xlix). These three methods consist of investigating (1) the "orderly" accomplishment of "inserted sequences" (Sacks 1992 I: 313–315) with which a newcomer is greeted and introduced or with which the group therapy is closed; (2) the "stable" use of "temporal and spatial indicator terms" such as "now", "later" or "here" across a longer stretch of talk (Sacks 1992 I: 462–463, 517–522); and, finally, (3) the deployment of "cover identities" – for example, "adults" and "teenagers" – which *maintain* the "partitioning" between constitutive categories of two "constant" alternative devices (Sacks 1992 I: 317, 590–96).[5]

Indicator terms and inserted sequences in a parent–child food-preparation setting

My participation in data sessions and discussions on founding papers of conversation analysis and ethnomethodology gave me several opportunities to discuss the issue of omni-relevance with regard to video extracts of parent–child interactions selected from my large video corpus featuring everyday family interactions. Inspired by my colleagues' invaluable observations and expertise (Bovet & Relieu 2014; Merlino 2018; Relieu 1994; Sormani 2014), the following analysis of parent–child food-preparation activities aims to unpack how participants' orientation to and reflexive constitution of the developmental scheme as an omni-relevant sense-making device is observable (or not) in the sequential turn-by-turn organisation of their interaction.

The following transcripts are taken from video-recordings featuring, in the one case, a mother and her two daughters making a cake (Transcripts 13.1–13.3) and, in the other, a father making a pizza with his son (Transcripts 13.4–13.7). As discussed above (third section), one analytic method of evidencing the omni-relevance of a category collection consists of demonstrating the interactants' stable use of indicator terms. An initial analysis of the transcribed recordings reveals the parents' frequent use of temporal indicators such as "d'abord/first", "maintenant/now" and "après/after" (Transcripts 13.1–13.7).

Transcript 13.1 (S2/ST2_10_00:02:55)

1 MO **alors d'abord j'vais vite séparer le::s chocolats/**
so first I'll quickly separate the::: chocolates/

Transcript 13.2 (S2/ST2_10_00:05:24)

1 MO **pis maintenant les oeufs.**
and now the eggs.

Transcript 13.3 (S2/ST2_10_00:08:14)

1 MO **alors maint'nant on va rajouter le lait**
so now we are going to add the milk

Transcript 13.4 (St3_07_ 00:04:59)

1 FA **alor:s (0.4) tout d'abord (1.3) on va faire la sauce**
so (0.4) first of all (1.3) we're making the sauce\

Transcript 13.5 (St3_07_ 00:08:35)

1 FA **maintenant on va mettre de l'ail.**
now we're going to put some garlic in.

Transcript 13.6 (St3_07_ 00:13:25)

1 FA **après il faut couper l'jambon encore.**
after we have to cut the ham also.

First, we can see that the parents' uses of "indicator terms" (Transcripts 13.1–13.6) are followed by their formulation of a food-preparation activity (Transcripts 13.1, 13.3–6) and/or of an ingredient (Transcripts 13.1–13.6). Second, the indicator terms are preceded (Transcripts 13.1–13.4) or followed (Transcript 13.6) by a particle "pis/and", "alors/so" or "encore/also" that the speaker uses to indicate that the turn is intrinsically related to what precedes and/or follows. Third, their use can be characterised as "stable" over a longer stretch of interaction as they systematically relate to an orderly unfolding of the process of making a cake (Transcripts 13.1–13.3) or a pizza (Transcripts 13.4–13.6). Fourth, it is systematically the parent who deploys the indicator terms. For reasons of space, the children's responses to their parents' invocations of indicator terms are not included in the above transcripts. As a result, my word with respect to this last point must suffice. The parents' stable use of indicator terms is never problematised or otherwise questioned by the co-present children; instead, they align with the sequential orderliness of the food-preparation process established by their parents' utterances, making an epistemic asymmetry between the two interactants available: the leading "expert cook" (the parent) sets the pace of the food-preparation activity, and the "assistant cook" (the young child) systematically aligns with the course of action established by the parent's invocation of indicator terms.

In summary, adopting Sacks's first method to evidence the omni-relevance of a category collection reveals that parents and children treat the collection "making a cake" (Transcripts 13.1–13.3) and "a pizza" (Transcripts 13.4–13.6) as an omni-relevant device for organising their food-preparation activities. With their stable interactive organisation of indicator terms, the participants display their orientation to the "food-preparation device" as implying an asymmetric relationship between the two constitutive categories – "expert cook" and "assistant cook" – that is characteristic of the developmental scheme device. Applying Sacks's second analytic method to test the omni-relevance of membership categorisation devices – the analysis of inserted sequences – will further nuance this observation.

The insertion of a pedagogical sequence in a parent–child food-preparation activity

In the following transcript (13.7), after finishing the sauce for the pizza (see Transcript 13.4 above), the father turns to the fridge to get the next ingredient and begins an utterance with the indicator term "now" (2), while the boy observes him silently (1). However, what follows the "now" takes a different form from what has been discussed so far.

In contrast to Transcripts 13.1–13.6, in which the indicator term is followed by a straightforward announcement of the next food-preparation activity or ingredient, in this transcript (13.7), the term is followed by a request that the father addresses to the boy (2). The request accomplishes two things at the same time. First, it asks the boy to name the next relevant ingredient for the pizza-making process. As such, it makes the omni-relevance of the food-preparation device available once more. Second, as we will see, it also launches a three-part pedagogical sequence (Tarplee 2010), which places the speaker and the recipient in two specific categories of the developmental scheme: "competent *natural language user*" versus "not-yet-fully competent *natural language user*" (see Watson 1997 on "turn-generated categories").

Transcript 13.7 (St3_07_ 00:10:34)

13.1

13.2

1		**(0.2)*(0.9)*(0.4)**
	fa	<<stands in front of fridge, looks for ingredient->
	el	<<stands on chair oriented to FA, monitors FA->
2	**FA**	***main'nan#t on met quoi Elio*?**
		now we put what Elio?
	fig	**#figure 13.1**
3		**(0.2)%(0.3)**
	el	%..........->
4	**EL**	**fazza%*ll+ieu: (0.2) %epfelletala#%**
		fazzallieu: (0.2) epfelletala
	fig	**#figure 13.2**
	el	....>%rh: points twds FA%follows FA's movement%
	fa	->*rh: grasps, holds mozzarella, shakes it->
	fa	+turns to EL approaches twds him->
5		**(%0.3)**
	el	%transforms pointing into reaching->

13.3

13.4

6 FA **quo#i:+?**
what?
fig **#figure 13.3**
fa +stands still in front of EL->
7 EL **+azzel%le#**
azzelle
fig **#figure 13.4**
el ->%rh: grasps mozzarella, directs it downwards->
8 **(0.3)**
9 FA **la mozzarelle.**
the mozzarella.

13.5

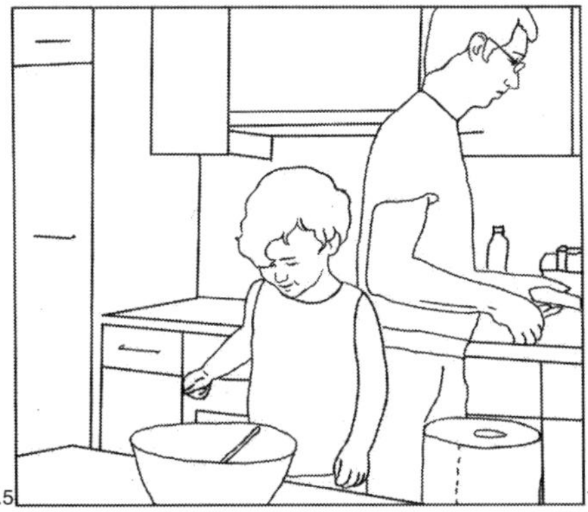
13.6

10 **(0.1)*%(0.5)+%#(0.5)**
fig **#figure 13.5**
fa *rh: directs mozzarella downwards->
el ->%rh: looses contact with mozzarella%
fa ->+moves to sink->
11 EL **>azzalle/<**
>azzalla/<
12 **#(0.2)£*+(0.2)***
fig **#figure 13.6**
el £looks down, at tomato sauce->
fa *lh: puts mozzarella down on sink*
fa +turns, moves back to table->>
13 EL **%pas lalelle=**
not lalelle=
el %rh: down->>
14 FA **=alors vie£ns**
=so then come
el £turns towards FA->>

During the silence (3) following the father's request (2), the boy identifies the target object in an embodied way (Mondada 2009: 334) by pointing to it with his right hand (Figure 13.2) and then grants his father's request by producing two words (4). Whereas the first word phonetically resembles the target word "mozzarella", the second one is difficult to identify as similar to this target word. At the same moment that the boy utters his first word (4), the father turns and walks towards him, directs the white package, which he holds in his hand, into the boy's field of vision and further highlights its relevance in an embodied way, shaking it slightly, while the boy produces the second word. The father thus deploys multiple embodied resources, which are usually used to pursue a response when the projected response is not forthcoming or is treated as unsatisfactory (Keel 2015). Interestingly, the boy interprets his father's behaviour as a giving gesture, transforming his own pointing (Figure 13.2) into a reaching and grasping gesture (Figure 13.4), thus orienting to the progression of the pizza-making process.

However, standing in front of the boy and looking at him, the father resists his grasping, thus pursuing the pedagogical inserted sequence instead of prioritising the food-preparation process. The father keeps the mozzarella in his hand and, uttering "what?" (6) with a rising intonation, asks the boy to give the production of the target item another go. This type of "open-class other-initiation" of correction leaves it to the recipient to find out what needs to be fixed and accomplish the actual correction (see Corrin 2010: 40). Immediately after its occurrence, Elio produces a corrected repetition of the first word of his initial response, deploying a falling intonation, "azzelle\", while grasping the mozzarella (7; Figure 13.4). Shortly after the boy's self-correction, the father responds with an other-correction, highlighting the target item. At the same time, he deploys a closing intonation: "the *mozzarella*." (9). Although the father's other-correction induces the child to produce another self-correction (11) and thus to continue practising the correct production of the target lexical, the child's accomplishment is not further followed up by the father. Instead, he prioritises the progress of the pizza-making process, turning towards the sink, putting the mozzarella down (Figure 13.6) and using an imperative to get the boy to join in the new course of action in line 14. The father thus closes the inserted pedagogical sequence and is followed by the boy, who grants his request by turning towards his father and allowing himself to be placed on a high chair so that he can chop the mozzarella (omitted from the transcription for reasons of space).

Analysing the interactive accomplishment of an inserted pedagogical sequence in detail makes it possible to evidence the omni-relevance of the developmental scheme in a more nuanced way. First, and most importantly for the discussion on omni-relevance, its interactive organisation shows that the omni-relevance of the developmental scheme needs to be accomplished locally and interactively, turn by turn. Second, its interactive realisation as an opportunity to teach the correct pronunciation of a word makes the interactive constitution of two *specific* categories of the developmental scheme available for inspection: "not-yet-fully competent natural language user" versus "competent natural language user".

Discussion

In this chapter, I focus on the "respecification of socialisation" as discussed by Garfinkel et al. (1982) and the notion of omni-relevance as introduced by Sacks in his lectures on group therapy (1992 I: 312–319, 515–522, 590–596). Using transcripts taken from recordings of parent–child food-preparation interactions, I argue that, independently of its omni-relevance, the orientation to and constitution of the developmental scheme must be analysed as a fundamentally local and interactive process. My analysis of Transcripts 13.1–13.6 shows that focusing on participants' use of indicator terms not only makes available the omni-relevance of a "food-preparation device", referring to the temporal orderliness of the process, but also reveals an orientation to this device as implying an asymmetric relationship between its constitutive categories: "expert cook" (parent) and "assistant cook" (child). However, I further argue that *in contrast* to Transcript 13.7, what seems at stake for the interactants in Transcripts 13.1–13.6 relates mainly and for all practical purposes to the orderly progression of food preparation rather than to its asymmetric dimension. In contrast, my detailed examination of Transcript 13.7 shows that launching and accomplishing a pedagogical labelling sequence in the middle of a food-preparation activity, which makes the developmental scheme relevant in a very particular way, not only requires the father to make the targeted object locally relevant at the beginning of the sequence, and so on, but also requires the boy to recognise that its accomplishment involves a (brief) pause in the food-preparation process to practise the correct production of a specific target word, rather than moving right on to preparing the next ingredient.

In this sense, taking the omni-relevance of the developmental scheme for granted would preclude recognising what specific constraints its interactive accomplishment involves and what its socialisation target consists of. Acknowledging the radical *gestalt switch* (Watson 1994: 177) involved in Garfinkel et al.'s working conjecture (1982) and in Sacks's (1992 I) proposal to test omni-relevance of "category collections" by contributing to a systematic analysis of participants' orientation to and constitution of the developmental scheme device has proven to be a productive way to better understand parent–child and everyday family interactions and these participants' pervasive accomplishment of specific socialisation practices.

Notes

1 Most notably, Sacks's lectures on a story fragment by a 3-year-old girl – "The baby cried. The mommy picked it up" – given in fall 1965 and spring 1966 (Sacks 1992 I: 223–266) and published as a paper in 1972; his lecture on the "Inference making machine" given in fall 1964 (Sacks 1992 I: 113–126) and published as a paper in 1985; and his lecture "Button button who's got the button", given in spring 1966 (Sacks 1992 I: 363–370) and published as a paper in 1982.

2 This unpublished research project, authored by Garfinkel, Girton, Livingston and Sacks (hereafter Garfinkel et al. 1982) was written after Sacks's death in 1975. However, it is essentially based on the lectures and oral presentations on children's interactions with others that Sacks gave in the 1960s, but which were only published much later (1972, 1982, 1985, 1992 I & II; see Garfinkel et al. 1982: 6).

3 The book *Participation et asymétries dans l'interaction institutionnelle* (Mondada & Keel 2017a, 2017b) addresses the embodied organisation of asymmetric interactions,

focusing on three distinct institutional settings: medical, political and business (Keel 2017; Mondada & Keel 2017a, 2017b).

4 Why the "omni-relevance" of the "developmental scheme" remains underexamined not only in conventional sociology and psychology but also in EMCA studies on parent/adult–child interactions is probably due to what Sidnell calls "the developmentalist hegemony", which is not only "pervasive but also naturalised and deeply entrenched in our ordinary and scholarly ways of thinking" (Sidnell 2010: 107).

5 For reasons of space, I will not be able to discuss this third method further here (but see Sacks 1992 I: 316–329, 590–596, and Schegloff's introduction in Sacks 1992 I: xix–xx).

References

Bovet, A., Gonzalez Martinez, E., & Malbois, F. (Eds.). (2014). *Langage, activités et ordre social*. Bern: Peter Lang.

Bovet, A., & Relieu, M. (2014). Assembling the collective experience of a serious game mediation as an interactional practice. Human–computer interaction. *Applications and Services Lecture Notes in Computer Science*, 8512, 571–580.

Butler, C. W., & Fitzgerald, R. (2010). Membership-in-action: Operative identities in a family meal. *Journal of Pragmatics*, 42, 2462–2474.

Butler, C. W., & Wilkinson, R. (2013). Mobilising recipiency: Child participation and "rights to speak" in mutli-party family interaction. *Journal of Pragamatics*, 50, 37–51.

Corrin, J. (2010). Hm? What? Maternal repair and early child talk. In H. Gardner & M. Forrester (Eds.), *Ethnomethodology and Adult-Child Conversation: Whose Development?* (pp. 23–41). Chichester, UK: John Wiley.

Cromdal, J. (2006). Socialization. In K. Brown (Ed.), *Encyclopedia of Language and Linguistics* (2nd ed., pp. 462–465). North-Holland: Elsevier.

Filipi, A. (2009). *Toddler and Parent Interaction: The Organisation of Gaze, Pointing, and Vocalisation*. Amsterdam/Philadelphia: John Benjamins.

Forrester, M. (2008). The emergence of self-repair: A case study of one child during the early preschool years. *Research on Language and Social Interaction*, 41(1), 99–128.

Forrester, M., & Cherington, S. M. (2009). The development of other-related conversational skills: A case study of conversational repair during the early years. *First Language*, 29(2), 166–191.

Forrester, M. A. (2013). Mutual adaptation in parent–child interaction: Learning how to produce questions and answers. *Interaction Studies*, 14(2), 190–211.

Forrester, M. A. (2017). Participation and engagement. Some possible challenges for research on early social interaction. *Research on Children and Social Interaction*, 1(1), 55–76.

Garfinkel, H., Girton, G., Livingston, E., & Sacks, H. (1982). *Studies of Kids' Culture and Kids' Talk*. Los Angeles: unpublished research project, University of California.

Keel, S. (2011). The parents' questioning repeats in response to young children's evaluative turns. *Gesprächsforschung*, 12(11), 52–94.

Keel, S. (2014). Des adultes et des enfants en situation d'interaction. Redécouvrir la socialisation. In A. Bovet, E. Gonzalez-Martinez, & F. Malbois (Eds.), *Langage, activités et ordre social. Faire de la sociologie avec Harvey Sacks* (pp. 139–163). Bern: Peter Lang.

Keel, S. (2015). Young children's embodied pursuits of a response to their initial assessments. *Journal of Pragmatics*, 75, 1–24.

Keel, S. (2016). *Socialization: Parent–Child Interaction in Everyday Life*. London: Routledge.

Keel, S. (2017). "Moi, j'aurais en tout cas pas voulu …": La participation du patient à la planification de sa sortie d'une clinique de réadaptation. In L. Mondada & S. Keel (Eds.), *Participation et asymétries dans l'interaction institutionnelle* (pp. 95–128). Paris: L'Harmattan.

Kidwell, M. (2005). Gaze as social control: How very young children differentiate "the look" from a "mere look" by their adult caregivers. *Research on Language and Social Interaction*, 38(4), 417–449.

Kidwell, M. (2009). Gaze shift as an interactional resource for very young children. *Discourse Processes*, 46(2), 145–160.

Kidwell, M. (2011). Epistemics and embodiment in the interactions of very young children. In T. Stivers, L. Mondada, & J. Steensig (Eds.), *The Morality of Knowledge in Conversation* (pp. 257–282). Cambridge: Cambridge University Press.

Kidwell, M., & Zimmerman, D. (2006). "Observability" in the interactions of very young children. *Communication Monographs*, 73(1), 1–28.

Laakso, M., & Soininen, M. (2010). Mother-initiated repair sequences in interactions of 3-year-old children. *First Language*, 30, 329–353.

Mackay, R. (1975). Conceptions and models of socialization. In R. Turner (Ed.), *Ethnomethodology* (pp. 180–193). Harmondsworth: Penguin Books.

Merlino, S. (2018). Assisting the client in aphasia speech therapy: A sequential and multimodal analysis of cuing practices. *Hacettepe University Journal of Education*, 33(Special Issue), 334–357.

Mondada, L. (2009). The embodied and negotiated production of assessments in instructed actions. *Research on Language & Social Interaction*, 42(4), 329–361.

Mondada, L. (2018). Multiple temporalities of language and body in interaction. Challenges for transcribing multimodality. *Research in Language and Social Interaction*, 51, 85–106.

Mondada, L., & Keel, S. (Eds.). (2017a). *Participation et asymétries dans l'interaction institutionnelle*. Paris: L'Harmattan.

Mondada, L., & Keel, S. (2017b). Introduction: Participation et asymétries dans l'interaction institutionnelle. In L. Mondada & S. Keel (Eds.), *Participation et asymétries dans l'interaction institutionnelle* (pp. 9–48). Paris: L'Harmattan.

Pomerantz, A. (1975). *Second Assessments: A Study of Some Features of Agreements/Disagreements*. Unpublished PhD, University of California, Irvine.

Pomerantz, A. (1984). Agreeing and disagreeing with assessments: Some features of preferred/dispreferred turn shapes. In M. Atkinson & J. Heritage (Eds.), *Structures of Social Action: Studies in Conversation Analysis* (pp. 57–101). Cambridge: Cambridge University Press.

Relieu, M. (1994). Les catégories dans l'action. In B. Fradin, L. O. Quéré, & J. Widmer (Eds.), *L'enquête sur les catégories. De Durkheim à Sacks* (pp. 185–218). Paris: Editions de l'école des hautes études en sciences sociales.

Sacks, H. (1972). On the analyzability of stories by children. In J. J. Gumperz & D. Hymes (Eds.), *Directions in Sociolinguistics* (pp. 325–345). New York: Holt Rinehart & Winston.

Sacks, H. (1982). Button button who's got the button. *Sociological Inquiry*, 50(3–4), 318–327.

Sacks, H. (1985). The inference-making machine: Notes on observability. In T. A. van Dijk (Ed.), *A Handbook of Discourse Analysis. Vol. III: Discourse and Dialogue* (pp. 13–22). London: Academic Press.

Sacks, H. (1992). *Lectures on Conversation* (Vols. I & II). Oxford: Blackwell.

Sidnell, J. (2010). Questioning repeats in the talk of four-year-old children. In H. Gardner & M. Forrester (Eds.), *Analysing Interactions in Childhood Insights from Conversation Analysis* (pp. 103–127). Chichester, UK: Wiley-Blackwell.

Sormani, P. (2014). *Respecifying Lab Ethnography. An Ethnomethodological Study of Experimental Physics*. Surrey, UK: Ashgate.

Speier, M. (1971). The everyday world of the child. In J. D. Douglas (Ed.), *Understanding Everyday Life: Toward a Reconstruction of Sociological Knowledge* (pp. 188–217). London: Routledge & Kegan Paul.

Speier, M. (1976). The child as conversationalist: Some culture contact features of conversational interactions between adults and children. In M. Hammersley & P. Woods (Eds.), *The Process of Schooling: A Sociological Reader* (pp. 98–103). London: Routledge & Kegan Paul.

Tarplee, C. (2010). Next turn and intersubjectivity in children's language acquisition. In H. Gardner & M. Forrester (Eds.), *Analysing Interactions in Childhood Insights from Conversation Analysis* (pp. 3–23). Chichester, UK: Wiley-Blackwell.

Walker, G. (2017). Young children's use of laughter as a means of responding to questions. *Journal of Pragamatics*, 112, 20–32.

Watson, R. (1992). Ethnometodology, conversation analysis and education: An overview. *International Review of Education*, 38(3), 257–274.

Watson, R. (1994). Harvey Sacks's sociology of mind in action. *Theory, Culture & Society*, 11, 169–186.

Watson, R. (1997). Some general reflections on categorization and sequence in the analysis of conversation. In S. Hester & P. Eglin (Eds.), *Culture in Action: Studies in Membership Categorization Analysis* (pp. 49–76). Washington, DC: University Press of America.

Wootton, A. J. (1981). The management of grantings and rejections by parents in request sequences. *Semiotica*, 37(1/2), 59–89.

Wootton, A. J. (1997). *Interaction and the Development of Mind*. Cambridge: Cambridge University Press.

Wootton, A. J. (2006). Two request forms of four year old. In P. Drew & J. Heritage (Eds.), *Conversation Analysis, Volume III, Turn Design and Action Formation* (pp. 103–116). London: Sage.

Wootton, A. J. (2007). A puzzle about please: Repair, increments, and related matters in the speech of a young child. *Research on Language and Social Interaction*, 40(2), 171–198.

Wootton, A. J. (2010). "Actually" and the sequential skills of a two-year-old. In H. Gardner & M. Forrester (Eds.), *Analysing Interactions in Childhood Insights from Conversation Analysis* (pp. 59–73). Chichester, UK: Wiley-Blackwell.

14 Sacks and the study of the local organization of second language lessons[1]

Ricardo Moutinho

This chapter builds on the work of Harvey Sacks to discuss how his contributions have influenced my research on second language (L2) classroom interaction and how this influence can be meaningful to the study of talk in educational settings. This discussion will be based on the emphasis Sacks always placed, in his lectures and articles, upon the importance of looking at the data in an unmotivated way or, as he himself would put, to let the materials 'fall as they may' (Sacks, 1995, vol. 1, p. 11). Because Sacks studied talk as an actual instance of our everyday practices, my aim here is to show how his influences made me look at classroom talk as a 'lived work' practice, which is carried out by members (not by analysts). To start, I will explore some of Sacks's ideas on context formulation and then explicate (through the analysis of a short excerpt) how members in an L2 class contextualize activities based on the categorial relationship they invoke.

One of the central discussions by Sacks is his observations on context, in particular in relation to data gathered from institutional settings. In his considerations in 'On Formulating Context' (1976),[2] Sacks points us towards an analytic understanding of how people establish relationships among participants in a setting and produce/define the context for their interaction. Sacks's observations, drawing on Garfinkel's (1967) notion of indexicality, place the definitional privilege of context onto the members engaged in any particular action or event. The emphasis then is to look at how participants provide context formulations/definitions for what they are engaged in. For example, within a setting such as a language class, there are activities done that are made relevant within the ongoing interaction of members in the setting. For members and participants within the setting, the categorization work made operative or invoked by them provides for what is done, and by whom, within the flow of social actions over the course of the lesson. Taking this on board, it is then possible to consider not only how people engage in a setting, but that their actions are oriented to contextual relevancies for the actions they are engaged in.

Part of the interactional work relies on participants' common-sense knowledge and competencies in relation to membership categories and how these are ongoingly configured and enacted within a setting. For example, when people are in a language class (or any other kind of social encounter), they are engaging both in a setting and in making that lesson happen (Payne, 1976), and they can display their orientation to the setting without necessarily having to specify or formulate it out loud (Sacks, 1976). That is, they can perfectly propose different activities without having to say: 'Now, we're going to do X'. However, despite not necessarily having to specify the context, they cannot, according to Sacks, engage in a 'merely-non-consequentially, non-methodically, non-alternatively' context (Sacks, 1976, p. F8). When participants engage in a setting, there are always consequences and some 'analyzable basis' for them to differentiate from another possible formulation, even without a necessary invocation. In other words, it is exclusively a member's concern and task to formulate what the context of a given speech encounter is. They do so by constantly repairing the essential indexicality of words and conduct through the use of particularization procedures and other methods. So, what matters for Sacks was how members themselves orient toward the context which they are in and the methods they are using in the process of producing it.

This means that, although people do not necessarily formulate context verbatim, they do establish relevant memberships and orient to the situational relevancies of the categories in this setting. Moreover, categories once established are not static, as the interactional tasks unfold, and participants are able to invoke, re-invoke or replace relevant categories made operative at any particular time. For Sacks, 'context' was the competence people bring and conjointly use to establish (and orient to) the relevant memberships invoked in the course of an interaction. This contextual apparatus was referred to as a membership categorization device (Sacks, 1995). This term points to the way members use methods to routinely and necessarily categorize people and conduct around them as they encounter situations. According to Sacks (1976), categorization phenomena can give us some analytic purchase on studying how participants invoke orderliness, without having to formulate the terms of that orderliness (i.e., who they are and what they are doing at that moment). The discussion below will explore how Sacks's ideas on membership categorization have influenced my studies of classroom data, and especially the ongoing contextual orientations in classroom activities.

Categories in context in classroom activities

Taking the idea of membership into consideration, Sacks proposed that some categories members invoke are *omni-relevant* (Sacks, 1976, 1995) – that is, members may orient to certain actions (or predicates) as being appropriately done by an omni-relevant category. During a classroom encounter, for example, 'teacher' is an omni-relevant category,[3] as the actions carried out by this member (teacher) are 'expectable' to happen in a classroom setting and, as such, constitute a 'default' orientation involved in the formulation of a specific context.

In other words, members recognize actions (especially utterances) that have priority to get done (Sacks, 1976), and they associate these activities with specific categories. So, for example, in a classroom setting, the utterance ‘Let’s open the book to page 45’ is an utterance/activity that has priority of use as it is done by reference to an ‘always-relevant’ category in that setting, teacher (Payne, 1976). Then, if the category ‘teacher’ is made relevant in a classroom setting, there is no way to exclude its operation (Sacks, 1976). Although this category can be temporarily ‘defeased’ or ‘put aside’ (as the simple fact that the participants are in a classroom does not mean they are always operating under the aegis of the same categories), ‘teacher’ can be invoked again at any next point during the course of the talk produced in that setting. A related category in this omni-relevant device is the category ‘student’, as it can also be invoked as a relational pair (‘teacher–student’) in the setting of classroom or teaching activities.[4]

Following Sacks (1976), the ways activities get run off can exhibit some categorization via devices that handle what is going on. These membership categorization devices are usually formed by a set of paired categories such as teacher–student. This means that categories are rarely invoked alone because, when they are invoked, they establish a relationship with other categories that are present in that setting.

Categories occur in any natural setting, and one does not need to look for specific moments in the interaction to analyze these phenomena. The simple use of a pronoun in natural conversation, such as ‘I’ or ‘you’, is done by reference to a certain category that the member is invoking (Watson, 1987). But these categorizations are not fixed: their meaning is produced in situ and occasioned for the action in the setting. For this reason, each occurrence is only valid for that specific moment that is being analyzed, for a particular situation and its ‘haecceities’ – that is, the ‘what it is’ of the ordinary, ongoing order produced by members and their actions.

Based on this, we can then take it that, although naturalistic data may seem disorganized and ‘fuzzy’, there is an order in all situations, and what we have to do (as analysts) is to find out how members are producing it.

By looking at order we can also see how people use the resources of a culture, and more specifically a ‘culture-in-action’ (Hester and Eglin, 1997). Consequently, we can also assume that, although we are looking at single situations, we are also looking at how people produce order and, in so doing, we are looking at how the world is seen to operate. Sacks (1984, p. 22) makes this point very clear:

> That sort of order would be an important resource of a culture, such that, for example, any members of the culture, encountering from their infancy a very small portion of it, and a random portion in a way (the parents they happen to have, the experiences they happen to have, the vocabulary that happens to be thrown at them in whatever utterances they happen to encounter), would come out in many ways much like everybody else and able to deal with just about anyone else. Were it important for nature to

ensure that if persons are to be workable things in a society they have an adequate sampling setup, then a culture might well be so arranged. And then, of course, research might employ the same resources: Tap into whomsoever, wheresoever, and we get much the same things.

Below, I discuss an example exploring the methods/resources people use to find and produce order with data taken from a class where an L2 (Portuguese) is being taught to Chinese students. The data were generated in the fifth meeting of the semester in a first-grade primary school in Macau, which has Portuguese as a second language in its curriculum.

Analyzing categories invoked by classroom participants

Transcript 14.1 depicts a moment in which the teacher starts using a pig-shaped glove puppet during one of the lessons, referred to in the analysis as 'Piggy'. What is of interest is how members orient to this new activity through the categorization work that they produce as the interaction unfolds. The analysis examines how children do the complicated work of formulating what is going on when the new participant, Piggy, joins in.

Transcript 14.1

13. Piggy	sim(.)olá:
	yes(.)hello:
14.	(1,0)
15. Ss	olá:
	helo:
16. Piggy	hoje eu vou apresentar(.)algumas(.)ah expressões
	today I'll introduce(.) some (.)ah expressions
17.	教 你 一 滴 句 子 哦 (1,0) 好 啦 (.) 好 啦
	gaau nei jat di geoi zi o (1,0) hou la (.) how la
	teach you some expressions(1,0) okay (.)okay
18.	知 唔 知 道 哩 张 图 画 讲 咩 啊?
	zi m zi dou lei zoeng tou wa gong me a?
	do you know what this picture means?
19. Ss	知 啊
	zi a
	I know it
20. T	知 咩?(.) 听 下 先
	zi me?(.) teng ha <u>sin</u>
	do you?(.)let's listen
21. Ss	((wait in silence whilst the teacher prepares the audio))

Sacks proposed that some activities are category-bound, and the way conversationalists categorize utterances is tremendously varied. As Sacks (1995, Vol.1,

p. 180) puts it, 'if somebody knows an activity has been done, and there is a category to which it is bound, they can damn well propose that its been done by such a one who is a member of that category'. In Transcript 14.1, we can see classroom phenomena taking place and participants engaging in an activity as an organized group. As in any social, organized event, the participants understand and recognize each other's actions and make sense of what is going on in the classroom interactive space. This organization makes the utterances flow as a logical sequence, and the participants categorize each utterance as belonging to a member of that setting. In other words, they know what is being talked and who is talking what.

However, as Sacks (1979, p. 13; 1995, Vol.1, p. 41) recognizes, in dealing with categories, we are not necessarily dealing with 'groups' or 'organized groups'. For example, the fact that we have an organized group does not mean that people in that group cannot apply the knowledge stored about a specific category to other participants who are not members of that group. We can see this in the extract above, where there seems to be a new challenge to the participants involved in this enterprise of identifying utterances as belonging to a certain category. A new participant (a 'proxy' member), Piggy joins in, and this has a number of consequences for the ongoing interaction. First, 'what kind of member' is the puppet?

In the sequence in Transcript 14.1, we can see how the puppet is introduced, and the way it is introduced tells us a lot about how the other participants categorize it. When the puppet is animated by the teacher at line 16, she uses the term 'hoje' ('*today*') at the beginning of this sequence, which was uttered in Portuguese at 16: 'hoje eu vou apresentar(.)algumas(.)ah expressões' ('*today I'll introduce(.)some (.)ah expressions*'). Here, the term 'hoje' is used as a marker towards which participants will then orient their actions in the ongoing development of the sequence. The use of this marker at the beginning of the sequence – 'today' in 'today I'll …' – brings the idea that a new activity of the day will take place. Looking again at the sequence – *today I'll introduce(.)some (.)ah expressions* – it is possible to see the kind of activity in which the students will be engaged. But not only this. It is also possible to see that this utterance was 'produced' by Piggy – that is, the puppet that was being animated by the teacher. One may, of course, be familiar with the use of puppetry as a routine technique teachers use to attract children's attention. It is, however, how these activities get done in detail that is of analytic interest and that draws on Sacks's ideas. For example, the puppet (at line 16), when using 'eu' (meaning 'I') in 'hoje eu vou apresentar …' (today I'll introduce …) as opposed to 'you' provides the combination of these two pronouns as 'interactionally paired' terms. This can be heard as referring to the affiliations or categorizations the participants are invoking while the puppet is being animated by the teacher. The pronoun 'eu' is associated with the puppet, who is going to introduce (or 'teach', as is said in line 17 in Cantonese: 'gaau') the students ('you', as also depicted at line 17 in Cantonese: 'nei') to some expressions. The relationship established between 'eu' (line 16) and 'nei' (line 17) refers to a pair of membership categories, a 'relational or categorial pair', which can be heard in this classroom situation as the pair teacher–student. However, as the teacher is animating a puppet (Piggy) in this sequence, one can see that this relationship is much more complex than that.

The sequence shows that the puppet will be used to work on a lesson topic with the students, which is [introducing new expressions in the target language]. The use of square brackets for the lesson topic is deliberate for the purposes of the analysis. The puppet is not only used as an instrument, it is a proxy member in that cohort who can be employed to partition out a particular activity as category-bound. Piggy is supposed to introduce (line 16) and teach (line 17) some expressions in the target language. In other words, Piggy will act as a teacher and also be used to partition out one categorization over any other. All the students can see that a puppet is talking (even if it is 'being talked' by the teacher). For all practical purposes, this complex relational pair can be heard, instead of as teacher–student, as 'puppet-as-categorized(by proxy)–student'. To make things simpler, however, I will use the term 'proxy–student' to refer to this complex categorial pair.

This configuration becomes clear if we look at the extract from the very beginning, at the moment when the puppet is introduced. Looking at the first utterance of this sequence (line 13), we will see how this new categorial pair (proxy–student) makes sense. At that line, the puppet greets the students with a recognized popular term in Portuguese ('Olá', meaning 'hello'). After some hesitation (line 14), the students reply to the greeting by repeating the same word at line 15. In replying to the greeting, the students can be heard to be producing an identifiable categorization that the one who is talking is the proxy-as-enacted-by-the-teacher, and not the teacher alone. The reason for this is, arguably, that it would not make sense if the teacher greeted the students by saying 'olá' ('hello') in the middle of the class. As Sacks (1995, Vol. 2, p. 534), notes, greetings 'can only go in some places in a conversation, i.e., their positioning is *restricted*' (emphasis in the original). So this adjacency pair ('olá–olá') only makes sense if it is produced by parties that are meeting for the first time during this event – that is, this lesson period. Licoppe (this collection) shows how greetings can occur in 'unusual' places when a new appearance happens – that is, when participants get oriented to the initiation of a new encounter, making the production of a greeting a conditionally relevant move. Thus, this 'olá' (line 13) could not have been produced by the teacher alone, but by the teacher's proxy, the puppet, who was joining in.

As the sequence develops, however, we can see the category 'proxy' is slowly being put aside. In lines 16 and 17, the puppet can be heard providing instructions about what will happen, as any teacher might normally do. As the sequence develops, we have more evidence of this relationship, which I will mention only briefly and return to later for a finer-tuned analysis. We can see at line 18 that the puppet starts to check comprehension, asking the students if they know how to identify (in the target language) what is being shown on a picture fastened on the board. After receiving a joint 'I know it' (line 19) from the students, the interlocutor does not give them the floor to answer, but plays the audio first so that the students can hear the answer in advance. All these steps show that the members are slightly moving away from the relational pair proxy–student to the 'omni-relevant' one, teacher–student.

Sacks (1995, Vol. 1, p. 180) states that, 'one of the ways one goes about making a problematic position accounted for is, for instance, to assign some category to its sayer'. He goes on to say: 'the category is, of course, important, because there can be some categories that are, for example, the categories of persons who are entitled to say such a thing' (1995, Vol.1, p. 180). In thinking of classrooms as places where members produce, recognize, and make sense of events that happen in that social encounter, what is being said and who is saying what require a great effort from the students, as they need to concentrate on the organization of the utterances to follow the sequence of events. And students show themselves to be very competent in this enterprise. How they do that is shown below in more detail.

At line 20, '*zi me? Teng ha sin*' ('do you? Let's listen') is heard as being spoken by the teacher, not Piggy. 'Let's listen' is a category-bound utterance that represents a command, usually uttered by someone who is in charge of the class, which in turn switches the focus of the interaction. Also note how the teacher stresses the last syllable of the expression '*teng ha sin*' ('let's listen'), changing the soft pitch she was using while animating the puppet. As a response, the students keep silent and wait for the teacher to play the audio to hear the correct answer (line 21). This is a method used during the previous lessons, and the participants are organized in a way that they recognize this method as a phenomenon of order, a technique that proves that they know how to interact in that situation. Here, however, we can ponder an interesting question: if the teacher was animating the puppet to conduct the class for a period of time, could she keep performing this move in the same way until the end? What I mean here is that commands such as 'Let's listen' (with a rising pitch in the end) are not types of methods that teachers frequently use when animating puppets. These commands are more hearable as belonging to a category that is visibly competent in that context to direct commands and manage the next steps of the interaction. As Sacks (1976, p. G6) puts it:

> there are actions which for them to be effective, need to be formulated via some particular Device. And then those actions invoke that Device. That is, the utterances which might do those actions can invoke that Device, though of course an utterance by someone who is not known, for example, to be that person, might well not do the activity: 'Who the hell do you think you are.' 'I'm So-and-So.' 'Oh excuse me.' Or whatever else.

However, the category 'teacher' is not here because 'Let's listen' is part of teacher's 'discourse', but because the hearers, who are the students, invoke categories whose actions represent predicates of a specific participant. The categories 'teacher' and 'student', then, represent a single categorization device – that is, the categorial pair teacher–student, which is always relevant throughout the interaction.

Therefore, although very complex in terms of categorization work, the teacher–student pair is what sustains the possibility of Piggy's participation, and this move does not seem to be a big problem for the students. This shows how students have competence in establishing new relationships and in recognizing classroom events as locally produced phenomena, as elements of organization that furnish the development of the sequence. The teacher did not need to mention that the puppet would be put aside to move to the other part of the activity [listening to the correct answer]. The category 'teacher' is, then, never made 'irrelevant'. Paraphrasing Sacks (1995, Vol. 1, p. 183), what occurs is good grounds for the teacher to do what she ought to do (stopping one activity and moving to the next part of the activity), and what students do is recognizing this action as category-bound, as an action belonging to the category 'teacher'.

For this reason, this is not a matter of discourse format, but a matter of agency, of competence that students showed themselves to possess in bringing off a social event. Instructions are part of the social life in any classroom, they are phenomena of order that work as a method to accomplish social tasks, rather than elements used participants just because they are in an educational setting. That is, it is not the format of the interaction that counts, but how participants make sense of what is said during the interaction and 'who' is saying it. What makes this dynamic layering of categorial pairs unproblematic to the participants is that the students are constantly working on the common-sense knowledge they have about relevant participants in the setting and themselves in relation to the ongoing categorial ordering of the setting. The sense that these participants made of the situation demonstrates this agency, that they are competent in that particular situation, even within an evolving, complex configuration that would make the interaction look 'fuzzy' to a non-competent participant – in this situation, the teacher animating a puppet and giving instructions while switching from the participants' mother tongue to a different language the students barely know. Here, the teacher orients to the potential difficulty by using the puppet, as one aspect of using this element, a 'single category' proxy, is to 'simplify' the class content for very young students.

Nonetheless, this potential simplification does not guarantee that the students will orient to this practice. As Sacks also mentions (1995, Vol. 1, p. 184; parentheses mine), 'the work of digging out what's being said is, then, the task of the hearer, and one (in this case, the teacher) can leave out what one knows the hearer has to fill in in a specific way'. But the students here do not only 'fill in a blank', because hearers do much more than that, as Sacks also argues. In this case, as mentioned before, the member who said 'Let's listen' takes the floor that was being taken by the students at line 19 and, for this reason, this could not be uttered by the proxy (the puppet). In that sense, knowing who is saying what and what action should properly follow what is being said (in this case, the silence in line 21, which shows that the students are ready for the next part of the activity) also involves a shift (even though more implicit than explicit) in the relational pair-in-operation at that moment (proxy–student), so that the other pair (teacher–student) could 're'-emerge. This shows us how teacher–student is not only observable as an omni-relevant pair, which can be re-invoked at any time in a classroom activity, but also how this is made operative, moment to moment, within the flow of the tasks. It is also interesting to note that, although the teacher is animating the puppet, it does not replace the category 'teacher'. Each category has its own predicates that become visible through the actions carried out by the participants. If the categorial pair teacher–student is shown to be omni-relevant, other categorial pairs (such as proxy–student) may be layered onto the omni-relevant one, which is shown by who gets to act as the teacher by proxy – that is, the teacher decides who gets to be the teacher. What is involved here, then, is a complex categorization work, its organization, and also what is known according to its use. This is the most complicated task the students are doing, and they seem to perform it extremely well.

Final remarks

As has been shown here, participants in a language class work together and rely on common-sense understanding of the organization of relevant categories in a sequence to understand what is said and who is saying what. And the way they do that is extremely important. It tells us a lot about how the world operates (Sacks, 1995, Vol.1, p. 185). That is, to examine how the world or society operates, it is important to look at it in its particulars in the specific interactional routine. Single occasions, such close examination, enable us to unpack and explore the cultural methods and sense-assembly techniques members use to make sense of what is happening around them and what is happening to them. My continuing interest is in the study of these methods and techniques in language educational settings, especially in environments where participants do not share the same linguistic skills (L2 classrooms). The difference in terms of language proficiency between teacher and students in these settings is evident at a first glance, but, when we examine how participants interact, we find that they share a sophisticated competence that is much more varied and versatile than their apparent linguistic skills or limitations. Sacks stated that there are 'alternative methods that persons use in going about doing whatever they have to do' (1995, Vol.1, p. 11). And, the most important thing: these methods are describable natural occurrences that may lead to more general phenomena. This 'machinery', as Sacks calls it, is worth exploring as it is tied up with the mundane abilities that participants show themselves to possess in different settings, such as in L2 classroom events.

Notes

1 This study uses data from the project 'Interactions in Portuguese as a Foreign Language classrooms and the building of contextual competence', coordinated by Roberval Teixeira e Silva (University of Macau). Many thanks to him for granting me access to his database. Special thanks are due to Richard Fitzgerald and Rod Watson

for their brilliant comments and insights on the earlier versions of this chapter. All mistakes that might persist, however, are entirely my responsibility.

2 Although with some differences in terms of data extracts and analysis, and a large discussion on 'omni-relevance' cut, a very close text is included in *Lectures on Conversation*, Volume 1, Winter 1967 (1995, pp. 515–522). I am indebted to Andrew Carlin for this key observation.

3 For recent work on omni-relevance, see, for example, Fitzgerald, Housley and Butler (2009).

4 However, 'student' is more generally invoked as a single category – as a cohort – rather than as an individual category for each pupil in a class, even in a setting where many students are present. For this matter, please see Payne and Hustler (1980).

Funding Acknowledgment

This work was supported by the Macau Science and Technology Development Fund (FDCT) grant # 0054/2019/A1.

References

Garfinkel, H. (1967). *Studies in Ethnomethodology*. Cambridge: Polity Press.

Fitzgerald, R., Housley, W., & Butler, C. W. (2009). Omnirelevance and interactional context. *Australian Journal of Communication*, 36(3): 45–64.

Hester, S., & Eglin, P. (Eds.). (1997). *Culture in Action: Studies in Membership Categorization Analysis*. Washington, DC: University Press of America.

Payne, G., & Hustler, D. (1980). Teaching the class: the practical management of a cohort. *British Journal of Sociology of Education*, 1(1): 49–66.

Payne, G. C. F. (1976). Making a lesson happen: an ethnomethodological analysis. In M. Hammersley & P. Woods (Eds.), *The Process of Schooling: A Sociological Reader*. London and Henley: Routledge & Kegan Paul with the Open University Press, pp. 33–40.

Sacks, H. (1976). On formulating context. *Pragmatics Microfiche*, 1(7): F5–G8.

Sacks, H. (1979). Hotrodder: a revolutionary category. In G. Psathas (Ed.), *Everyday Language: Studies in Ethnomethodology*. New York: Irvington Press, pp. 7–14.

Sacks, H. (1984). Notes on methodology. In J. M. Atkinson & J. Heritage (Eds.), *Structures of Social Action: Studies in Conversation Analysis*. Cambridge: Cambridge University Press, pp. 21–27.

Sacks, H. (1995). *Lectures on Conversation, Volumes I and II*. Edited by G. Jefferson with introduction by E. A. Schegloff. Oxford: Blackwell.

Watson, R. (1987). Interdisciplinary considerations in the analysis of pro-terms. In G. Button & J. R. Lee (Eds.), *Talk and Social Organisation*. Clevedon, PA: Multilingual Matters, pp. 261–289.

15 Categorisation practices, place, and perception

Doing incongruities and the commonplace scene as 'assembled activity'

Robin James Smith

My first engagement with Harvey Sacks 'in his own words' came in the form of his treatment of the 'Bullock's Department Store' story (Sacks, 1986). I was already familiar with the 'Formal Structures' paper (Garfinkel and Sacks, 1970) and had already had Sacks's methodological approach introduced to me by David Silverman (1998). Yet, as I imagine might be the case for many others, directly reading the wildly engaging and original analytic style and sensibility of Sacks was a transformative experience. I came to that piece of analysis while trying to get to grips with 'place talk' during my doctoral studies. Since then, I have become increasingly interested in the use of 'place' and 'space' categories as deployed in ordinary activities as more general organisational resources beyond their recognised, if still underdeveloped, role in talk. In this chapter, I trace something of my work on the mutually reflexive character of setting, activity, and category as it draws from, overlaps with, and develops what appears to be a continued curiosity that Sacks himself had with place terms and the categorisation of space. The curiosity surfaces across various lectures, rather than being attended to as a specific 'topic'. This is important in its own right, and I do not intend to treat 'space' and 'place' as topics here, as might a professional social scientist (Laurier, 2001). Spatial categories appear, as with other collectivities (Coulter, 1996), to be a resource for the organisation of various activities such as telling stories (this was Sacks's original interest) and a whole range of others, such as driving and cycling on the road or walking in a public space, in a way that is also bound up with the local practical accomplishment of perception. Sacks hints at this possibility in the early lecture 'On Exchanging Glances', where he describes, among other things, the seeing of an incongruity as an 'assembled activity'. He returns at various points to the 'eerie' significance (1995[I]: 758) that (available categories of) space and place seem to have for members' activities. This chapter traces that curiosity through related materials and analyses in the lectures on storytelling in which categorisations of space and place have a recurrent relevance for participants' accomplishments of possible descriptions.

What I am particularly interested in, in this chapter and in my work in general, is how the organisation and use of spatial and place categories in talk might give insights into the organisation of situated activities as they are produced/recognised in their occurrence in actual settings, rather than as described in stories and accounts. To put things another way, everything happens somewhere, and 'somewhere' is finely organised matter implication in the production/recognition[1] of action within a given gestalt contexture. The payoff of an attention to local uses of categorisations of space and place is, I suggest, that Sacks's analytic sensibility provides a means for the specification of 'context' as ongoingly, finely, locally assembled accomplishment. This might also contribute to a continued attempt to avoid decontextualisation, abstraction, and reification in the pursuit of the description of categorisation practices as members' practices located in the locally, ongoingly, produced world of members.

The girl with the pipe: glances, incongruities, and categorisation practices

The lecture on 'On Exchanging Glances' (Sacks, 1995[I]: 81–94) lays out some foundational aspects of what later becomes 'membership categorisation analysis' (henceforth MCA; see Jayyusi, 1984; Hester and Eglin, 1997a, 1997b; Housley and Fitzgerald, 2002, 2015; Hester and Francis, 2003; Stokoe, 2012; Watson, 2015) and the possible role that Sacks acknowledged for categorisation practices in the organisation of perception (for further elaboration, see Hester and Francis, 2003; Lynch, 2013; Smith, 2019). In the lecture,[2] Sacks makes two key propositions for the use of categorisation practices in the 'standardised' character of members' procedures for observing commonplace scenes and 'doing an incongruity'.

Sacks begins the lecture by discussing an observational exercise in which his students were tasked to record (by fieldnote) instances of two unacquainted persons exchanging glances about a third. They are asked to 'write down the class' of the people they observe. A student asks how they should 'know the class'. Should they ask the people observed? Sacks's response is that they should 'figure it out', insisting that they do *not* ask the observed parties who they are.[3] After some back and forth about the possibility of the task, Sacks (1995[I]: 82) provides an anecdote of the sort of thing he assumed his students would be able to see:

> I was walking down the hall the other day, to give an exam to one girl. She was standing, leaning up against the wall. In between us walks another girl. She passed this girl first, and then me. And the girl who was standing leaning against the wall looked at me and gave a shrug of her shoulders with a big smile, which I returned. And I don't think it was a big puzzle over what was going on. The girl who walked by was smoking a pipe.

The exercise was not simply identifying glances being exchanged – part of the point, after all, is that *anyone* can see it – but to consider the *possibility* and *organisation* of the observation. In other words, the analytic task is to take something 'trivially obvious' (p. 87) and aim to build a 'machinery' that gives you back your observations: the massively routine availability of the thing that is 'odd', the sharing of that observation through the shrug and the smile, and the recognisability of both the action and the relevant category of the parties doing the exchanging for the observer. Sacks proposes three core elements for consideration: the availability of the classes and the way they 'permit you to see what's there'; how members might 'know what someone else is thinking'; and, the activity with which the bulk of this chapter is concerned, the 'decomposability' of commonplace scenes.

'The classes allow you to see'

The possible and occasioned availability of the classes of the 'glancers' to the observer will be recognisable to those familiar with Sacks's work on categorisation practices and the subsequent development of MCA, and is sufficiently available elsewhere to avoid repeating here. Still, the lecture on glances provides both an early formulation of the use of categories for 'viewing' person categories, but also how categorisation practices are more diffuse. For a start, Sacks notes:

> the sorts of things you've reported suggest that what persons see is a class member, for whole collections of classes. You see 'a girl,' 'a Negro,' 'a such-and-such.' *That is, the class permits you to see what it is that's there. It permits you to see.*
>
> (1995[I]: 86; emphasis added)

The well-known point made here is that members do not see, and are not viewed as, 'individuals' but as representatives of classes and categories (Sacks, 1995[I]: 40–41). Significantly, the notion that the 'class permits you to see what it is that's there' is reformulated shortly after (following a further example from Proust, whom Sacks calls 'an incredible sociologist') as 'the classes and their categories permit you to see' (p. 87). For Proust, 'it is the explanation that opens our eyes', but, in Sacks's treatment of viewing and categorisation practices, 'knowledge' is not so much an *explanation* (that once you are given some bit of information you will view a scene differently) but is a reflexively constituted *resource*. In this sense, occasioned categorisation practices form a resource for the local organisation of knowledge in the situated viewing of a scene and the elements thereof as 'normal', 'unusual', 'deviant', and so on (see also Pollner, 1987). 'Knowing' and 'viewing' are thus emergent and intertwined properties of action. A 'viewer' thus accomplishes-in-use categorial and sequential resources to provide for what they are viewing as orderly (Sacks, 1995[I]: 260) with a preference for it to be viewed, first, as 'ordinary' (Sacks, 1984).

In the exchanging of glances and in the seeing of the classes, nothing needs to be *said* by any of the parties. Sacks was quite unconcerned with the actual *word* that the students wrote in relation to what they observed, but was concerned rather that they *could* categorise the parties observed in such a way that was procedurally relevant for the task at hand. Additionally, and as emphasised by Hester and Francis (2003), 'context' is significant in and for viewing in that any 'observer' always observes from somewhere and within some flow of ongoing activity (for example, from the car, when searching for a parking space; Laurier, 2005). Their elucidation of the 'observer's maxim' adds situatedness and context to Sacks's more disembodied and decontextualised 'viewer' and 'hearer'. To return to Sacks's own anecdote above, person categories can be seen as 'belonging together' ('professor' and 'student'), the activities can be viewed as 'bound' to those membership categories (the giving of an exam), and these 'viewings' are recognisably accomplished in and as a particular context (a university setting). The categories allow you to see. And the same, or at least very similar, practices are involved whether you where there in the hall or reading the anecdote as a 'professional text' (Watson, 2009b).

One way of taking some of these foundations forward is to treat Sacks's proposition that 'the classes and their categories permit you to see' in a literal sense. Doing so may provide for a primarily *sociological* orientation to perception-in-action that aims to specify the still problematic gloss of 'context'. As noted by Liberman (2013: 147):

> Speaking of 'context' is usually too general a way to speak about it and may only obscure the radical reflexivity that is in play. To be sure, there are 'contextual processes' but 'contexutalize' serves as a gloss for immensely detailed practical activities of speakers that remain to be identified.

How members 'contextualise' activities and, indeed, organise and display orientation to 'context' remains problematic. Drawing on Sacks's analyses, however, we might find ways to gain technical access to the methods through which 'context' is finely assembled, and disassemble-able.

The decomposability of commonplace scenes

A key practice that provides for how a glance can be an action is the question (one that Sacks claims not to have figured out) of how members 'do an incongruity'. When challenged by a student to differentiate his analysis from what Goffman had already written, Sacks (1995[I]: 92) replies: 'Goffman's told us about incongruities but not how they are done'. He goes on to suggest that he has 'the beginning of how it is that you do it'. A central component of that beginning was 'a notion that what Members' see is decomposable by them.' He goes on:

> That members can decompose some event, situation, complex, whatever you want to call it, is no surprise at all, given the sorts of things we've

> been considering. … The question then is, having taken something apart, how do they put it back together again so as to find what it is that's strange. *The way they do this involves treating something that they see as a combination of parts, some of which have names. And to those nameable parts are affiliated standardised procedures for producing those objects in some combination.*
>
> (1995[I]: 89; emphasis added)

The sense in which 'viewing' is an 'assembled activity' is significant, as is the reflexive organisation of the situated procedures for assembling and disassembling the scene and its describability. This, then, points to a particular class of activities that bear a reciprocal relation to talk, but which in no way rely upon verbalisation. The statement is also an example of Sacks's insistence on the recovery of members' practices that provide for the orderly appearances of the world. In distinguishing his approach, Sacks takes it as insufficient to simply suggest that an incongruity 'emerges' from or against some background of normal appearances – as another 'undescribed' aspect of social action. An incongruity is a 'by-product' of members' practical procedures and, as such, it is necessary to recognise that the categorial practices for 'viewing' are themselves irrevocably endogenous to the scene viewed (Watson, 2015, inter alia).

That members can and do decompose and assemble the commonplace scene in various ways, in and through routine activities, is sporadically attended to by Sacks but, as noted above, not systematically developed. The question of *how* such matters are organised in practice remains to be seen, and the empirical elusiveness of this aspect of the machinery may have been cause enough for Sacks to drop it. There are, however, moments across the lectures where Sacks's interest in how categorisations of space and place operate in talk appears to point to some ways forward.

Space in the place: procedures for the assembly and decomposability of the commonplace scene

Sacks returns to matters of the organisation of the commonplace scene, and the accountability and story-ability of observed incongruities, across a number of lectures. For instance, in the lecture on 'settinged activities', Sacks (1995[I]: 515–522) considers, briefly, how place categories and their devices might form a resource for members' treatments of the spatial and temporal order of a given setting:

> The matter of space in the place is, of course, another thing, and, at least within this culture, things that arise, arise within 'this room' or arise in 'other rooms;' there are battles over who's chair is which, and things like that. And there's talk of territorial rights, territorial distribution, etc., which can apparently go on in a room as well as in anything else formulatable as

> a 'setting,' perhaps? … the idea is that whenever people can set up and maintain the fact of a setting, there's an enormous amount that they can get going for them.
>
> (Sacks, 1995[I]: 522)

Although 'space in the place' is treated, here, as 'another thing' rather than a central topic, Sacks's remarks indicate how spatial categorisations form a massively prevalent mundane concern for members. Put another way, if activities always happen somewhere, a fine-grained situated sense of the 'somewhere' might be of relevance for the discoverable order of the activity and relevant moral order.[4] One of the things that members might be able to 'get going for them', or, indeed, might use in the formulation of a setting, is the placing of activities in relation to 'nameable' parts of that location. Something of this device appears to be at work in relation to the use made of place and setting terms in the organisation of storytelling.

Although the later lectures on storytelling are better known for Sacks's increasing focus on sequential organisation and participants' own orientations to category use in conversation (see Fitzgerald, this volume), there is a continued space given to categorial matters; of course, incongruities make for good stories. The lecture on 'Topic' (Sacks, 1995[I]: 752–763), for instance, includes remarks in relation to the Bullock's Store story[5] in which Sacks shows how, 'Where a place is is a great vehicle for presenting an orientation to a topic' (p. 754). Sacks then turns to talking about members' attentiveness to 'discriminative class uses', using the contrasting example turns of 'I was at County Line yesterday' and 'I went surfing yesterday'. Sacks considers how the former formulation provides, for 'colleagues' who can hear 'County Line' as a location where surfing happens, an occasion for further talk about surfing ('How was the surf?'), whereas the latter might be generative of talk about other topics ('Nice. I went for a ride'). So, a geographic place name *can* be hearable as bound to an activity by members of that 'community', and such category use is one which in such membership is routinely displayed.[6] There are, however, other classes of 'setting categories' that appear to have a more general applicability across a 'culture' in such a way that can be routinely viewed as having activities 'bound' to them.

Something of this kind of category work is found in the unproblematic hearing of a story told about the 'witnessing'[7] of an auto wreck. The data excerpt analysed in a lecture on 'Story Organisation, Tellability; Coincidence, etc.' reads:

> *A*: Say did you see anything in the paper last night or hear anything on the local radio, Ruth Henderson and I drove down to Ventura yesterday,
> *B*: Mm hm
> *A:* And on the way home we saw the:: most gosh awful wreck.
>
> (Sacks, 1995[II]: 229)

Sacks's analysis (pp. 229–241) is concerned with the sequential organisation of the telling of the story; for example, how the 'mm hm' may provide for the recognition by B that the first turn of A is not the story, but a preface to it. A good deal of the lecture is devoted to the design and hearing of the story as a local news story and how the placing of the story – temporally and spatially – does a good deal of that work. Sacks notes that, 'drove down to Ventura' is 'terribly useful' as it 'sets up where the event took place, i.e. on the freeway, or something like the freeway – which never has to be said in the storytelling … [it] locates where the thing took place', thus forming a key element for the 'massive *economy*' of the story and storytelling more generally (Sacks, 1995[II]: 236). What Sacks does not draw out further is *how* 'drove down to Ventura' provides for the event taking place 'on the freeway, or something like the freeway'. It seems that Sacks himself would be unsatisfied with 'it just does' as a solution.

The availability of the wreck taking place, and it being 'witnessed' on the freeway, might be said to be simply organised through 'what everyone knows' in relation to the named activity of driving (or, at least, travelling by car). Yet, how that knowledge is organised locally in the telling and hearing of the story appears to get done through a more extensive device than the 'County Line' example and is one case of how members appear to be able to find that certain activities are hearable or viewable as 'bound' to, or 'belonging in' a particular setting. A procedural consequence of this relation of activity-to-setting for the story might also be that it provides for the consistency of hearing 'wreck' as an automobile wreck and not, say, a ruined building, a ship, or, indeed, a person in emotional distress.

Perhaps the clearest example of the ways in which members can use the 'boundedness' of some activities to specific settings in interaction, and the way setting and place terms can, in Sacks's words, be 'peculiarly useable' is found in the 'crude sort of fact' that 'lots of intended announcements of activity are not done via activity names but via place or setting names, e.g. "I'm going to the bathroom"' (Sacks, 1995[I]: 759). Again, Sacks does not develop this further, and moves on to talk of the relationship between place and place categories as mnemonic devices, but it seems that the same device is employed for the hearing of the wreck being seen on the road and not somewhere else. Sacks (1995[I]: 462) discusses this elsewhere in a lecture on 'place reference' in which 'the place reference serves to indicate in one or another way, and not name, the activity or class of activities that are to be done, that are done there'. An example is, 'they went to bed'. Indeed, the asking of 'what for?' as a response to someone saying 'can I use your bathroom?' would likely be taken as a joke or some form of breach. In the lecture, Sacks goes on to say: 'Now what's involved in those, I don't know; why those places are picked out, I don't know, but it's something that one might give some attention to'.

In giving attention to why those places are picked out, we might consider how, much like with the relationship between categories and 'bound' activities, one aspect can be inferred when not made explicitly available. The sorts of possibilities outlined above might, I suggest, be the by-product of an aspect of the categorial machinery that I have called elsewhere the 'category-relevant setting device' (Smith, 2017). In considering this further, the local categorial work that provides for the relevance of a nameable setting for some activity appears to be similarly organised to the distinction between 'categorically-bound' and 'categorially-open' activities and predicates (Coulter, 1996: 343); that is, some categories are available through some named activity (for instance, talk of 'sentencing' provides for the category 'judges'), whereas for other activities ('thinking' or 'sleeping') they are not. In much the same way, some activities are not 'bound' to a setting ('I was thinking'), whereas others can be heard or seen as properly done in relation to a setting, a setting that is usually designed or built up for that activity and the categories to which it can be 'bound' (giving a lecture, for example, or, indeed, passing sentence). This seems a simple and rather central operation for doing certain kinds of incongruity. In returning to Sacks's exercise of 'writing down the class', it seems that some incongruities can be produced using minimally referential person categories and setting categories alone.

What we have, so far, is the seemingly 'trivially obvious' recognition that the locally accomplished relationship, relevancy, and 'bounded-ness' of categories to nameable spaces and settings can be a resource for 'assembling' observations of the commonplace scene via the combining of 'parts that have names' and their standardised affiliated procedures. Such a procedure also appears rather central to the organisation of activities in a whole range of settings, and perhaps particularly so in 'public' spaces, where unacquainted members come to be using the material, 'name-able' elements of a scene together. This form of (spatial) category work that demonstrates the accountable reflexivity and mutually constitutive character between category (of person), activity (whether 'bound' or 'tied' or 'predicated'; see Reynolds and Fitzgerald, 2015), and what we might call 'category-relevant setting' is readily observable in the local organisation and accomplishment of the 'traffic system' (Goffman, 2010[1971]). Indeed, members can be found applying such procedures in the use and accomplishment of the traffic system in which 'deviant actions' are often available in and through some 'part that has a name' and the apparent misuse or 'mis-orientation' to it. A readily available case is disputes between cyclists and drivers that turn on the topicalisation of the 'correct' positioning of a bicycle in relation to 'nameable parts' of the scene such as cycle lanes (Smith, 2017). In the case below, the categorial organisation of 'bicycles' in and through the 'road user' device or 'traffic system' collectivity is accomplished relationally with the scenic 'parts with names'. The dispute takes place on a dual-laned road with a 'double red line' next to the kerb and a broken line marking an area of road marked with painted cycle symbols. In the dispute that follows, 'cycle lane' comes to be invoked as the space in which bicycles should properly be found, thus providing for an 'incongruity' from the perspective of the driver in and through their initial, aggressive actions toward the cyclist (lines 1–2 occur as the car is overtaking the cyclist).

Transcript 15.1

1.Dr: *horn sounds* (1.1)
2. get in the fucking cycle lane you moron
3.Cy: ((Reads number plate aloud))
4. (15)((car is stopped at lights))
5. ((Cy pulls alongside L hand window))
6.Cy: what was that about a cycle lane
7.Dr: get in the cycle lane
8.Cy: what if I'm overtaking someone
9.Dr: you're overtaking
10. well I'm going to fucking knock you off
11. your bi er bike
12. ((unclear)) that
13.Dr. I'm overtaking someone
14.Dr: do you want me to knock you off your bike
15.Cy: why?=
16.Dr: =then stay in [the fucking cycle lane]
17.Cy: [You've got two]
18. lanes(.)you've got-
19.Dr: and look how many how many cars there are
20. and there's four cyclists
21.Cy: yeah I'm-
22.Dr: jus stay behind each other

Here, the 'bicycle lane' is invoked as a moral object, locally bound to the activity of 'cycling' which consequently provides for the 'driver' to topicalise the 'cyclists'' problematic spatial position relative to that of the car. In this instance, quite beyond any sense of formal rules of the road, 'cars' and 'drivers' are bound to the 'road', whereas 'cyclists' and 'cycling' are bound to the visually available 'cycle lane'. Although such incidents can be glossed as having to do with 'territory' (Goffman, 2010[1971]) and a sense of entitlement to the road that drivers of cars have, I would suggest that such claims rely on the possible assembly of scenes in such a way that finds categories and 'bound-activities' also bound to available 'name-able' parts – such as bike lanes – which is at least one way in which members appear to 'do an incongruity' (see also Lloyd, 2019).

Such an assembly is made explicit in talk in such disputes, but, importantly, analyses of the organisation of mobility in and through and as a commonplace 'traffic scene' also display the procedural relevancy of such 'standardised procedures' for, in Sacks's words, viewing 'illegitimate combinations'. There is no good analytic or practical reason that such a procedure would be limited to combinations of categories of person. Beyond incongruities, there is also no good reason to assume that the procedures for viewing a scene without incongruities are differently accomplished. The 'normality' of a scene is, after all, a situated accomplishment of assembled activities (Sacks, 1984). In drawing out the continued interest that Sacks had in 'space', the discussion demonstrates an aspect – one among many – of how categorisation practices go beyond person descriptions and might be central to the organisation of perception and social action more generally (Hester and Francis, 2003). Categorisation practices should not be treated as 'imposed' by individual members upon an external world in order to make that world make sense; rather, such practices are endogenous to, and inextricable from, the settings in and through which categories are found to be relevant in the course of some activity. This begins to sound a little like a theory, a decontextualised 'structure' of categorisation practices. Yet, I trust that the seemingly trivially obvious observations made in this chapter are recognisable enough to any 'native' reader, and *that,* as Sacks repeatedly demonstrated, is the place to start. Further examination of such 'standardised affiliated procedures' for formulating category, activity, and setting is required. An attention to such practices should, at least, serve as a way of further explicating how members go about organising, producing, and recognising action within and without talk in actual settings. Settings where, not only do the 'parts have names', but the assembly of those names mirrors the local building of 'collections' and 'context' in such a way that has an observable operational relevance for a given activity.

Conclusion

Drawing inspiration from Sacks's wide-ranging remarks on the 'eerie significance' and 'peculiar usability' of categories of space and place, this chapter has aimed to outline how categorial relationships are often treatable by members as *spatialised* relationships, and that those relationships are often accomplished in and through situated uses made of the settings that members inhabit. A key point, then, made across this chapter is that categories are not just for talking (Edwards, 1991) but are for *organising.* This, again, is to return to the sociological manner in which Sacks was addressing talk as an available, 'good enough' means of accessing an aspect of the local accomplishment of culture and social organisation. Indeed, Sacks's methodological dictum of 'building a model' of the members' machinery that gives the analyst back their own observations poses some analytic questions for the ethnomethodological notion of 'context' as an assembled activity (an activity which is part and parcel of the radically locally assembled, mutually elaborative whole) and provides some foundations for paying sustained attention to the spatial organisation and perceptual availability of members' activities.

Harvey Sacks possessed and practised what was at once a uniquely creative, yet uniquely systematic, sociological imagination in which the 'scientific' and the 'creative' were in mutual dialogue. The *Lectures*, in my reading at least, remain a relatively untapped resource for the *doing of sociology* writ large in such a way that might encourage contemporary researchers to regain something of the 'indeterminacy' and 'vertigo' that characterised Sacks's original insights and ideas, which inspired and supported the systematic and empirical approach. So, while recognising the importance of the development of sequential analysis for the analysis of conversation and, subsequently, multimodal interaction (see,

Mondada, this collection), Sacks's work and ideas encapsulate a unique understanding of social organisation and the analytic treatment thereof, while also providing additional inspiration for 'natural' observational social science more generally. Harvey Sacks remains the most creative and systematic sociological mind; it is his legacy that we who would follow keep a hold of *both* elements of his work.

Notes

1 I write 'production/recognition' in this way as a gloss for a longer discussion relating to difficulties in separating the 'two sides' of the cultural coin from the perspective of members' methods (see Watson, 2009, 2015).

2 A lecture comprising three sessions, the transcript of which, unlike the majority of others, includes questions and comments from students. It is perhaps the inclusion of this dialogue that adds to the 'work in progress' quality of the lecture and its appeal.

3 This orientation, of course, signals a distance from dominant sociological approaches – then and now – that can barely imagine handling the significance of some observed scene, or remark made in interview, without having demographic criteria to hand in order to provide a significance, while also raising its own troubles as regards the 'promiscuity' of categories. A second insistence is that the observers should not 'play the alien' or 'feign ignorance' of things that one can see perfectly well as members (see Mair and Sharrock, this collection; see also Livingston, 1987: 59–64), an orientation surely of significance for all ethnographers. There is far more to be said on what a 'Sacksian' ethnography might look like. Rod Watson's work is instructive in this regard (for example, 1999, also 2015). See also Andrew Carlin's chapter, this collection.

4 The influence of Goffman, and environmental psychology via Goffman, seems apparent here, albeit respecified in typically Sacksian style.

5 See also Whitehead, this collection, for further elaboration.

6 As further elucidated by Drew (1978) in relation to 'religious geography' and McHoul and Watson's (1984) discussion of the use of common-sense geographical categories for the teaching of 'formal' geographic knowledge in the classroom.

7 This lecture also contains a typically profound yet 'obvious' methodological observation by Sacks. He says it took him a year and a half of observation to notice that the 'witness' of the wreck did not witness the wreck at all, but, rather, was able to 'find the story' of the wreck itself in the available traces of what they actually saw (crumpled cars, bodies covered over on the pavement).

References

Coulter, J. (1996). Human practices and the observability of the 'macrosocial'. *Zeitschrift für Soziologie*, *25*(5): 337–345.

Drew, P. (1978). Accusations: the occasioned use of members' knowledge of religious geography in describing events. *Sociology*, *12*(1): 1–22.

Edwards, D. (1991). Categories are for talking: on the cognitive and discursive bases of categorization. *Theory & Psychology*, *1*(4): 515–542.

Garfinkel, H., & Sacks, H. (1970). On formal structures of practical actions. In J. C. McKinney & E. Tiryakian (Eds.) *Theoretical Sociology* (pp. 338–366). New York: Appleton Century Crofts.

Goffman, E. (2010[1971]). *Relations in Public. Microstructure of the Public Order.* New York: Harper & Row.

Hester, S., & Eglin, P. (Eds.) (1997a). *Culture in Action: Studies in Membership Categorization Analysis*. Washington, DC: University Press of America.

Hester, S., & Elgin, P. (1997b). Membership categorisation analysis: an introduction. In S. Hester & P. Eglin. (Eds.) *Culture in Action: Studies in Membership Categorization Analysis* (pp. 1–23). Washington, DC: University Press of America.

Hester, S., & Francis, D. (2003). Analysing visually available mundane order: a walk to the supermarket. *Visual Studies*, *18*(1): 36–46.

Housley, W., & Fitzgerald, R. (2002). The reconsidered model of membership categorization analysis. *Qualitative Research*, *2*(1): 59–83.

Housley, W., & Fitzgerald, R. (2015). Introduction to membership categorisation analysis. In R. Fitzgerald & W. Housley (Eds.) *Advances in Membership Categorisation Analysis* (pp. 1–22). London: Sage.

Jayyusi, L. (1984). *Categorization and the Moral Order.* London: Routledge & Kegan Paul.

Laurier, E. (2001). Why people say where they are during mobile phone calls. *Environment and Planning D: Society and Space*, *19*(4): 485–504.

Laurier, E. (2005). Searching for a parking space. *Intellectica*, *41*(2): 101–115.

Liberman, K. (2013). *More Studies in Ethnomethodology.* New York: SUNY Press.

Livingston, E. (1987). *Making Sense of Ethnomethodology.* London: Routledge.

Lloyd, M. (2019). The non-looks of the mobile world: a video-based study of interactional adaptation in cycle-lanes. *Mobilities*, *14*(4): 500–523.

Lynch, M. (2013). Seeing fish. In P. Tolmie & M. Rouncefield (Eds.) *Ethnomethodology at Play* (pp. 89–104). Farnham: Ashgate.

McHoul, A., & Watson, D. R. (1984). Two axes for the analysis of 'commonsense' and 'formal' geographical knowledge in classroom talk. *British Journal of Sociology of Education*, *5*(3): 281–302.

Pollner, M. (1987). *Mundane Reason: Reality in Everyday and Sociological Discourse.* Cambridge: Cambridge University Press.

Reynolds, E., & Fitzgerald, R. (2015). Challenging normativity: re-appraising category, bound, tied and predicated features. In R. Fitzgerald & W. Housley (Eds.) *Advances in Membership Categorization Analysis* (pp. 99–122). London: Sage.

Sacks, H. (1984) On doing 'being ordinary'. In J. M. Atkinson & J. Heritage (Eds.) *Structures of Social Action: Studies in Conversation Analysis* (pp. 413–429). Cambridge: Cambridge University Press.

Sacks, H. (1986). Some considerations of a story told in everyday conversation. *Poetics*, *15*: 127–138.

Sacks, H. (1995). *Lectures on Conversation.* (Vol. I). Edited by G. Jefferson with introduction by E. A. Schegloff. Oxford: Blackwell.

Silverman, D. (1998) *Harvey Sacks: Social Science and Conversation Analysis*. New York: Oxford University Press.

Smith, R. J. (2017). Membership categorisation, category-relevant spaces, and perception-in-action: the case of disputes between cyclists and drivers. *Journal of Pragmatics*, *118*: 120–133.

Smith, R. J. (2019). Visually available order, categorisation practices, and perception-in-action: a running commentary. *Visual Studies*, *34*(1): 28–40.

Stokoe, E. (2012). Moving forward with membership categorization analysis: methods for systematic analysis. *Discourse Studies*, *14*(3): 277–303.

Watson, D. R. (1999). Driving in forests and mountains: a pure and applied ethnography. *Ethnographic Studies*, *3*: 50–60.

Watson, D. R. (2009a). Constitutive practices and Garfinkel's notion of trust: revisited. *Journal of Classical Sociology*, *9*(4): 475–499.

Watson, D. R. (2009b). *Analysing Practical and Professional Texts: A Naturalistic Approach*. Farnham: Ashgate.

Watson, D. R. (2015). De-reifying categories. In R. Fitzgerald & W. Housley (Eds.) *Advances in Membership Categorisation Analysis* (pp. 23–50). London: Sage.

16 On Sacks and the analysis of racial categories-in-action

Kevin A. Whitehead

As a new graduate student with an interest in using CA to study race, I was quickly directed by my mentors to read Harvey Sacks's (1984, 1986) analyses of "the Bullock's story." These analyses were compiled by Gail Jefferson for publication some years after Sacks's death, based on materials from several lectures he delivered in 1970 and 1971. They have rightly been lauded for their foundational observations with respect to storytelling in conversation, the normative bases of experience, and the interactional management of rights and responsibilities relating to knowledge, or "epistemics" (Heritage and Raymond 2005). However, an under-appreciated feature of these analyses, and one that was revelatory for my intellectual project, is his discussion of the storyteller's use of a racial person reference in the course of the telling. In this chapter, I discuss the penetrating analyses Sacks offers in this regard and some important observations with respect to (racial) categories in talk-in-interaction to which they give rise, and which inspired the research I produced as a graduate student and in subsequent years. I then offer a further contribution to this work in the form of an analysis of racial self-categorizations produced in the course of complaint sequences.

Racial person reference in the Bullock's story

This story, shown in Transcript 16.1,[1] was told by a speaker named Ellen in a telephone conversation with her friend Jean. This conversation, and the story told by Ellen in its course, was occasioned by an incident Ellen witnessed while driving past the department store, Bullock's, at which Jean was employed.

Transcript 16.1

[Sacks 1984, 1986]
1 Jean: Hello,
2 (0.4)
3 Ellen: Jean.
4 Jean: Yeah.
5 (0.4)
6 Ellen: Well I just thought I'd- (.) re-better report to you
7 what's happened at Bullock's toda:y=

Jean: =What in the world's ha:ppened. [hhh
Ellen: [Did you have
the day o:ff?
Jean: Ya:h?
(0.3)
Ellen: Well I: got out to my car at fi:ve thirty I: drove
arou:nd and of course I had to go by the front of
the sto:re,=
Jean: =Yeah?=
Ellen: =And there were two (0.2) police cars across the
street en leh-e colored lady wanted to go in
the main entrance there where the si:lver is and
all the [(gifts and] things).
Jean: [Y e a h,]
(0.4)
Ellen: A:nd, they wouldn't let her go i:n, and he, had
a gu::n,
(0.2)
Ellen: He was holding a gun in his hand a great big
lo:ng gu::n?
Jean: Yea:h?
Ellen: And the over on the other side, I mean to the
right. of there, where the (0.2) employees come
ou:t, there was a who:le, oh:: must have been ten
uh eight or ten employees standing there, because
there must have been a:, it seemed like they had
every entrance ba:rred. I don't know what was
goin[g o:n.
Jean: [Oh my Go:d,

In the course of recounting what she saw happening outside the store, Ellen singles out a "colored lady" (line 18), who she reports was trying to enter the store and was prevented from doing so by a police officer (lines 23–24). In his analysis of the story, Sacks describes how Ellen's elaboration of the "main entrance" of the store, describing it as the place "where the ↓si:lver is'n all the (gifts and things)" (lines 19–20), allows her to make the inference that "the colored lady wanted to go in to where the silver is and all the gifts and things" (Sacks 1986: 133). Simply by explicitly referring to the race of the person at the door ("colored lady") and elaborating her description of the entrance to the store, Ellen "works to put in information relevant to seeing what was happening" (Sacks 1986: 134). Thus, the identification of the woman as "colored," when combined with her position outside a particular entrance of the store, provides for the inference (on the part of both Ellen and her recipient) that she is engaged in the activity of trying to rob the store. By contrast, an alternative categorical formulation of the woman as "an employee," for example, would not have provided for this type of inference. In this way, with respect to both what Ellen saw as happening on the scene as she observed it and in her subsequent recounting of the events, the identification of the woman as a member of a racial category serves as a tacit account for the woman's observed and reported actions (Sacks 1986).

Importantly, and as Sacks (1984: 422) notes, "This lady is not designing a rightwing report. All she is doing is reporting what she saw." Ellen thus designs her account "not in a nasty fashion" (Sacks 1986: 134), but simply in the service of achieving a recognizable description – and, likewise, there is no hint that Jean treats Ellen's use of a racialized account as in any way problematic. Nonetheless, the way in which Sacks's analysis problematizes her actions, criticizing their essentially racist character, shows how the treatment of race as an account for action is vulnerable to sanctioning. Specifically, Sacks (1986: 133) notes how Ellen assumed that the woman was "involved in a robbery of the store" while having

> no idea that the colored lady had any idea what was in behind the main entrance, or that she was going through the main entrance to get to what was right in the main entrance area; where for all anybody knows, she was going into the store, up to the second floor.

Moreover, Sacks (1984: 423, 1986: 137) notes how Ellen singles out this particular lady for "non-witness, party-to-the scene status," in contrast to the "eight or ten employees" (line 32) she describes later in her telling as being present at the scene, and in contrast to the confidence she displays that she herself was at no risk of being assigned a similar non-witness status[2] (Sacks 1984, 1986). These observations are driven home by a subsequent conversation between Jean and a third person, who was present in the store at the time of the incident, and who reveals that the lady was in fact an employee and was having a friendly conversation with the police officer, rather than being prevented by him from entering the store (Sacks 1984: 423).

In sum, Sacks's analyses of this story provide for at least three important observations regarding uses of racial categories in talk-in-interaction, namely, that (1) using a (racial) category in referring to an actor can serve to tacitly provide an account for their actions, grounded in what recipients can be taken to know about the category; (2) in this way, racial (and other) categories, and the common-sense knowledge associated with them, can be reproduced as a "by-product" of whatever else participants are doing, even if it ostensibly does not involve race and/or race has not been directly topicalized; and (3) speakers who use racial categories in these ways may become vulnerable to sanctioning or criticism of their conduct as effectively racist. In combination with his largely convergent, but more widely recognized, work on membership categorization devices, or MCDs[3] (Sacks 1972a, 1972b, 1992), these observations were profoundly important for my efforts to develop a conversation analytic approach to examining uses and management of racial categories in everyday interactions (Whitehead 2009, 2011, 2012, 2013a, 2013b, 2015, 2018b, 2020; Whitehead and Lerner 2009). It is also worth noting that these features of the analyses also obliterate the subsequently propagated myth that conversation analysis is poorly suited to, or even incapable of, contributing to critical or politically engaged research, providing a brilliant demonstration of the use of a technical analysis of everyday talk-in-interaction as a basis for political commentary and critique (also see Schegloff 1992: xxii–xxiii) – something that I have similarly sought to demonstrate in my own work.

In the remainder of the chapter, I build on this work by examining some ways in which speakers producing complaints on South African radio call-in shows claim membership in a racial category implicated as an object of the complaint. I begin by briefly describing some of the conversation analytic research on intersections between complaint sequences and membership categories that informs this analysis.

Complaints and categories[4]

Schegloff (1995, 2005) describes the following canonical trajectory for complaint sequences:[5]

1. A first pair part in the form of a complaint, or mention of a "complainable."
2. A responsive, and either aligning or disaligning, second pair part, such as an expression of sympathy, apology, agreement or disagreement, remedy or offer of remedy, excuse or account, and so on.
3. Uptake of the response in third position, such as acceptance or rejection of the response.

The actions produced in the unfolding of these sequences implicate a set of situated participant categories, including a complainer, one or more complaint recipients, and the object(s) of the complaint or complained-about party/ies[6] (also see Edwards 2005).

While complaints can easily be recognized as implicating some kind of moral failing on the part of the object(s) of the complaint (Drew 1998; Edwards 2005), they can also, through what Edwards (2005) refers to as the *subjective side* of complaining, index morally implicative characteristics of the complainer. Thus, the production of complaints can occasion evaluations of "the propriety or fairness or justice or accuracy with which we have reported some (external) events, or our motives in doing so" (Drew 1998: 295–296), and may result in a complainer's actions being treated as complainable in their own right, as well as implicating particular dispositions on the part of the complainer (Sacks 1992; Edwards 2005). In addition to this speaker indexicality potentially resulting in a complainer being seen as (for example) a "dispositional moaner" (Edwards 2005: 24), complaints that implicate a particular (racial) category as their target can, as my analysis shows, index the complainer's (racial) category membership (also see Whitehead 2009, 2013a, 2020).

My analysis thus also builds upon a broader body of conversation analytic research on the relationship between category membership and complaint sequences, with Sacks's early work again planting the seeds of much of what has followed. For example, Sacks (1992: Vol. I, 599–600) observed the role of membership categories in distinguishing between "safe" and "unsafe" complaints, with unsafe complaints being those that may implicate other people who could be categorized under the same membership category as the object(s) of the complaint. Sacks (1992: Vol. I, 417) also described how "intentional misidentification" (i.e., identifying someone using a category of which they cannot properly be claimed to be a member) can be used as a way of producing complaints, by treating someone's actions as being category-bound to the category of which they have been misidentified as a member. Building on Sacks's work on membership categorization, Schegloff (2005: 452) notes that the "complainability of some form of conduct can be contingent on the identity of the agents and the recipients of the conduct – identities often grounded in category memberships." That is, the degree to which someone's conduct is treated as complainable may depend on the category of which they are seen to be a member in producing the conduct, and on the category membership of those observing the conduct. In a related analysis, Laforest (2009) examines how members of different categories (specifically, children versus parents) are treated as having differential rights to complain about one another.

Also noteworthy is the heightened nature of the abovementioned delicacy and moral implications associated with complaints in cases where particular categories of people are made relevant, especially when the categories at hand are politically sensitive ones, as is the case with racial categories (Whitehead 2009). A substantial body of research has examined the range of practices that speakers may employ in such cases in order to avoid appearing prejudiced or racist in the course of talking, and particularly complaining, about people of particular racial categories (see reviews in Augoustinos and Every 2007; Whitehead 2018a).

Racial self-categorization in complaint sequences

A first instance of a speaker displaying his co-membership in a category of which he has treated the objects of his complaint as incumbents is shown in Transcript 16.2. Just prior to this excerpt, the host and caller have collaboratively complained about executives who help companies to engage in illegal or unethical financial practices. As he continues this complaint, starting in line 1 of the transcript, the host claims that these companies recurrently hire "some black guy" to serve as "the face" of the company (c.f Shrikant 2019), thereby taking the blame for their unethical practices or financial failures (lines 1 and 3–5). The host then shifts from complaining about the companies who engage in these racialized scapegoating practices to complaining about the specific individuals who agree to take these positions and, in the process, he uses the pronoun "we" (line 7) to refer to this collectivity, thereby including himself in the category of people about which he is complaining (cf. Sacks 1992; Lerner and Kitzinger 2007, Shrikant 2019).

Transcript 16.2

[237 – SAfm, 5-12-08]
Host: They do that a lot. .hh[h=pt When a company's looking
Caller: [(Can he)
Host: to go down or looking really ugly, .hh they think "Whoa!

4 You can't put a >blonde blue eyed person there,"< .hh
5 they ge[t some black guy, and he's the face everywhere.
6 Caller: [(Wow.)
7 Host: .hhh But how do we say "nye:s" to that, I wonder? <Maybe
8 it's the paycheck?
9 (0.8)
10 Caller: Hey, ya, now, hey we- we in big trouble, I'm
11 tel(h)l[ing (you!)
12 Host: [Huh huh!

It is also significant that, in aligning with the host's complaint (following a pause at line 9), the caller similarly uses the collective pronoun "we" (line 10). Assuming that neither the host nor the caller has actually personally taken on the scapegoat position for the type of company being complained about, either or both of them could have instead distanced themselves from the group of people criticized by the host by using the alternative pronoun "they." Their use of "we" thus apparently indexes their co-membership with the objects of the complaint in a racial category, rather than claiming co-incumbency of a professional category. As such, it is recognizable as the outcome of a choice between (at least) two alternatives, with the chosen outcome serving to treat inclusion in a complained-about category as preferred over exclusion from it.

While the speakers' uses of pronouns in Transcript 16.2 enabled their displays of co-membership in a complained-about category to be seamlessly integrated into their turns-in-progress, Transcript 16.3 shows a case in which such a display is more overtly exposed through being produced as an increment to a possibly complete turn. Here, a caller who has just complained about a lack of action being taken in response to a series of violent xenophobic attacks that were being carried out at the time produces a follow-up complaint about those whom he treats as primarily culpable for the violence. In doing so, the caller singles out members of a particular racial and citizenship category ("black South Africans" – line 3) for criticism, reaching a possible completion of his turn constructional unit (see Sacks, Schegloff, and Jefferson 1974) at the end of his utterance of this category, before quickly adding the pronoun "Us" (line 3). The caller thus retrospectively includes himself in the category he has criticized, having not done so initially. The caller then continues with his complaint, with the work done in producing this pronoun thereby becoming observable as temporarily halting the progressivity of the complaint (cf. Whitehead 2020).

Transcript 16.3

[234 – SAfm, 5-12-08]
1 Caller: .hh The- the problem here is, (0.4) I- I don't think
2 there is e- enough is- education <es↑pecially (.) for-
3 for black South Africans.=Us. [.hh Because we seem not
4 Host: [Mm.
5 Caller: to understand the continent.
6 (0.5)
7 Caller: We- we- we seem to: to think that we are the best in the

8 continent <and we are no:t.
9 Host: (pt) Ja, you see .hh we are >n- n- n-< not educated and
10 are hung- ah=our stomachs are empty.
11 (1.0)
12 Caller: .hh You kno[w- I- I-
13 Host: [It's a bad combination.

In continuing his criticism following his production of this increment, the caller uses the pronoun "we" on several further occasions (see lines 3, 7, and 8), thereby continuing his display of co-membership in the category he is criticizing in much the same way seen in Transcript 16.2. In addition (and again similarly to Transcript 16.2), the host, in his agreeing response to the caller, produces his own display of co-membership in the racial category of the objects of the criticism through his use of the pronouns "we" (line 9) and "our" (line 10). Moreover, he does this even though it involves implicitly making a dubious claim that the attributes he mentions (e.g., "uneducated" and "empty stomach") apply to him in the way that he is claiming they apply to other members of the category.

It is also worth noting that both the caller and the host display an orientation to their actions as delicate (also see Lerner 2013). This can be seen in the brief pauses and restarts produced by the caller just prior to his formulation of "black South Africans" (lines 7–8), and in the host's numerous restarts prior to agreeing with the caller's claim that "we" are "not educated" (line 14). This provides further evidence for the possibility that speakers' self-inclusion in a category being targeted for complaint or criticism may be a way of orienting to and managing the potential for sanctioning in response to their actions.

In a final and more complex case, shown in Transcript 16.4, a caller initially does not claim co-membership in the category about which he has complained, but then explicitly racially self-categorizes as an apparent way of managing what he thereby treats as the possible racial implications of his complaint. The caller launches the complaint by noting a recent discussion of "the skills shortage" by the deputy president of South Africa (lines 1–2), before suggesting that this problem was one of the ANC (African National Congress) government's own making (lines 5–6).

Unlike in the excerpts above, the recipient of the complaint in this case does not immediately align with the complainer, with the host remaining silent during a relatively lengthy (0.4-second) pause at line 7. Whereas pauses of this sort recurrently occur in my data as a result of hosts orienting to allowing callers to take extended turns in order to say whatever they have called in to say (cf. the 1.0-second pause at line 3, followed by the host prompting the caller to continue at line 4), it is noteworthy that the pause at line 7 comes at a place at which the caller has explicitly solicited a response from the host through his use of the tag question ("hey?") at the end of his turn in line 6. As conversation analytic research on preference organization (as described by, e.g., Schegloff 2007a) has shown, silences in places prepared for an aligning or disaligning response are recurrently treated by participants as indicative of an incipient disaligning (or "dispreferred") response, while also providing speakers with opportunities to do further work in pursuit of alignment and/or to forestall or mitigate the potential disalignment. Consistent with these findings, following the pause at line 7, the caller pursues alignment from the host by producing an upgraded reaffirmation of the complaint he has just produced (line 8), but the host continues to withhold a response during an even longer (0.8-second) pause at line 9. This second pause provides a further, and stronger, indication of incipient disalignment on the part of the host, and, in the face of this evident trouble, the caller first denies being a member of the category "white person" and then claims membership in the category "black person" (line 10).

Transcript 16.4

[573 – 702, 4-23-08]

```
 1 Caller:  Uh look, uh: thee: deputy: °president° uh:: (0.5) was
 2          talking about the skills shortage.
 3          (1.0)
 4   Host:  Mm [hm?
 5 Caller:     [>The thing is=is< the ANC government has made a
 6          <helluva mess> hey?
 7          (0.4)
 8 Caller:  And there's no doubt about it.
 9          (0.8)
10 Caller:  I'm not a white person, °I'm a° black person.
11          (.)
12 Caller:  .hhhh Number one, they decided to close down=hh
13          most (.) of the nursing colleges.
((22 seconds omitted as caller continues complaint))
14 Caller:  So we've messed it up there.
15          (.)
16 Caller:  Alright, okay. .h We mess it up with education,
17          we('ve) now gotta import thirty thousand teachers,
18          ((continues))
```

By producing these racial self-categorizations, the caller orients to his complaint about the government as potentially implicating a complaint about the racial category "black," and as thereby indexing his own racial category membership (cf. Edwards 2005; Whitehead 2009, 2020). Moreover, he thereby overtly treats complaining as a member of a racial category implicated as the object of a complaint as being less potentially problematic – and thus less likely to result in a full-blown realization of the interactional trouble that has thus far been only incipiently projected – than complaining as a non-member of the category (also see the analysis of a strikingly similar case of the use of racial self-categorization as a way of managing incipient disalignment, although not in the context of a complaint sequence, in Whitehead 2015: 378–381).

When the host still does not respond during a further brief pause at line 11, the caller launches a series of more specific claims in support of his complaint (and possibly in further pursuit of an aligning response), starting in lines 12–13 and continuing through a non-transcribed portion of the call thereafter. Then, importantly, in formulating the upshot of these claims (as marked by his use of the word "So" in line 14; see Raymond 2004), the caller claims co-membership in the category of people he is complaining about through (as in Transcripts 16.2 and 16.3) multiple uses of the pronoun "we" (lines 14, 16, and 17). Thus, having oriented to the possibility that his complaint was being treated as problematic by virtue of coming from a non-member of the complained-about category,[7] and having used racial self-categorization as a way of addressing this possible hearing, the caller subsequently shifts to consistently displaying his co-membership in the category about which he is complaining.

Concluding remarks

In the cases I have examined above, and across my data, participants appear to be systematically oriented to the maxim, *if you can claim membership in a category about which you are complaining, then do*. This orientation serves to reflect and reproduce the relevance of category-based entitlements in the production of everyday actions; specifically, it constitutes category (co-)membership as a basis for differential entitlement to complain.

In addition to the analyses of these cases drawing in many respects upon Sacks's work, broadly construed, these findings also build more specifically on the abovementioned observations afforded by Sacks's analyses of the Bullock's story in a number of ways. First, and consistent with my Sacks-inspired analysis of "categorizing the categorizer" (Whitehead 2009), this analysis demonstrates a way in which, in addition to tacitly accounting for the actions of a referred-to party, membership categories can provide for differential understandings of the actions of the party doing the referring. That is, in this case, complaining as a co-member of a category implicated as an object of the complaint is treated as meaningfully different from complaining as a non-member of the category (also cf. Schegloff 2002, 2007b). Second, although race is more overtly topicalized in some (but not all) of the cases in my data than it was in the Bullock's story, this analysis nonetheless extends the observation afforded by Sacks's analyses of the Bullock's story regarding the reproduction of race as a "by-product" of whatever else participants are doing. Specifically, race is made relevant in the process of participants' engagement in the "main business" of complaining about a diverse set of matters (events, actions, personal attributes, etc.), with racial categories thereby produced in situ as intersecting both with these matters and with categories from other MCDs (profession, citizenship, political party, etc.; cf. Whitehead 2012, 2013b). Third, these findings build on the observation regarding the vulnerability to sanctioning that may result from speakers' uses of racial categories, with participants' displays of co-membership in a category implicated as an object of a complaint evidently serving as a way in which participants may address the potential trouble that may arise from their production of the complaint. That is, participants treat complaining as an "insider" as less risky for self–other relations than complaining as an "outsider," and they may deploy category (co-)membership as a resource for managing the potential relational consequences of complaints (cf. Whitehead 2013a, 2018b, 2020).

Conducting detailed examinations of these sorts of everyday uses of racial categories constitutes an important component of efforts to describe the operation of race as a form of social organization and the mechanisms through which it is (re)produced as such. This is in keeping with the spirit, abundantly evident in so much of Sacks's pioneering work, of observing the features of so-called "macro" social structures in the details of "micro" interactions, rather than treating these as fundamentally distinct levels of social organization and analysis (also cf. Schegloff 1987). This, in turn, is underpinned by close attention to the fine-grained details of the production of ordinary actions-in-interaction, including the ways in which they are enabled by the types of generic interactional practices and structures (e.g., pronoun use, turn constructional units and increments, sequencing and preference organization, etc.) evident in the data I have examined here. More generally, my work to this end, and my intellectual agenda as a whole, owes an immeasurable debt to Sacks, whose rare genius left a legacy that is more vital than ever, more than 45 years after his untimely passing.

Acknowledgements

Earlier drafts of portions of this chapter were included in a presentation at the National Communication Association Convention in 2016 as part of a panel in honor of Gene Lerner, which in turn was based on a part of my Ph.D. dissertation. As alluded to at the outset of the chapter, this work – and indeed all the work I have done since beginning my graduate studies at UCSB – owes a debt to the enthusiastic encouragement and guidance provided by Gene Lerner and Geoff Raymond.

Notes

1 There are some differences between the transcripts of this conversation included in Sacks's 1984 versus 1986 analyses, including in the pseudonyms allocated to the speakers and in some of the details of the talk transcribed. The transcript included here largely follows the (more detailed) 1984 version, while also including some features present only in the 1986 version.

2 Although Sacks never explicitly mentions Ellen's own racial category, he does implicitly make it relevant by contrast with those of other racially identified potential observers of this scene, noting that, "if this action took place in a black neighborhood, watched by black people, then 'the very same scene' would perhaps turn into, for the perception of the parties, an altogether different phenomenon" (Sacks 1984: 421, 1986: 136). In addition, Sacks (1984: 422, 1986: 137) suggests that Ellen's "massive comfort in her innocence, and in the legitimate audience status that she has" is so taken-for-granted for her that "she can have no sense of an empathy with, for example, a kid in the ghetto." These aspects of his analysis thus serve as a remarkable early example of how implicit features of whiteness can be identified and critiqued on the basis of a technical, empirically

grounded analysis of participants' conduct and orientations in talk-in-interaction. In Whitehead (2020), I provide a detailed demonstration of the use of CA in conducting analyses of these phenomena.

3 Given that this work has received substantial attention elsewhere, I provide no further elaboration of its details here; readers are directed instead to useful introductions by Schegloff (2007b) and Stokoe (2012). It is potentially noteworthy, however, that, although much of Sacks's work on membership categorization predates the lectures in which he discusses the Bullock's story, he does not mention this work in his analyses of the racial categorization in this story. Although any attempt to account for this would be speculative, it may simply be reflective of the focus of the lectures during the period in question. That is, the lectures that focused on membership categorization were largely delivered in the 1964–1968 period, and the lectures during the 1970–1971 period that included analysis of the Bullock's story focused primarily on storytelling, the overall structural organization of conversations, sequence organization, and turn-taking (also see Schegloff 1992).

4 There is some overlap between this section and Whitehead (2013a: 187–190), as a result of their related respective analyses and their common origin in a chapter of my dissertation.

5 See Schegloff (2007a) for a more comprehensive treatment of the organization of sequences of action-in-interaction more generally. As Edwards (2005) notes, it can be difficult to distinguish complaining from related actions, such as criticizing, denigrating, accusing, and so on. However, these related actions share important features with complaints, most centrally the display by a participant of a negative stance towards an object, and a similar set of interactional contingencies associated with producing or responding to them (Edwards 2005). As such, the distinctions between complaints and other related actions are not crucial for the purposes of the analysis that follows.

6 Although the object(s) of a complaint need not always be (a) person(s), the collection of complaints on which my analysis below is based consists entirely of complaints that target either specific persons or collectivities (e.g., categories or groups of people, institutions or organizations, etc.).

7 It is possible that the host's withholding of responses to the caller's complaints may reflect his orientation to his own membership in the racial category "white," rather than arising from a misattribution of the caller's racial category. That is, the host may have declined to align with the caller on the basis that co-implicating himself in a complaint about the government could make him vulnerable, as a white person, to inferences or accusations of racism. However, rather than the question of whether the host really did misattribute the caller's racial category, what is crucial for the purpose of the present analysis is the caller's evident orientation to the host as having disaligned on this basis.

References

Augoustinos, Martha, and Danielle Every. 2007. "The Language of 'Race' and Prejudice: A Discourse of Denial, Reason, and Liberal-Practical Politics." *Journal of Language and Social Psychology* 26 (2): 123–41.

Drew, Paul. 1998. "Complaints About Transgressions and Misconduct." *Research on Language and Social Interaction* 31 (3&4): 295–325.

Edwards, Derek. 2005. "Moaning, Whinging and Laughing: The Subjective Side of Complaints." *Discourse Studies* 7 (1): 5–29.

Heritage, John, and Geoffrey Raymond. 2005. "The Terms of Agreement: Indexing Epistemic Authority and Subordination in Talk-in-Interaction." *Social Psychology Quarterly* 68 (1): 15–38.

Laforest, Marty. 2009. "Complaining in Front of a Witness: Aspects of Blaming Others for Their Behaviour in Multi-Party Family Interactions." *Journal of Pragmatics* 41 (12): 2452–64.

Lerner, Gene H. 2013. "On the Place of Hesitating in Delicate Formulations: A Turn-Constructional Infrastructure for Collaborative Indiscretion." In *Conversational Repair and Human Understanding*, edited by Jack Sidnell, Makoto Hayashi, and Geoffrey Raymond (pp. 95–134). Cambridge, UK: Cambridge University Press.

Lerner, Gene H., and Celia Kitzinger. 2007. "Extraction and Aggregation in the Repair of Individual and Collective Self-Reference." *Discourse Studies* 9 (4): 526–57.

Raymond, Geoffrey. 2004. "Prompting Action: The Stand-Alone 'So' in Ordinary Conversation." *Research on Language and Social Interaction* 37: 185–218.

Sacks, Harvey. 1972a. "An Initial Investigation of the Usability of Conversational Data for Doing Sociology." In *Studies in Social Interaction* (pp. 31–74), edited by D. N. Sudnow. New York, NY: Free Press.

———. 1972b. "On the Analyzability of Stories by Children." In *Directions in Sociolinguistics: The Ethnography of Communication* (pp. 325–45), edited by John J. Gumperz and Dell Hymes. New York, NY: Holt, Rinehart & Winston.

———. 1984. "On Doing 'Being Ordinary'." In *Structures of Social Action* (pp. 413–29), edited by J. Maxwell Atkinson and John Heritage. Cambridge, UK: Cambridge University Press.

———. 1986. "Some Considerations of a Story Told in Everyday Conversation." *Poetics* 15: 127–38.

———. 1992. *Lectures on Conversation* (Volumes I and II, edited by Gail Jefferson). Oxford, UK: Blackwell.

Sacks, Harvey, Emanuel A. Schegloff, and Gail Jefferson. 1974. "A Simplest Systematics for the Organization of Turn Taking in Conversation." *Language* 50: 696–735.

Schegloff, Emanuel A. 1987. "Between Micro and Macro: Contexts and Other Connections." In *The Micro-Macro Link* (pp. 207–34), edited by Jeffrey Alexander. Berkeley, CA: University of California Press.

———. 1992. "Introduction." In Sacks, Harvey, *Lectures on Conversation* (Volumes I and II, pp. ix–lxii), edited by Gail Jefferson. Oxford, UK: Blackwell.

———. 1995. "Discourse as an Interactional Achievement III: The Omnirelevance of Action." *Research on Language and Social Interaction* 28 (3): 185–211.

———. 2002. "Accounts of Conduct in Interaction: Interruption, Overlap and Turn-Taking." In *Handbook of Sociological Theory* (pp. 287–321), edited by J.H. Turner. New York, NY: Plenum.

———. 2005. "On Complainability." *Social Problems* 52 (4): 449–76.

———. 2007a. *Sequence Organization in Interaction: A Primer in Conversation Analysis*. Cambridge, UK: Cambridge University Press.

———. 2007b. "A Tutorial on Membership Categorization." *Journal of Pragmatics* 39: 462–82.

Shrikant, Natasha. 2019. "'Who's the Face?': Communication and White Identity in a Texas Business Community." *Ethnic and Racial Studies*, 42 (2): 254–271.

Stokoe, Elizabeth. 2012. "Moving Forward with Membership Categorization Analysis: Methods for Systematic Analysis." *Discourse Studies* 14 (3): 277–303.

Whitehead, Kevin A. 2009. "'Categorizing the Categorizer': The Management of Racial Common Sense in Interaction." *Social Psychology Quarterly* 72 (4): 325–42.

———. 2011. "An Ethnomethodological, Conversation Analytic Approach to Investigating Race in South Africa." *South African Review of Sociology* 42 (3): 1–22.

———. 2012. "Racial Categories as Resources and Constraints in Everyday Interactions: Implications for Non-Racialism in Post-Apartheid South Africa." *Ethnic and Racial Studies* 35 (7): 1248–65.

———. 2013a. "Managing Self/Other Relations in Complaint Sequences: The Use of Self-Deprecating and Affiliative Racial Categorizations." *Research on Language and Social Interaction* 46 (2): 186–203.

———. 2013b. "Race–Class Intersections as Interactional Resources in Post-Apartheid South Africa." In *Social Inequality and the Politics of Representation: A Global Landscape* (pp. 49–63), edited by Celine Marie Pascale. Newbury Park, CA: Sage.

———. 2015. "Everyday Antiracism in Action: Preference Organization in Responses to Racism." *Journal of Language and Social Psychology* 34 (4): 374–89.

———. 2018a. "Discursive Approaches to Race and Racism." In *The Oxford Encyclopedia of Intergroup Communication* (pp. 324–39), edited by Howard Giles and Jake Harwood. New York, NY: Oxford University Press.

———. 2018b. "Managing the Moral Accountability of Stereotyping." *Journal of Language and Social Psychology* 37 (3): 288–309.

———. 2020. "The Problem of Context in the Analysis of Talk-in-Interaction: The Case of Implicit Whiteness in Post-Apartheid South Africa." *Social Psychology Quarterly* 83 (3): 294–313.

——— and Gene H. Lerner. 2009. "When Are Persons 'White'? On Some Practical Asymmetries of Racial Reference in Talk-in-Interaction." *Discourse and Society* 20 (5): 613–41.

17 Harvey Sacks, membership categorization and social media

William Housley

The complexity and richness of Sacks's ideas lend themselves to thinking about and approaching social media as a conspicuous site of everyday methods and practices. Of course, these practices are realized in and through platforms that are algorithmically configured, networked and distributed socio-technical artifices. As ethnomethodologists, we certainly need to peer into the machine and respecify the occupational narratives and sales pitch associated with contemporary platform capitalism and marketing that surrounds and accounts for disruptive digital technologies. However, a concern with human practices associated with text and talk (and hybrid forms such as interactive text and threads) provides a good starting point for approaching the question of what people are actually *doing* on social media (Brooker et al., 2017). This is an important consideration, given the overwhelming framing of social media activity as a source of big and broad social data for formal analytic enterprise, the generation of social accounts from 'a one thousand feet view' and the reincarnation of abstract positivism in the guise of social data science (Housley and Smith, 2017; Housley et al., 2017a). Yet, the routine *ethnomethods* associated with these data-generative, networked and algorithmic environments remain largely taken for granted – at least by social scientists.

My own introduction to the work of Sacks was realized through my doctoral work, supervised by Stephen Hester, and engagement with the ethnomethodological community based in Manchester during the 1990s. Of particular interest was Sacks's commentary on membership categorization practices and how this had been approached and developed by my supervisor and some of his colleagues. This involved long debates and extensive reading around topics that included the relationship between category and sequence in conversation, membership categorization and context and wider ethnomethodological themes (Hester and Eglin, 1997). From my perspective, Sacks was primarily a sociologist who was approaching the question of social order and organization in a particularly novel and empirically robust way. While acknowledging and embracing the diversity of Sacks's concerns, the main focus in this chapter will be on membership categorization practices and how they might inform a consideration of mundane digital practices associated with social media. Furthermore, I will attempt to reflect on how Sacksian concerns can continue to stimulate and inform relatively new interactional fields and recognizable orders of ordinary socio-technical action in and through the study of members' practical activities.

Social media exhibit a degree of variety in and through different platforms. The way in which interactive text, visual and audio content combine can be understood to be a significant expression of platform architecture, as are the means by which information is shared, publicly assessed and responded to. The way in which these virtual resources present themselves, to members, routinely and as an ordinary order of action suggests that they would have very likely been of interest to Sacks. The accompanying architecture and organizational consequences of algorithms, likes and retweets may have also been of interest, especially through the ways in which members navigate these everyday online socio-digital facts-as-accomplishments. However, we will leave a detailed discussion of mundane metrics for another time.

As has been well established, Sacks relayed his discussions of membership categorization practices through reference to texts, such as newspaper headlines, stories and conversational exchanges. In terms of reflecting on Sacks's work, some consideration of social media (such as Twitter, for example, a well-known microblogging platform) provides an opportunity to reconsider and apply Sacksian ideas surrounding membership categorization and their development through the work of key ethnomethodologists such as Watson (1997) and Hester and Eglin (1997). In doing so, perhaps we can begin to trace some continuities in new forms of communicating and interacting, as well as important differences and discontinuities. To do so, therefore, is not out of any interest in social media per se, but rather because social media lend themselves to scrutiny, owing to the social fact that they are nothing less than networked membership categorization machines whose affordances, driven by human input, rage in the well-trodden paths, wilds and frontiers of everyday digital cultures. Consequently, this chapter claims that a pertinent feature of social media is the proliferation of membership categorization practice and work. In many respects, this has been one of my key interests and sources of inspiration that has influenced my sociological reading of Sacks's work. One of the striking things about social media is the ubiquity of networks, the role of algorithms and platform architecture and the disruption of late modern communication and communicative practices. However, from a Sacksian vantage point, these disruptive innovations have enabled a proliferation in categorization practices, the description of populations' groups, strategies for moral evaluation and the mapping, contestation and invocation of myriad forms of predication and the bounding of activities, associations and attributions to particular devices in threads, posts and visual formats. We have only just begun to scratch the surface of this form of life, and Sacks's ideas and concerns have much to offer the practical understanding of members' work in the digital age.

Precedents

In order to initiate our consideration of social media in terms of membership categorization practices, it is perhaps worth identifying some precedents in

Sacks work. The first includes 'Sociological Description' (1963), which outlines some of the features of the 'commentator machine'. In this paper, Sacks examines everyday description as a topic of inquiry and attempts to show how it is central to the routine accomplishment of social reality. In 'Notes on Police Assessment of Moral Character' (1972a), Sacks explores the relationship between appearances and mundane moral inference. Through reference to police patrols in neighbourhoods, Sacks suggests how this can be seen to operate in relation to the identification of outlier behaviours that may signal or warrant further investigation within specific spaces and places. 'On the Analysability of Stories by Children' (1972b) expresses an ongoing concern with the sociology of description, moral assessment, and the everyday machinery for routine social inference through a consideration of storytelling by children. This is developed through the language of membership categorization device (MCD) analysis. During the course of this chapter, the notion of MCD, the economy rule and duplicative organization are introduced alongside related ideas and concepts. These ideas are developed significantly and find expression in later publications that include 'An Initial Investigation of the Usability of Conversational Data for Doing Sociology' (1972c), during the course of which an apparatus for MCD analysis is developed in more detail. In addition to this, Sacks, through his own unique perspective, considers the role of categories in relation to social control and social change. 'Hotrodder: A Revolutionary Category' (1979) outlines the way in which membership categorization in relation to discrete acts has moral and practical consequences for specific groups, where actions are seen as applicable to members of specific categories and not merely in terms of how an *individual* acted or did not act.

According to Sacks, descriptions in talk could be understood to be organized in terms of MCDs and categories. This forms a further dimension to Sacks's ideas concerning categories and culture – namely, that displays of categories in conversation, he argued, were organized into specific cultural and socially situated devices. Sacks introduces us to questions of categorization and intelligibility through the use of a simple story (*Lectures in Conversation* Vol.1 and II, 1992: 236). Namely, 'The baby cried. The mommy picked it up'. The question for Sacks here is, how do we make sense of the story? How do we understand that the categories can be routinely heard to go together and be tied, unproblematically, to particular actions? One way of answering this question is that we hear the two categories as going together owing to their mutual relation to the device 'family'. Of course, this leads to further questions and an important observation about how different categories of membership are routinely tied to each other and underpinned by sets of possible descriptions of social action 'that make sense' within a specific cultural context, a particular setting or site of situated action.

The framework of membership categorization was also complemented by some rules of application. These are the economy rule and the consistency rule. The economy rule states: 'if a member uses a single category from any device then he can be recognised to be doing adequate reference to a person'. The consistency rule states that, once one membership category of a device has been used, 'other categories of the same collection may be used to categorise further members of the population'. From the consistency rule, Sacks (1992) derives a corollary, which he calls the Hearer's Maxim: 'If two or more categories are used to categorise two or more members of the same population and those categories can be heard as categories from the same collection then: Hear them that way' (p. 247). The extent to which these 'rules' are occasioned phenomena is an important consideration, and there is considerable reflexive and accountable work in how categories (including visual, conversational and textual category assemblages) are brought together in making sense of local settings and situated practices.

Sacks also states that some categories have a strong cultural association. He calls these standardized relational pairs (e.g., father–daughter, mother–baby, doctor–patient). A further culturally available (and frequently used) device is the stage-of-life device (e.g., young man, elderly women, mature person). One of the key features of these forms of membership categorization is that they exercise descriptive and moral control of who or what is allocated where. Furthermore, standardized relational pairs can be seen to be operative within particular situations, such as the activity of giving or providing help. These types of standardized relational pair form what Sacks calls 'Collection R', in which specific rights and obligations are attributed between specific category pairings such as husband and wife, daughter and mother, or parent and child. In situations where help is required, the absence of one of these categories from these types of pairing is recognizable and morally notable. This relates to what Sacks calls 'programmatic relevance', where, 'if R is relevant, then the non-incumbency of any of its pair positions is an observable'. Consequently, persons attributable to these relevant standardized relational pairs are expected, for example, to help one another. A related set of standardized relational pairs, 'Collection K', consists of specific distributions of knowledge that are tied to particular categories and persons, when dealing with problems and troubles. This collection may include experts and the public, medical professionals and patients, or counsellors and clients. The core issue here is the way in which Sacks begins to unpick the base concept of common-sense knowledge and identify ways in which it can be understood to be organized and operate as a context-sensitive machinery for providing socially adequate descriptions of events or for accounting for anomalous behaviour.

Given that the above represent an important array of ethnomethods for organizing and making sense of activities, it is worth reflecting on how these might make sense of some aspects of social media interaction as a practical and social accomplishment. Of course, membership categorization has also been explored in relation to Sacks's concern with sequences in conversation, turn taking and recipient design (Hester and Eglin, 1997; Watson, 1997). However, I will assume that readers are already acquainted with these particular matters (if not, see Housley and Fitzgerald, 2015); my concern is to remind us of some basic membership categorizational features and consider, albeit briefly, how they inform the world of social media practice – or at least some of the mundane ways in which humans routinely seek to influence and communicate with others through networked platforms and machines. In the following sections of this chapter, I provide three examples derived from social media as a means of illustrating the way in which the study of membership categorization practices is central (although not exclusively so) to these forms of socio-technical frames of action and life.

Membership categorization and social media?

For the purpose of this chapter, I will draw from publicly available communications derived from social media platforms. One of these platforms was Twitter, a micro-blogging site that enables open and public networked communication between followers and followed in ways that can facilitate varying degrees of public and global broadcast. In each case, these materials were derived from research projects subject to ethical approval and a framework for social media research (Webb et al., 2017).

One of Twitter's early advertising slogans exhorted people to 'broadcast themselves'. Along with the incorporation of the hashtag, the '@' function and the use of condensed links to other online content, this provided a 140-character 'micro-blog' through which to push promotional content, engage with other users and participate in an exchange of views in ways that some early commentators described as an emerging digital public sphere or 'agora'. Nowadays, with the rise of 'naturally produced' and automated antagonistic content within these environments, the analogy is less deployed in general commentary than in the recent past. Yet, there is something public about Twitter – it takes place on the digital street. Of course, who inhabits this street and how they inhabit it are deeply anthropological aspects – in this sense, despite its anonymity and networked, despatialized and temporally distantiated qualities, it has become an important site of membership and membership categorization.

Example 1: membership categorization and Twitter formulations

In terms of 'broadcasting oneself', social media cultures include a variety of types, roles and communicative practices. Examples of types and roles routinely encountered on micro-blogging sites such as Twitter include the celebrity antagonist, political pundit and anonymous troll. The occasioned and routine interplay between these aspects can be understood to produce recognizably distinct social media roles that are realized and accomplished through social media accounts. Communicative practices associated with these role-bounded 'accounts' – especially those associated with a significant number of followers (i.e. those with 'high network capital') – include the use of category-based formulations that might announce 'news' or generate interest through provocation or antagonism (see Housley et al., 2017a,

2017b). It comes as little surprise that these are often 'category-rich' phenomena, and that, in turn, this inference-rich design is a key feature of social media practice as a textual, interactional and communicative accomplishment. For example, Figure 17.1 draws on tweets produced by a well-established 'celebrity antagonist'. These can be understood as membership category formulations that are designed to generate interest, controversy, antagonism and, ultimately, social media traffic.

The first formulation (Tweet 1) makes reference to 'babies', which can be heard to act as an MCD in this instance, as well as a membership category of the wider device of 'family'; in this sense, we can hear it as being duplicatively organized (Watson, 2015). In this formulation, the membership category 'babies' is predicated in terms of hair colour, in this case 'ginger'; this provides the grounds for generating an additional membership category population of 'ginger babies'. The second part of the formulation invokes the consistency rule in relation to the membership category in question but stipulates an exceptional category-bound (predicate-based) feature: namely, that they are 'so much harder to love'. This formulation makes use of a contrast class (regular babies vs ginger haired babies) and forms of moral downgrading and an extreme case formulation through which to degrade a population group. In doing so, this serves to produce an 'antagonistic formulation' that is designed to provoke a response in and through the generation of online controversy via a popular and 'public' micro-blogging platform.

The second formulation (Figure 17.2) is one that was produced by the account in question earlier in the timeline of social media postings gathered within the data set. Of interest here is the difference in the number of responses, which may be tied to the design of the MCD formulation. First, the target membership category is referenced in a more economical manner – that is, 'ginger babies' (as opposed to ginger haired babies) – and the formulation is broken down, through the use of punctuation, into a clear three-part list, a well-established rhetorical device (Atkinson, 1984). This combination of design features – that is, contrast, use of a three-part list, economy, and a downgrading form of emotional attribution – can be read as a refined version of the antagonistic formulation initially presented in the prior example (Figure 17.1). These illustrative examples not only provide further insight into how membership

Katie Hopkins
@KTHopkins

Ginger haired babies. Like regular babies just so much harder to love.

Retweets 6 Likes 5
3:56am – 31 Mar 2013

Figure 17.1 Tweet 1 (14 responses).

Katie Hopkins
@KTHopkins

Ginger babies. Like a baby. Just so much harder to love.

Retweets 1065 Likes 371
6:11 pm 4 Jul 2013

Figure 17.2 Tweet 2 (181 responses).

categorization is central to the work of generating controversy and normative disruption in social media spaces, by certain social media actors (e.g., celebrity trolls), but they also shed some practical illumination on how formulations are routinely optimized, honed and tested against social media metrics and thread-based responses for controversial impact.

Example 2: Corrective memes

Our second example, shown in Figure 17.3, involves an 'alternative correction' of a prominent headline. This form of practice (among many others) is often used to breach or context the framing of news events or high-profile social media communications in particular ways. Again, this practice mobilizes membership categorization as a common resource that can be used to subvert, index or provide alternative readings on social media platforms where knowledge claims, political views and the framing of events are routinely and noisily contested.

Of interest here is the notion of 'fixing' particular categorical framings evident in newspaper headlines. Indeed, this example, as with other examples of this type of practice routinely found in social media exchanges and debates, makes recognizable the inference-rich character of newspaper headlines. Through the provision of an alternative predicate attribution, 'fighting for their future because governments aren't', readers are invited not only to see the contingent nature of the original framing, but also to identify with the morally or

THE AUSTRALIAN

Headline: Climate kids ~~mere pawns in a bid to undermine capitalism~~ fighting for their future because governments aren't

Accompanying picture: Greta Thurnberg giving speech in Hamburg

Figure 17.3 'Fixing' headlines.

politically 'fixed' alternative. This displays the contested character of headlines and the framing of political topics where categories and categorization are key features for dispute within and through social media platforms.

Example 3: Mundane deconstruction, interactional threads and countering derogatory speech

One of the innovative interactional features of social media platforms is the ability of 'users' to respond to and engage with specific posts and subsequent comments in and through a thread format. This can facilitate text-based responses to particular posts sequentially and through a 'skip connect' form of response enabled by the use of the @ function or similar, where different accounts within a thread (or, indeed, elsewhere on the network) can be referred to and signalled. In previous papers (Housley et al., 2017a, 2017b), we have noted how threads can exhibit a hybrid conversational form that incorporates features associated with both text and talk. For example, within social media threads (such as those associated with Twitter), there are strong observational grounds for suggesting that recipient design and adjacency are often in operation, although this is complicated by the networked characteristics of the platform, which may allow for a variety of interlocuters to contribute to an open thread and exchange where turn-taking procedures are routinely (although not exclusively) seen to be in operation. Social media threads produced within 'open' environments and sites are often multi-party interactions that also provide for a variety of responses, including links to visual media, other websites or text. The following social media thread is presented for illustrative purposes:

Social media thread

1. User1: I mean, I'm not racist but even you can't deny it. X people make everything scarier. Don't even try to deny it
2. User2: @User1@YesYoureRacist -haha- does that apply to Disney movies? [–] What about birthday parties?
3. User3: @User1 Y people have that effect too
4. User4: @User1 @YesYoureRacist You have a lot of life yet to live #Civiltown
5. User5: (emoji)@User 1:I mean, I'm not racist but even you cant deny it. X people make everything scarier. Don't even try to deny it
6. User6: @User1 oh honey … *vomits all over you*
7. User7: @User5 @User 1 'I'm not racist'
8. User5: @User7 @User 1 literally the best omg
9. User7: @User5 @User1 idiot lol
10. User8: @User1 Y people make schools and cinemas scarier!
11. User9: @User1 @YesyoureRacist I mean, #asshats just make everything stupider. Don't even try to deny it

12. User10: @User1 @YesyoureRacist I guess what your saying is u would feel more comfortable if X people didn't exist Fascinating #Hitlermuch
13. User11: @User1 @YesyoureRacist not ridiculous at all
14. User12: @User1 @YesyoureRacist Don't even start a sentence with 'I'm not racist but.' Not only is it cliché, it doesn't work
15. User12: @User1 @YesyoureRacist 'I'm not racist but … ' is admitting that you're being offensive whilst trying to avoid consequences
16. User13: @User1 @YesyoureRacist I know I get scared when I see Y people in movie theaters, shopping malls, schools …
17. User 14: @User1 @YesyoureRacist Wow.
18. User 13: @User1 maybe you're just a pussy

In this example, the antagonistic formulation consists of an 'I'm not racist but …' disclaimer (Stokoe and Edwards, 2007) or 'sin license' (Hewitt and Stokes, 1975), followed by the membership categorization and attribution that 'X people make everything scarier'; this is followed by a clause, 'Don't even try to deny it' (a clause proffered as part of the disclaiming work produced at Line 1 of the social media thread). At Line 2, User 2 asks a series of questions that mock the racist formulation offered at Line 1 while also '@' the relevant 'Yes You are Racist' sentinel site. The use of 'laughter particles' and questions invoking various scenarios of activity and possible membership category inferences (e.g., birthday parties or Disney movies) displays category complexity, as a means of downgrading the assertion that this predication of X people is salient or ubiquitous – there are other activities and membership categories that may also invoke fear or other responses to being scared. Moreover, this downgrading work invokes scenarios and possible membership category imputations that we might associate with stage-of-life categories and activities such as being young or immature. In this way, the counter formulation is provided alongside a provocation that makes use of both these methods for responding to antagonistic content in membership category terms.

At Line 3, a distinct (and contrastive) counter formulation is produced (Y people have that effect too). As with other examples, these formulations deal in the stock and trade of membership categorization work not merely as responses, but as interpretive resources that provide the inferential apparatus for the practical deconstruction of racist formulations. Furthermore, these formulations have been designated and recognized as potentially racist by the members of the social media speech community; this is evidenced by the action of alerting the relevant sentinel site. In this way, the thread examined here may provide insight into the way a social media community negotiates and manages antagonistic content at an interactional level.

At Line 4, the framing introduced by User 2 at Line 2 is alluded to – 'you have a lot of life yet to live'; this recognizes possible imputations of immaturity and naivety (introduced at Line 2), but also sets up further inferences. This counter formulation is concluded with the hashtag '#Civiltown'. In this way, the topical frame is shifted to include a recent event that has been understood in relation to police violence, the shooting of young men from a specific ethnic group, civil reaction and disturbance. Lines 7–9 present a chorus of provocation formulations. At Line 10, another example of category substitution is provided as a design strategy for counter speech that is directed to User 1 through the @ function 'Y people make schools and cinemas scarier!' (Line 10). Lines 12, 14, 15 and 16 consist of further counter-speech formulations.

At Line 16, we can see a further example of category substitution as a strategy for countering mundane racist logics: 'I know I get scared when I see Y people in movie theatres, shopping malls, schools.' It also makes available further possible inferences, including mass shootings by non-X members of the community. However, at Lines 15 and 16, the use of a disclaimer – 'I'm not racist but …' – by User 1 at Line 1 is topicalized by Users 12 and 13: both question its use and effectiveness as a form of moral licensing for antagonistic and racist views. In this way, we can see how counter-speech formulations can question the mundane use of rhetoric and specific forms of account structure associated with racist text and talk.

Digital hotrodders – revolutionary and transformational category work on social media

In terms of the horizons in and through which members routinely engage with social media, it is worth reflecting on the extent to which social media provide a space through which revolutionary categories can be generated, applied and tried out, in the sense that counter-categories are not formally recognized by standard agents of social control – that is to say, membership and associated attributes and activities are not always available on first viewing to standard agents associated with social control practices, particularly if they are the situated product of a chain of mundane online innovation and category 'testing' within online environments. As a consequence, the accountable architecture through which social media operate can be a source of trouble, in the face of transparency and intelligibility, for concerned and interested others such as parents, teachers, social workers or law enforcement, particularly if it is a source of unintelligibility and normative variance.

However, in addition to providing a space for the acceleration of revolutionary categories, platforms such as Twitter, also provide a space for digitally cultivated and accomplished *transformational* categories. Social media provide an environment through which multiple and networked 'crowd responses' can provide verification and mundane testability for new forms of membership categorization in the service of particular topics, campaigns or debates. They also provide a networked means for reproducing new forms of membership categorization and mundane predicate mapping rapidly, and in ways that allow for networked communities to promote, propagate or ignore mundane innovations in membership categorization. From a Sacksian perspective, this provides an interesting window on the making of culture-in-action, moral praxeology and normative contestation that is characteristic of social media environments. The mundane metricized environment, alongside the potential for broad mass response through a variety of recipient-signalled verification and response functions (e.g., the use of the @ function, the emergence of threads and response lines and the more general hashtag function), provides a plethora of material and everyday data that can be used by members of digital cultures to advance or accomplish various activities that are subject to mundane refinement and augmented everyday optimization. A good example here can be found through the examination of 'trolling' practices and the generation of antagonistic content in the pursuit of building responses (and, thence, network capital) around particular topics in order to advance or denigrate specific world views and persons.

Social media as a digital 'street'

These illustrations provide a limited practical reflection on some of the possibilities of approaching social media as a socially organized and ethnomethodologically resonant setting.[1] Although we have no way of knowing, it is a fair bet that Harvey Sacks would have viewed social media as an important site for observing everyday routine practices for accomplishing, assessing and describing social life. Recent work on the Sacks archive (Fitzgerald, 2019) reveals Sacks's interest and use of multiple cultural artefacts that were drawn upon in order to develop systematic ways of analysing and thinking about the routine accomplishment of social and cultural life.

In one sense, social media represent a site for reapproaching Sacksian concerns, and in ways that resonate with, but do not match neatly, the relatively advanced state that ethnomethodology and conversation analysis now find themselves in. For example, social media can combine a spectrum of orders of ordinary action, including text, visuals and the spoken word. The way in which these ordering practices are routinely brought together and made sense of forms the basis through which Sacksian principles can be extended to the study of social media in action (Housley et al., 2018). In more general ethnographic terms, social media can be understood to be analogous to a digital street characterized by routine forms of activity, character types, presentations of 'self', forms of life, scenes, settings and ways of speaking and seeing the world. Of course, this analogy will get us only so far. Sacksian principles can take us a little further and in ways that provide granular detail to some of this world's organizational features and characteristics at 'street level'. An important dimension associated with these spaces of digital life, especially in the context of Web 2.0 and the interactive web, includes the increased visibility of vernacular analysis and mundane reason distributed across comment boards and threads that routinely refer, for example, to controversial artefacts associated with You Tube video content, specific social media postings and online news items.

What types of things can be observed and analysed by ordinary members on the streets, alley ways, footpaths, highways and byways associated with social media and related platforms? Clearly there are ways of doing things, of accomplishing interest, controversy or indeed amplification through antagonism and related strategies for visibility and attention generation. The practical expertise of the social media troll is predicated on an understanding of recipient design, turn-taking, category formulation and associated interpretive procedures. There exist a range of methods, perfected through a networked order of interaction, that are deployed on different platforms to advance particular views or context, antagonise or generate interest and 'clickability'. Indeed, as this chapter has argued, it represents a space in which a panoply of interactive and platform architectural metrics can help verify, confirm and feed back on social media category content in the service of particular activities. In this way 'doing it for the likes and the lolz' can be a rich 'verification' resource through which certain techno-methods, inclusive of the membership category organization of specific social media content, can be refined, optimized and automated in the service of particular activities and objectives. Indeed, the use of mundane metrics is a key feature here and one that next-generation EM/CA will have to consider as a routine dimension of everyday digital ethno-technical methods and practices.

Note

1 An additional and related challenge for ethnomethodological work in this field of human and technical practices is its networked character. Nekvapil and Leuder's (2002) respecification and application of dialogical networks as a conceptual tool provide a possible avenue for thinking about the relationship between situated action, mediation and networks.

References

Atkinson, M. (1984). *Our masters' voices: The language and body language of politics*. London: Routledge. Psychology Press.

Brooker, P., Dutton, W. and Greiffenhagen, C. (2017). What would Wittgenstein say about social media? *Qualitative Research*, 17(6): 610–626.

Fitzgerald, R. (2019). The data and methodology of Harvey Sacks: Lessons from the archive. *Journal of Pragmatics*, 143: 205–214.

Hester, S. and Eglin, P. (Eds.) (1997). *Culture in action: Studies in membership categorization analysis*. Washington, DC: University Press of America.

Hewitt, J.P. and Stokes, R. (1975). Disclaimers. *American Sociological Review*, 40 (1): 1–11.

Housley, W. and Fitzgerald, R. (2015). Introduction to membership categorisation analysis. In R. Fitzgerald and W. Housley (Eds.), *Advances in membership categorisation analysis* (pp. 1–22). London: Sage.

Housley, W. and Smith, R.J. (2017). Interactionism and digital society. *Qualitative Research*, 17(2): 187–201.

Housley, W., Webb, H., Edwards, A., Procter, R. and Jirotka, M. (2017a). Digitizing Sacks? Approaching social media as data. *Qualitative Research*, 17(6): 627–644.

Housley, W., Webb, H., Edwards, A., Procter, R. and Jirotka, M. (2017b). Membership categorisation and antagonistic Twitter formulations. *Discourse & Communication*, 11(6): 567–590.

Housley, W., Webb, H., Williams, M., Procter, R., Edwards, A., Jirotka, M., Burnap, P., Stahl, B.C., Rana, O. and Williams, M. (2018). Interaction and transformation on social media: The case of Twitter campaigns. *Social Media+ Society*, 4(1): 2056305117750721.

Nekvapil, J. and Leuder, I. (2002). On dialogic networks: Arguments about the migration law in Czech mass media in 1993. In S. Hester and W. Housley (Eds.), *Language, interaction and national identity* (pp. 60–101). Aldershot: Ashgate.

Sacks, H. (1963). Sociological description. *Berkeley Journal of Sociology*, 8(1): 1–16.

Sacks, H. (1972a). Notes on police assessment of moral character. In D. Sudnow (Ed.), *Studies in social interaction* (pp. 280–293). Glencoe, IL: Free Press.

Sacks, H. (1972b). On the analyzability of stories by children. In J.J. Gumperz and D. Hymes (Eds.), *Directions in sociolinguistics* (pp. 325–345). New York: Holt Rinehart & Winston.

Sacks, H. (1972c). An initial investigation of the usability of conversational data for doing sociology. In D.N. Sudnow (Ed.), *Studies in social interaction* (pp. 31–74). New York: Free Press.

Sacks, H. (1979). Hotrodder: A revolutionary category. In G. Psathas (Ed.), *Everyday language: Studies in ethnomethodology* (pp. 7–14). New York: Irvington Press.

Sacks, H. (1992). *Lectures on conversation: Volumes 1 & 2* (edited by G. Jefferson with introduction by E.A. Schegloff). Oxford: Blackwell.

Stokoe, E. and Edwards, D. (2007). 'Black this, black that': Racial insults and reported speech in neighbour complaints and police interrogations. *Discourse & Society*, 18(3): 337–372.

Watson, D.R. (1997). Some general reflections on categorization and sequence in the analysis of conversation. In S. Hester and P. Eglin (Eds.), *Culture in action: Studies in membership categorization analysis* (pp. 49–76). Washington, DC: University Press of America.

Watson, D.R. (2015). De-reifying categories. In R. Fitzgerald and W. Housley (Eds.), *Advances in membership categorisation analysis* (pp. 23–50). London: Sage.

Webb, H., Jirotka, M., Stahl, B.C., Housley, W., Edwards, A., Williams, M., Procter, R., Rana, O. and Burnap, P. (2017, June). The ethical challenges of publishing Twitter data for research dissemination. In *Proceedings of the 2017 ACM on Web Science Conference* (pp. 339–348). ACM.

Index

Note: Locators in *italics* refer to figures.